ABANDONED

ABANDONED

America's Lost Youth and the
Crisis of Disconnection

Anne Kim

NEW YORK
LONDON

Requests for permission to reproduce selections from this book should
be made through our website: https://thenewpress.com/contact.

Published in the United States by The New Press, New York, 2020
Distributed by Two Rivers Distribution

ISBN 978-1-62097-500-8 (hc)
ISBN 978-1-62097-568-8 (ebook)

CIP data is available.

The New Press publishes books that promote and enrich public discussion and
understanding of the issues vital to our democracy and to a more equitable world.
These books are made possible by the enthusiasm of our readers; the support
of a committed group of donors, large and small; the collaboration of our many
partners in the independent media and the not-for-profit sector; booksellers, who
often hand-sell New Press books; librarians; and above all by our authors.

www.thenewpress.com

Composition by dix!
This book was set in Fairfield LH

Printed in the United States of America

2   4   6   8   10   9   7   5   3   1

Contents

ABANDONED

Introduction

In June 2018, a then twenty-eight-year-old former waitress rocked the American political establishment with her surprise defeat of a nine-term veteran congressman in the Democratic primary election in New York's 14th Congressional District.[1] Alexandria Ocasio-Cortez's victory over Rep. Joseph Crowley was instantly hailed as the beginning of a tectonic generational shift in the country's political leadership. Now in her fledgling tenure as one of the youngest members of Congress ever elected, Ocasio-Cortez has been shaping the national debate while challenging old-guard politics.

In the same month as Ocasio-Cortez's first momentous political victory, high school students from Parkland, Florida, survivors of a massacre at Marjorie Stoneman Douglas High School that killed seventeen people, launched a nationwide bus tour to advocate for gun control legislation.[2] The students had already racked up a major victory in their home state, when Florida passed its first gun control bill in two decades in defiance of the National Rifle Association.[3]

America's young people are rising. And as young leaders like Ocasio-Cortez and the students from Parkland are proving, their energy and idealism are a transformational force. In technology, culture, the economy, and politics, young adults in both the millennial and post-millennial generations are making their mark as the most diverse, connected, and best-educated populations the nation has ever seen.[4] Sixty percent of millennials, for instance, consider themselves entrepreneurs, according to Britt Hysen, editor-in-chief of *Millennial* magazine,[5] and examples abound of twenty-somethings who have already founded multimillion-dollar ventures or visionary social enterprises with global reach.[6]

But while America's young people are rising—they are not all rising together.

A significant share of young people are not keeping up with their peers. Rather, they are disconnected from the mainstream of opportunity and disengaged from education and employment, or are at risk of being so. In 2017, as many as 4.5 million young people—or a stunning 11.5 percent of young people ages sixteen to twenty-four—were neither in school nor working, according to the Social Science Research Council.[7] For millions more, their hold on school and work is shaky at best as they struggle to make their way in communities that are left behind or to overcome the personal and family obstacles life has thrown their way.

The young people who ultimately lose their foothold in education and employment are variously known as "disconnected youth," "opportunity youth," or, as the Europeans call them, NEETs—"not in employment, education, or training."[8] Whatever the label, they represent the twin tragedies of societal failure and wasted potential. Their large numbers are moreover a warning sign of deeper underlying challenges that could cut short the potential of these upcoming generations.

For the vast majority of young adults in America, the transition to independence is a time of not only nerve-wracking anxiety but also excitement and possibility. Leaving home. Going to college. A first job. A first apartment. And down the road, perhaps, a partner, marriage, and family.

For most young people, this leap into adulthood is also cushioned by a web of connections to families, teachers, coaches, pastors, and other caring adults who can smooth an often tumultuous transition. Mentors like these provide young adults with advice as well as resources—emotional, financial, and professional—to navigate challenges and, importantly, help them bounce back from mistakes. Most young people also arrive at the threshold of adulthood armed with an education, emotional resilience, and other assets imparted to them by the "village" that raised them.

I remember arriving in Washington, D.C., during the mid-1990s at the age of twenty-four, a freshly minted law school graduate ready to start the first "real" job of my career. I was terrified of failure. But I also had enormous advantages in my favor, which I took for granted at the time. Despite a high five-figure student debt, I had a car, a credit card, and some money in the bank. As scared as I was of my new bosses, I'd had internships and summer jobs that had taught me how to behave (more or less) in a professional environment. And while my home life was far from perfect, I knew I could find refuge with my mom in Kansas City, Missouri, if my life completely cratered. As precarious as my professional, emotional, and financial situation seemed to me then, I had a net below me in case the ladder broke or I slipped.

The importance of these kinds of supports has only grown as the runway to independence has become more protracted and fraught with obstacles earlier generations didn't face. Young people today must invest more time in school than they once did if they want a job that pays a living wage. Escalating housing prices in many parts of the country mean that young adults often can't afford to live on their own with an entry-level salary. As one result, parental support now plays a larger and longer role in many young people's lives than it did in generations past. Middle-class parents increasingly recognize that their children's young-adult years are a chance to cement the advantages that will carry them through their adult lives. That's why they save for college, help their children find internships, and often welcome them back home before their final launch into independence. In 2015, as many as one in three young people ages eighteen to thirty-four were living at home with their parents, according to the U.S. Census Bureau.[9]

But many young people—especially those who are lower

income—do not have the benefit of this extended support. For them, their entry into adulthood is not so much a guided journey into independence as an abrupt abandonment.

"Rochelle" is one such young person whose journey into adulthood has been rocky. When I met Rochelle in the spring of 2018, she was twenty-three years old and had just enrolled in a program at CASES, a nonprofit offering education and job training and alternatives to incarceration for both youthful and adult offenders in New York City. She had brought her three-year-old daughter, Egypt, who was outfitted in pink from head to toe. We punctuated our conversation with "I Spy" breaks for the three of us out the window of CASES' offices on Adam Clayton Powell Boulevard in Harlem, Manhattan. We saw green double-decker tourist buses and the red marquee of the historic Apollo Theater, just a few blocks down the street.

Rochelle had come to CASES to finish her education and find a job. "I want to study as hard as I can, obtain my GED, and eventually move out of the shelter to my own apartment," she said.

Her prospects, however, were tenuous, despite her ambitions. At the time we spoke, Rochelle and Egypt had just moved into a nearby shelter for homeless families after six months in another shelter for victims of domestic violence. Her older sister and the aunt who had raised her were back in the Bronx, her aunt working the night shift as a housekeeper while her sister worked in security.

Rochelle had also just lost her most recent job, at a drugstore, when her bosses refused to give her time off for a mandatory appointment with her welfare caseworker. Not wanting to risk losing her benefits, she went to her appointment anyway. She was fired. "I had that job eight months," she said. "That's the longest I kept a job."

As extreme as her circumstances seem to be, Rochelle's story is all too common. America is facing a crisis among its young adults—one that public policy is woefully neglecting.

Millions of young people are navigating communities where

poverty is endemic, jobs are scarce, and opportunities weak, with parents and peers struggling just as much as they are to keep themselves afloat. Some have been pushed out by the institutions charged with their well-being—such as schools and the child welfare system—without adequate skills, education, or resources. Others have lost their parents to the ravages of substance abuse or domestic violence or to the maw of the criminal justice system. Some have been incarcerated themselves and then spit back out onto the street. Often, the systems and institutions that are supposed to help these young people have instead sabotaged their chances of success, exacerbating the hardships they already face.

Rochelle, for instance, was arrested at age sixteen—"I was in the wrong place at the wrong time with the wrong people," she said—and spent the prime years of her young adulthood in juvenile detention and mental health facilities, during which time her father passed away from cancer. She didn't get the chance to go back to high school, and then she became pregnant with Egypt. Despite the intense involvement of the four systems that have shaped the trajectory of her life—the child welfare system, the public schools, the juvenile justice system, and now the public safety net that is helping to support her and her child—Rochelle feels alone in her current struggles. "I'm doing everything," she said. "I'm by myself."

Alarmingly, many of the young people left alone to find their way end up like Rochelle, untethered to either education or employment through their young-adult years, leaving them at a severe disadvantage throughout their lives. Left without rescue, some of these young people could end up permanently severed from the broader fabric of society. In the worst instances, their ultimate fate could be to wind up among the chronically homeless adults who populate shelters and street corners; the repeat offenders who spend their lives behind bars; or the members of the dependent poor, unable to break from the prison of public benefits into a self-sufficient life.

It doesn't have to be this way, and this book is about how to help young people like Rochelle stay connected to their communities and to the opportunities they need to make the most of their lives.

Among the greatest triumphs of public policy over the last several decades is the recognition of early childhood as a critical developmental period in children's lives. This realization has led, among other things, to key programs such as Head Start and Early Head Start, support for policies such as universal pre-K, and pioneering innovations such as home visiting.

A similar revolution should be happening for young adults. Growing evidence—including new research from the field of adolescent brain science—shows that "emerging adulthood" is just as crucial a developmental period in people's lives, and that young adults have unique needs that current public policies do not yet meet. Compared to the attention paid to early childhood and at the other end to adults, youth policy has received relatively scant notice. This means young adults are shoehorned into adult programs that don't meet their specific needs, if there are programs at all.

We do, however, have a good sense of where we need to be. Thanks to an array of programs developed over the last couple of decades, we know what works to keep young people engaged in work and school and to ensure that even those who face the harshest of circumstances have a shot at a productive adulthood. We also know the kinds of reforms we need in the systems that touch young people's lives so that their challenges aren't magnified.

Much of this work has been achieved over the last twenty years, through an emerging movement for "opportunity youth" that has elevated the voices of young adults, developed new policies tailored to their challenges, and advocated on their behalf. These advocates have opened up a new frontier in public policy focused on the needs of young adults: (1) to ensure young people get the right support up to and through their early adult years and not just to age eighteen, when many current supports end; and (2) to provide each young person, at every step of the way, a caring adult who can help navigate the transition to independence.

This book aims to bring this emerging discipline of youth policy into the mainstream of our policy and political discussion. As troubled and as polarized as our current politics now seem, creating better opportunities for our young people—in rural America as well as in cities—is a priority that everyone can and should agree on.

In part I, I lay out the contours of the challenge of youth "disconnection"—how many young people are facing circumstances like Rochelle's. I also survey the evolution of the young-adult years in America and the increasing recognition of emerging adulthood as a distinct phase of development, including from the perspective of recent developments in neuroscience. This evolving understanding bolsters the case for a new dimension of public policy aimed specifically at disadvantaged young adults and their needs.

Part II explains the various forces and factors that can push a young person to become disconnected. I also look at the specific ways in which current public policy now fails to meet the needs of young adults, such as those involved in foster care and the justice system, and in many cases leaves them worse off. Given the many excellent works on the failings of the child welfare and justice systems, I do not attempt to replicate that research and instead offer a synthesis of what should be happening when young adults leave these systems.

Part III profiles just a few of the extraordinary programs that are working to provide young people in often difficult circumstances with the positive supports they need to establish a lasting connection to work and school and, ultimately, to achieve self-sufficiency. Among these are a "transitional living" program in Fairfax County, Virginia, that provides intensive support to homeless young moms; an extraordinary mentorship program in Washington, D.C., that provides young people support from ages fourteen to twenty-four; and a South Texas school district that has transformed itself from having one of the worst high school dropout rates in the country to becoming a pioneer in "early college" and other strategies to connect kids from school to career.

These efforts are also representative of the thousands of programs that now exist to serve young people—it is impossible to survey them all. While there's still much we don't know about the best ways to help young people, especially those who face the greatest barriers, understanding these programs can provide a window into the most promising practices and provide a template for more programs across the country.

Part IV lays out a blueprint for a youth agenda aimed at bipartisan appeal.

Throughout this book, I share the stories of young people like Rochelle, as well as the stories of the adults—many of whom have overcome similar trauma and hardship in their own lives—who have dedicated their lives to creating opportunities for America's young people.

If there are common threads among the stories of the young people I talked to in the course of researching this book, it is their optimism, their resilience, and, above all, their unshakable sense of agency. Despite the difficult circumstances they have survived or still find themselves in, they do not see themselves as victims. Nor do they blame the institutions that maltreated them, even if that blame would be more than justified.

"I did have a troubled childhood, but I would never use it as an excuse," said Rochelle. "I will always use it to better myself. When my father passed away, one of the only things he wanted me to do was get my high school diploma. He was able to see my sister graduate but not me, so that right there is motivation. Maybe he's smiling down on me. I've got to make him proud as if he was still here."

With so many young people like Rochelle ready and willing to do their share to make a better life for themselves, we too must do our part to make those opportunities possible.

PART I

Embarking

1

Emergence and Divergence

When exactly do you become an "adult"?

If you were a young man of a certain class in ancient Rome, your passage into adulthood was as clear as the clothes you wore. Sometime during your fifteenth or sixteenth year, in a ceremony held by your family, you would take off the purple-hemmed tunic worn by all highborn Roman boys and exchange it for the pure white toga—the *toga virilis*—emblematic of the citizens of Rome.[1] The transition was more than symbolic. When a young man was "bestowed a toga," he was also bestowed with all the rights and responsibilities of citizenship. He was officially enrolled on the Roman census and had the right to vote—a duty the ancient Romans took seriously. He also became eligible to hold public office and serve in the military. He could go into debt and transact business in his family's name.

In America today, the demarcation into adulthood is much more ambiguous. Legally, for instance, the lines of "adult" responsibility are wildly inconsistent across the fifty states. While teenagers typically can't get a driver's license until age sixteen, half of the states have no minimum age at which children can marry.[2] And while young people need to be eighteen to vote and twenty-one to (legally) drink, some states allow children as young as ten to be transferred out of juvenile court and tried as adults if they commit a crime.[3]

These varying legal thresholds are in part the result of historical accident, politics, and practical considerations, as well as shifting attitudes about the privileges and responsibilities "adulthood" should carry. In the late 1960s, for instance, young people opposed to the Vietnam War rallied behind the motto, "Old enough to fight, old enough to vote," to lower the voting age from twenty-one to eighteen.[4] The result was the 26th Amendment.

However, the question of how old is "old enough" has no hard and fast answer. Americans see adulthood as a process, rather than a terminal event, with a set of common milestones along the way: finishing school, working full time, earning enough to support a family, moving away from home, and being financially independent. According to the 2012 General Social Survey, a majority of Americans see these particular achievements as "extremely important" or "somewhat important" to "becoming an adult," with smaller numbers saying marriage and having a child are important threshold events.[5]

What's clear, however, is that becoming an adult is taking longer than it used to, and with important benefits for the young adults who can take the most advantage of this extended runway.

The Benefits of "Adultolescence"

Fifty years ago, young adulthood meant finding a job, setting up a household, and starting a family. Back then, those events were the starting points of people's adult lives. Today, those milestones are the culmination of a long period of preparation aimed at laying the financial, educational, and emotional foundations for adult success. Young people are increasingly taking zigzag paths toward their adult selves: they're switching jobs, switching majors, taking gap years, moving back home, dating the wrong people, experimenting—and occasionally falling flat.

In the past, this would have been called "failure to launch." Today, it's called "emerging adulthood." In an influential 2004 book that first described the phenomenon and coined this term, psychologist Jeffrey Jensen Arnett argues that today's young people are experiencing a "new and historically unprecedented period of the life course" made possible by more years in school and, consequently, more years before marriage and family.[6] Whereas in 1970 the typical young woman was married at twenty-one and a mother the same year, young women in 2017 were a median of twenty-seven years old when they married and twenty-six at the birth of their first child.[7] These extra years, Arnett argues, give today's young people "unprecedented freedom" to explore different paths for themselves before they settle down—freedom that's also shifted young people's expectations about what their early twenties should bring.

"Your twenties are about forming your identity and figuring out what to do with the rest of your life," says Ben, a colleague of mine who is twenty-six.

"Young people of the 1950s were eager to enter adulthood and settle down," Arnett writes. "Perhaps because they grew up during the upheavals of the Great Depression and World War II, achieving the stability of marriage, home and children seemed like a great accomplishment to them." Today's young people, on the other hand, see these milestones as capstone events that spell the "end of spontaneity [and] wide-open possibilities."[8] The trials and errors of young adulthood, Arnett argues, are both normal and even necessary for young people to set themselves on the right course. By getting a chance to practice adulthood, young people are better equipped in the long run for self-sufficiency, and are happier to boot. Emerging adulthood, as Arnett writes, "is . . . when hopes flourish, when people have an unparalleled opportunity to transform their lives." And at the end of this process, young people should be ready to embrace the obligations of self-sufficiency—"taking responsibility for yourself, making independent decisions and becoming financially independent."[9]

Making space for this transition is one rationale behind the growing popularity of the so-called gap year—an intentional time-out before college that's become fashionable among upper-middle-class young adults to defuse the pressure-cooker years of high school and the college admissions race.

Perhaps the most famous recent "gapper" is President Barack Obama's daughter Malia, who made news when she announced her plans to defer her freshman year at Harvard University. Though the intense public scrutiny of eight years in the White House likely influenced her decision, Obama was also joining an emerging trend among affluent young adults.

Although the exact number of gappers is hard to pin down, according to the Gap Year Association (yes, there is such a thing), a burgeoning industry of gap-year program providers and advisers attests to its growing appeal.[10] You can, for instance, spend $15,000 for a three-month odyssey in the Himalayas to "trek above 16,000 ft., study traditional arts with a local master, and sit for a 10-day Buddhist meditation retreat."[11] Obama's school, Harvard, in fact "encourages" students to defer their attendance for a year and reports that between 80 and 110 students do so annually.[12]

Though some students spend their gap year working and saving money, proponents argue that its principal purpose should simply be for young people to take time for themselves. According to Harvard's admissions office, its gap-year students explore such activities as "drama, figure skating, health-care, archeological exploration, kibbutz life, language study, mineralogical research, missionary work, music, non-profit groups, child welfare programs, political campaigns, rebuilding schools, special needs volunteering, sports, steel drumming, storytelling, swing dance, university courses, and writing."[13] Malia Obama reportedly spent the year traveling extensively and interning for movie mogul Harvey Weinstein's (now very defunct) production company.[14]

As indulgent as they seem, gap years may also have important physiological benefits—they're good for the brain.

While it's by now axiomatic that a person's early childhood experiences help set the stage for long-term success in life, neuroscience is also beginning to show that early adulthood could be just as important a period for the brain's physical development. What infant brains have that is so important is "plasticity," or the ability to physically mold themselves—including the ability to learn, re-member, and process information.[15] Infant brains can form more than one million new connections per second.[16] The quality of that wiring, however, depends heavily on a child's experiences, which is why you'll find shelf after shelf of items devoted to baby and toddler toys aimed at "early development" when you walk into any Tar-get or Walmart. These toys are designed to stimulate young brains with different textures, sounds, and colors, introduce them to their numbers and ABCs, and help them practice motor skills by stack-ing cups, pushing buttons, or shoving blocks through different-shaped holes.

Although early childhood may be when the brain enjoys its highest levels of plasticity, scientists have discovered that teen and young adult brains are almost as facile. Teenage brains, says neuro-scientist Frances E. Jensen in her book *The Teenage Brain*, "are only about 80 percent of the way to maturity."[17] The missing pieces are the connections yet to be laid between the frontal lobes—where reason and higher-order thought occurs—and the rest of the brain. The process of building the necessary neural connections contin-ues throughout the teen years and into a person's early twenties, and it isn't until a person is about twenty-five that the adult brain is more or less a finished product, according to Jensen's research.

The discovery of this continuing phase of development helps explain much of the impulsivity and drama that tends to charac-terize adolescence. Young adults behave the way they do because the rational parts of their brains are literally disconnected in sig-nificant ways from the parts of their brains that are emotional, thrill-seeking, and hormonally overloaded. But, more critically, it underscores the importance of young adulthood as a time when people can change, adapt, and reinvent themselves. "Many young adults find that their learning skills are much better at this age than when they were in high school," Jensen writes. "Organizational skills improve, as does the ability to abstract. Judgment, insight, and perspective all improve as a result of more accessible frontal lobes."[18] Young adults who have the chance to stretch themselves intellectually during this crucial time period are acquiring skills that will benefit them the rest of their lives.

Divergence—"Gap Years" Versus Gaps in Years

The invention of phenomena such as the gap year is a testament to the affluence of our society—that we can afford to have a significant chunk of our citizens remain relatively unproductive, economically, for an extended period of time. It's also a testament to the relative affluence of today's parents compared to generations past. A century ago, households depended on young people, even children, to work on farms and in factories from the day they were able to pick up a pitchfork or stand in an assembly line. Arnett, for instance, interviews in his book a twenty-three-year-old young man named Steve, who was waiting tables, still unsettled in his career but also unworried about his future. "My dad, when he was 15, moved out and basically had to find a way to support himself and eventually his family, and I'm not having to go through that," he tells Arnett. "My dad is in a position where he can help me out more than he got helped."[19]

The extension of young adulthood is, however, also widening disparities in the experiences of young adults, depending on the supports and resources at their disposal. Not everyone is as lucky as Steve. In fact, emerging adulthood, as Arnett describes it, is increasingly a preserve for the elite.

It's no surprise that young people with access to lavish parental attention are also the ones most likely to succeed in adulthood—or at the very least not allowed to fall too far. These fortunate young adults are enjoying more years of parental support, more time to get an education, build up savings, and find a job. While the longer runway to adulthood may be a boon to young adults, it's also another way for the middle and upper classes to cement their advantages over everyone else.

Even among those who skip an exotic gap year, the typical middle-class child will already have enjoyed innumerable advantages over her less-wealthy peers by the time she reaches age eighteen.

She would have been surrounded by Baby Einstein toys since infancy and listened to Mozart in the womb. By age three, as researchers Betty Hart and Todd Risley famously discovered, she would have heard 30 million more words than a child growing up in poverty, much of it in the form of encouragement and praise.[20] Studies find that middle-class babies tend to hear many more words than lower-income ones, and disparities in vocabulary between the children of highly-educated and less-educated parents appear as early as eighteen months.[21]

By kindergarten, she would likely already have been enrolled in soccer classes aimed at teaching teamwork and karate classes aimed at instilling self-discipline. Throughout her school years, her parents would have continued what sociologist Annette Lareau has called the "concerted cultivation" of children's talents and skills by middle-class parents—perhaps through chess club, piano lessons, and enriching summer camps that teach her self-reliance as well as how to waterski.[22] All of these activities will help her learn how to talk to adults and deal with authority figures constructively. She will have, as Lareau writes, a "robust sense of entitlement" and the ability to navigate institutional settings—such as school and work—to her benefit.[23]

Her advantages won't end at her high school graduation. If her parents can afford it, they'll finance her gap year if she takes one. Otherwise, her parents will kick in a lot to pay for college, which is likely to be a four-year school, where she'll live on campus. In 2017, for instance, according to Sallie Mae, parents with household incomes of more than $100,000 a year contributed three times more on average to their children's college costs than parents earning $35,000 or less—about $6,400 versus $1,600.[24] As a consequence, her student debts will make up a smaller share of her total college costs than if she'd come from a low-income family, and she will be less likely to default on her loans.[25] She will also be less likely to have to work through school. She will be more likely to graduate.[26]

After school, she can expect to make about $62,000 (the median for bachelor's degree holders) or as much as $85,000 if she majored in engineering or computer science, thereby setting herself on track to provide the same advantages she enjoyed to her own kids.[27]

In decades past, her parents might have expected to wean her from the family purse at this point—once she donned her mortarboard and picked up her diploma. But today, as an "emerging adult," the support she gets from her parents will likely continue far into her twenties and even beyond.

One 2005 study by Robert F. Schoeni and Karen E. Ross, for instance, estimated that of all the money parents spend to raise their kids, more than a fifth is now spent to support them as young adults, from ages eighteen to thirty-four. In 2001 dollars, this amounted to an average of $38,340 in financial help per young person. And among the top half of households, the average amount of help was a whopping $70,965.[28] Inflated to 2017 dollars, that's $53,979 per young person and $99,911 for the richest half.[29] A 2015 survey of young workers ages eighteen to twenty-four by the Federal Reserve also found that many young people get substantial financial support from their parents, including help with "miscellaneous bills" (30 percent), health care costs (24 percent), and car payments (24 percent).[30] Another survey, in 2018, found that more than half of Americans age twenty-one to thirty-seven have received some sort of financial help from a parent or other family member, such as help with cell phone bills, groceries and gas, or rent.[31]

Among the biggest benefits middle-class young adults are likely to get from their parents is free housing. According to the U.S. Census Bureau, as many as one in three young adults between the ages of eighteen and thirty-four and more than half of young millennials ages eighteen to twenty-four lived with their parents in 2015.[32]

During the Great Recession, moving back home took on the tinge of necessity and even desperation. The popular stereotype was of unemployed college graduates unable to find even low-level jobs while their student-loan payments were coming due. Today, however, the vast majority of young people living at home—81 percent in 2015—are actually in school or working. Moreover, more than two-thirds of these young adults at home report that they are "very happy" with their current arrangements.[33]

Living at home may in fact now be a key ingredient of the modern "emerging adulthood" experience. Home is a way to save costs while going to college. Young adults can also enjoy a much higher standard of living than they otherwise would on an entry-level salary, particularly as housing costs continue to escalate.[34] They can also accumulate savings for the day when they eventually leave the nest. And, crucially, as during the recession, home can be a safety net when things go wrong.

Parental support is also crucial to what's become another signature experience of middle- and upper-middle-class young adulthood: the internship. As the Brooking Institution's Richard Reeves ably chronicles in *Dream Hoarders*, internships have become an important career on-ramp for one-percenters in training.[35] Research finds, for instance, that college students who intern are more likely to find a full-time job when they graduate, the likely result of connections made or recommendations proffered. Students also say that internships helped guide their majors or even prompted a change in direction, thereby saving them valuable time and money in school.[36] Internships can also often serve as a pipeline to entry-level employment in elite reserves such as Capitol Hill. When I worked for a member of Congress, for instance, every new crop of interns was a talent pool for potential new staffers, and many of the legislative correspondents and staff assistants we hired were former interns. This was also the case at the *Washington Monthly*, where the first place we looked for new editors was among our former interns.

The catch is, of course, that many of these internships are either unpaid or poorly paid, which means parents must spend thousands of dollars subsidizing the chance for their children to sort through a congressman's mail or escort tourists on tours of the Capitol. One study finds that Capitol Hill interns spend an average of $6,000 for this privilege.[37] This also means, of course, that lower-income students are virtually shut out from these opportunities. Many internships are furthermore secured through parental connections or other networks, which also disproportionately favors higher-income students.

In 2018, the advocacy group Pay Our Interns successfully persuaded Congress to allocate nearly $13 million for paid internships beginning in 2019, which is an enormous first step.[38] Nevertheless, the reality is that even a paid internship is likely out of reach for many young people without some level of parental subsidy, particularly in places like Washington, D.C., or New York. In one egregiously tone-deaf and unintentionally parodic piece published by refinery29.com, a career and finance site aimed at young women, a twenty-one-year-old marketing intern chronicles the hardships of living in New York on $25 an hour, plus a $1,000 monthly allowance from her parents. (Among other things, she is reduced to eating $23 wraps to save money.) It turns out that her budget is also vastly understated—her parents also paid $2,100 for her share of the rent as well as her health insurance and her phone. In addition, she used her parents' Netflix, Spotify, and Amazon accounts (though she did manage to pay for her gym membership on her own).[39]

Another Thumb on the Scale

Internships are just one of the myriad ways in which wealthier parents perpetuate privilege for their young. As Reeves points out, there are many instances of what he calls "opportunity hoarding" by America's upper-middle class, such as through legacy college admissions, expensive tutors, and exclusive private schools.[40] He also documents yet another avenue through which better-off parents are able to gain advantages for their kids: public policy.

Exclusionary zoning ordinances, for instance, "have become important mechanisms for incorporating class divisions into urban physical geographies," Reeves writes. Not only can wealthy households build gated communities so they can live with people like themselves, they can keep out "undesirables" that could dilute their experience.

At the same time, federal tax policy—namely, the home mortgage interest deduction—generously subsidizes the ability of wealthy families to afford their expensive homes in these exclusive neighborhoods. "[W]e are using the tax system to help richer people buy bigger houses near the best schools," writes Reeves.

As the nonprofit Prosperity Now has documented, the lion's share of benefits in the federal tax code accrue to wealthy families who least need them. In 2013, for instance, $319 billion in tax incentives for savings went to the top 20 percent of earners, while a mere $91 billion went to the remaining 80 percent.[41] Among these perks are such boondoggles as 529 college savings accounts, which almost exclusively benefit affluent families. According to the Government Accountability Office, 47 percent of families with 529 accounts earned more than $150,000 a year.[42]

Even the child and dependent care tax credit, ostensibly aimed at lowering child-care costs for "working families," principally benefits upper-income earners. According to the Congressional Research Service, 35 percent of the benefits went to the top 20 percent of earners in 2014, while just 1 percent went to families in the bottom quintile.[43]

Groundbreaking research by Harvard University's Raj Chetty and colleagues finds that the American Dream of moving from rags to riches is, for the most part, just that—a dream. For the vast majority of Americans, the arc of their lives is rags to rags, or riches to riches, depending on the parents they were fortunate (or unfortunate) enough to have. According to Chetty and his colleagues, a child born to parents in the poorest fifth of Americans has just a 7.5 percent chance of rising to join the top 20 percent.[44]

Children "inherit" their future income prospects from their parents in the same way they might inherit their parents' blue eyes or curly hair. At the same time, the share of children doing better than their parents has fallen dramatically over the last half century, meaning that for many children, that inheritance is not so much a legacy but a doom. Chetty and his team find that while 90 percent of children born in 1940 ended up earning more than their parents, only 50 percent of children born in the 1980s are achieving the same.[45]

Research is beginning to dissect the determinants of this inequality. Robert Putnam, for instance, vividly describes the divergent futures of families living on opposite sides of the railroad tracks in his hometown of Clinton, Ohio, in his book *Our Kids*.[46] Chetty's work also finds strong connections between geography and economic mobility—children living in places with lower incomes, more racial segregation, poorer-quality schools, and less social capital (measured by characteristics such as the share of people who vote or belong to a church) are much less likely to move up the ladder.

So as much as childhood matters and geography matters, young adulthood matters too. And there, the disparities go beyond simply the vast differences in the amount of investment that wealthy parents can make in their young-adult children versus low-income ones. Public policy heavily favors the advancement of affluent young adults by subsidizing the ability of their parents to swaddle them in every advantage—well-funded schools, tax breaks for college, and nice homes in fancy neighborhoods.

But at the same time that government policies are making it easier for wealthy parents to support their kids to and through a productive young adulthood, they are making it harder for low-income young adults to catch up to their more affluent peers. If public policy is supporting middle-class kids, it is abandoning lower-income ones and accelerating the divergence in both young people's experiences of their transition to adulthood and their future prospects.

Public policy has yet to recognize young adulthood's importance as a turning point in the trajectory of individual lives. Rather, government is all too eager to shed its responsibilities toward vulnerable young people the day they turn eighteen, or in some cases at twenty-one, but in many instances before they're ready to be self-sufficient. Many public assistance programs, for instance, consider young people at age eighteen to be no longer part of the "family" eligible for benefits. This means an eighteen-year-old in poverty could lose Medicaid coverage in states that didn't opt to cover low-income adults under the Affordable Care Act.[47] Her parents can no longer claim her as a "dependent" for welfare benefits or public housing, and she may even need to move out to maintain her parents' eligibility for those programs.[48] She would also only qualify for three months of food stamps (now the Supplemental Nutrition Assistance Program [SNAP]), unless she had a child of her own or complied with work requirements—increasingly stringent in many states—now applicable to her.[49] Unless she is ready to succeed in college or can find a living-wage job, both iffy propositions, a young person growing up in poverty faces long odds of economic success. If she is leaving foster care or the criminal justice system, her prospects are even more dire. She might be literally pushed out into the streets the day she "ages out" or her sentence is over, and chances are good that she will end up homeless or back in jail.

This abandonment not only worsens the divergence in the individual fortunes of young people but also contributes to the widening gaps in income, wealth, and opportunity that have increasingly become a concern for policymakers. Economist Stephen Rose of the Urban Institute has found that rising inequality is not just about "the rich" getting richer but is also about the rising economic clout of the educated upper-middle class as well. Rose finds that the "upper-middle class"—whom he defines as households with annual incomes between $100,000 and $350,000—has more than doubled in size as a share of the U.S. population, from 12.9 percent of American households in 1979 to 29.4 percent in 2014. Rose also finds that the rich and upper-middle class now control 63 percent of all national income, compared to 46 percent in 1979. Meanwhile, the respective shares of national income going to the middle class, the lower-middle class, and the poor have all diminished—in the case of the lower-middle class and poor by nearly half.[50]

It's not hard to see the connection between rising inequality and the fortress of advantage that upper-middle-class parents have built for their young-adult children. The privileges affluent young adults enjoy not only cement their future standing but also insulate them from sliding too far down the economic ladder if they fall into misfortune. It's why just 8 percent of Americans born in the top quintile end up in the bottom fifth of incomes as adults.[51]

It's certainly not government's place to deprive parents of their right to bestow what advantages they can on their kids. Nor is it realistic for government policies to try to equalize the opportunities available to all young adults. But what government can do is stop sabotaging the prospects of vulnerable young adults by failing to provide the basic supports they need when they most need them. Government can also do a far better job of ensuring that more young people are better equipped to stay connected to jobs and schooling (or both) so they start off their young adulthood on a solid footing. Unfortunately, we are currently failing at both, with the result that far too many young people are disconnected from the mainstream of opportunity. This disconnection is the product not just of profound structural inequities in access to education and employment but also of deliberate policy choices that make it impossible for some of the nation's most vulnerable young people to succeed.

2

An Epidemic of Disconnection

Trevor is a twenty-six-year-old young man with liquid eyes, mahogany skin, and a soft voice that belies his solid build. On the day we met, he was about to leave for a part-time job he had just secured at a cosmetics store downtown.

Trevor is also homeless and has been on the streets of Washington, D.C., since his grandmother died four years ago. "She did everything for me," he says of her. He doesn't mention his parents. Many days, you can find him at the Latin American Youth Center (LAYC)'s drop-in center, a brightly painted row house in the Columbia Heights neighborhood of northwest D.C., about a half hour's drive from the U.S. Capitol.

Once the heart of D.C.'s black middle class, Columbia Heights was ravaged by three days of riots after Martin Luther King Jr.'s assassination in 1968 that left thirteen people dead and hundreds of businesses destroyed.[1] Photos of the period show buildings gutted by flames, broken glass in the streets, and police in gas masks using tear gas in their efforts to break up the crowds.[2] Left to its ruin for decades, the area is now enjoying a renaissance, swept up in the successive waves of gentrification that have remade D.C. over the past twenty years. There are hip new luxury condos and a Target nearby, along with infinite places for craft-brewed beer and artisanal coffee.

The LAYC, however, opened its doors in the 1970s, when

Columbia Heights was at the height of its post-riot devastation, plagued by poverty, drugs, and crime. Its aim was to be an oasis of hope for the neighborhood's young people—a mission it still pursues.

The drop-in center is one of just two places in the city where homeless young adults can find a safe place to stay during the day. Young people can get something to eat, take a shower and brush their teeth, talk to counselors, get help finding a job, and even do some laundry. The center's two sets of washers and dryers are in constant use, with sign-up sheets that are always full. On one fall day in 2017, the week before Thanksgiving, a young man was standing at the washer in the center's front room, carefully separating his clothes by color. Wafting over the smell of detergent was the aroma of a turkey roasting in the center's communal kitchen upstairs.

The center's director is John Van Zandt, a sandy-haired man in his thirties who began his career as a high school Spanish teacher in North Carolina but realized that many of his students needed much more than Spanish lessons. He says that about thirty to thirty-five young people come in every day. Most are regulars, like Trevor, but about one hundred or so every month are first-timers, newly homeless or passing through. All told, the center was serving about six hundred young people every month.

Nationally, as many as one in ten young adults ages eighteen to twenty-five—or 3.5 million young people—experience homelessness over the course of a year, according to 2017 research by Chapin Hall at the University of Chicago led by sociologist Matthew Morton.[3] They are perhaps the acutest symptom of the epidemic of "disconnection" afflicting the nation's young adults—a clear and tragic indication of just how badly the nation has abandoned its most vulnerable young people.

According to Chapin Hall's research, about half of these homeless young adults are "literally" homeless, sleeping in shelters, cars, bus stations, or wherever they can find. The other half are "couch surfing," staying with friends or family members in a merry-go-round of unstable arrangements.[4] That's why Van Zandt allows his clients to use the center as their mailing address. "We have two huge mailboxes upstairs full of mail," says Van Zandt. "Hundreds of youth use this as their permanent address—packages, checks, you name it. I'm sure the DMV is wondering why there are so many people who say they live at 3045 15th Street."

The instability of their circumstances means these young people are often vulnerable to exploitation. Nearly one-fifth of homeless young people have been victims of human trafficking; many more have resorted to "survival sex"—trading sex for food or a place to stay.[5] Some young people sell themselves on sites like Backpage .com, which was accused by federal authorities of being an online marketplace for prostitution and shut down in 2018.[6] "We'll have youth who get a call, go outside, disappear for an hour, and come back with $150," says Van Zandt. "It's clear what they're doing."

Many roads lead to this address. About 40 percent of the center's clients identify as LGBTQ and have been kicked out of their homes, says Van Zandt. "We [also] have a lot of young trans youth here," he says. Others are runaways or young parents. "Their parents tell them, 'If you're old enough to have a baby, you're old enough to be on your own,'" relates Van Zandt. Some young people have been incarcerated but were then released with no place to stay, while others are fleeing backgrounds of domestic violence or substance abuse or are aging out of foster care. Still others are what Van Zandt calls "generationally homeless," with parents who are homeless, too.

Deborah Shore, founder of Sasha Bruce YouthWorks, runs the other drop-in center for homeless young people in D.C. She has been working with homeless youth for more than thirty years and says the problems her clients face today are much more complex than they were when she first began her work. "In the early days, there were a lot of young people where with a relatively light intervention with the families and getting people to talk to one another, we were able to help young people go back home and be pretty stable," she says. "It's not so simple any more. So often, we're seeing young people where a parent has died, a parent is jailed, is mentally ill, or there's been toxicity like abuse." Many of the young people who show up at the Sasha Bruce drop-in center are pushed out of their homes the day they turn eighteen. "It's like parents are done," Shore says.

Back at the LAYC drop-in center, kitchen bags and paper sacks filled with clothes and random belongings are piled up against the walls of Van Zandt's basement office—all left with him for safe-keeping by the center's clients. Each pile is a young person's story.

"That hamper down there is a boy who's in jail," says Van Zandt, pointing to a white plastic basket filled with sweatshirts and other clothing. "So we're hanging on to his stuff till he comes back."

The Hidden Crisis of Disconnection

When you visit a place like LAYC, the desperation of young adults like Trevor is obvious and overwhelming. But to most policymakers and the public, the struggles faced by millions of young adults are still largely invisible, as is the underlying crisis of their estrangement from the mainstream of economic opportunity.

As many as 4.5 million young people between the ages of sixteen and twenty-four were neither in school nor working in 2017, according to the Social Science Research Council's Measure of America project, while millions more were in danger of becoming so.[7]

This is the crisis of "disconnection," a word that vividly describes both the economic and social isolation young people are likely to experience if they have no foothold either at work or in school. Consider the web of professional and social linkages enjoyed by people established in their communities and careers—alumni networks in both high school and college; office colleagues; spouses and partners; neighbors; fellow congregants at the church, synagogue, or mosque or fellow members at civic organizations or social clubs; the other parents at a kids' soccer game. Each of these contacts in turn has his or her own network that could become a source of further connection.

The popular concept of "six degrees of separation" (whether to actor Kevin Bacon or anyone else) shows how we intuitively understand the value of these interconnections. Scholar Mark S. Granovetter theorized its empirical worth in a famous 1973 paper distinguishing between the value of "strong" ties and "weak" ones in people's access to opportunity.[8] Granovetter's paper, titled "The Strength of Weak Ties," defines "strong" ties as close relationships such as those among family members and good friends, and "weak" ties as those such as acquaintances and friends of friends. Perhaps counterintuitively, "weak" ties are more valuable because they create bridges to opportunities outside someone's immediate circle— you are much more likely to hear about a new job opportunity from a friend of a friend than from a buddy who knows the same people you do. And if you land that job, you are ideally positioned to learn about even more opportunities in the future. "When a man changes jobs, he is not only moving from one network of ties to another, but also establishing a link between these," writes Granovetter. "Such a link is often of the same kind that facilitated his own movement."

Granovetter's insights are now conventional wisdom. It's why people go to professional conferences and happy hours to "network," and why people want to connect with you on social media sites such as LinkedIn, which even tells you how many common connections you have with someone, how distant those connections are, whether they've worked at the same employers or gone to the same schools. You might accept an invitation from someone you don't actually know if you've gone to the same schools or have the same circle of professional acquaintances, because these commonalities lead you to trust this person implicitly. It's difficult to overstate how important these networks have become, particularly as sites such as LinkedIn have formalized their value. One survey of hiring recruiters found that close to nine in ten use social media networks like LinkedIn to find candidates, while nearly four in ten said they often get their best candidates via referrals from their current employees.[9]

All of this, however, presupposes that you have an entry point into these vast networks of opportunity to begin with. This means a job in the formal economy or formal schooling through which you're earning or have earned some sort of credential with recognized value in the job market. To be connected means that you might have a boss who can vouch for your skills, colleagues who can keep you abreast of new or better opportunities, a mentor who can help you navigate through the early stages of your career, or teachers and parents who can coach you and provide advice. But if you are not in school nor working—disconnected from both principal avenues of participating in the mainstream of economic life—your world and your prospects narrow if not diminish altogether.

This disconnection, moreover, can be a permanent handicap throughout adulthood. Researchers Kristen Lewis and Rebecca Gluskin of Measure of America found that people who experience an episode of disconnection in their young adulthood earn, on average, substantially less than someone who was never disconnected, and that this wage gap is as high as $31,000 a year fifteen years later. Formerly disconnected individuals are also much less likely to be homeowners, much less likely to be employed, and significantly more likely to be in poorer health than people who stayed connected to school or work throughout their young-adult years.[10] As one consequence, people who were disconnected as young adults are also much more likely to be dependent on public programs than to be self-sufficient, at great cost to the public purse.

Despite the economic, social, and fiscal significance of young-adult disconnection and its linkages to poverty and inequality, recognition of this phenomenon is still fairly recent. For instance, there's still actually very little data about the fates and fortunes of America's young people as a distinct group in need of particular attention from public policy.

The Census Bureau's poverty statistics, for instance, dissect the extent of poverty by race, gender, age, and education and various combinations thereof. But while it publishes separate figures on poverty rates among children under eighteen and seniors sixty-five and over, its principal analyses don't specifically consider young adults. Rather, young people are swept into the broad category of adults aged eighteen to sixty-four, despite the fact that young adults have little in common economically with older adults in the prime of their careers.[11] Young adults are not yet a recognized subpopulation worthy of separate analysis.

There is also no official measure or definition of "disconnection," despite the liberal use of this term throughout this book—at least not in the United States. As in other realms of social policy, America is lagging the rest of the world with its inattention to struggling young adults. Both the Organisation for Economic Co-operation and Development (OECD) and the International Labor Organization (ILO), for example, track youth who are so-called NEETs ("not in employment, education, or training"), and in 2013, the ILO issued a report warning of a global crisis in youth unemployment (more on this later).[12] The U.S. Census Bureau, however, does not formally keep track of young people not in school or not working, nor does the Bureau of Labor Statistics.[13]

Here in the United States, the leading research organization tracking youth disconnection is the Social Science Research Council's Measure of America project, whose work I've already cited extensively. Lead researcher Kristen Lewis says the paucity of available data was, in fact, what prompted her interest in this topic a little more than a decade ago. "At the beginning, we were surprised the data weren't out there," she says.

The Many Faces of Disconnection

What we do know about young people who are disconnected is that they face major disadvantages compared to their "connected" peers who are in school or working.

Trevor's story, for instance, is a microcosm of the challenges that many disconnected young people face. He had once enrolled in the University of the District of Columbia but dropped out after a semester. "I wasn't psychologically ready," he says. Over the past several years, he's also been battling an alcohol addiction, brought on by grief over his grandmother's death. Though sober and now working, he has no family and no place to call home. While he spends his days at LAYC, he spends his nights at Casa Ruby, a nearby homeless shelter for LGBT youth. His part-time retail job won't pay him nearly enough to afford an apartment in D.C.

But while Trevor's story is common, it is not necessarily typical. Despite some commonalities, disconnected youth are a perhaps surprisingly diverse group. Among the findings from Measure of America's research:

Young people in rural areas are more likely to be
disconnected than young people in cities.
While the number of disconnected young adults in cities is greater, due to sheer population density, the prevalence of disconnection is higher in rural areas than in urban ones. Nearly one in five young people living in rural areas was neither in school nor working in 2017 versus about one in six young adults in urban centers (18.7 percent versus 12.3 percent). In some rural counties, the rate of disconnection was as high as 75 percent (more on this in chapter 5). The lowest rates of disconnection were in the suburbs.

Where you live really matters.
Measure of America's Sarah Burd-Sharps and Kristen Lewis found that rates of disconnection vary enormously from city to city and from state to state—which is yet another indication that structural factors might play the biggest role in whether a young person gets connected to opportunities or not. Among the biggest metro areas, for example, the disconnection rate ranged from a low of 5.6 percent in Grand Rapids, Michigan, to a high of 18.0 percent in Memphis, Tennessee.[14] By and large, young people living in the South were more likely to be out of school and out of work than their peers in other parts of the country.

Disconnected young people are handicapped by
poverty, disability, and lack of education.
Disconnected young people are twice as likely to live in poverty and three times as likely to have a disability than their connected peers. In 2017, 33.8 percent of disconnected youth lived below the poverty line, compared to 12.3 percent for the population as a whole.[15] More than one in four (27.1 percent) also have less than a high school education, and only 8.5 percent have a college degree.

By comparison, 88 percent of Americans are at least high school educated, and 33 percent have a bachelor's degree or more.[16]

African American young people are twice as likely to
be out of school and out of work than whites are.
In 2017, 17.9 percent of black youth were out of school and out of work, compared to 9.4 percent of whites. Latinos fell in between, with a 13.2 percent rate of disconnection in 2017, while Asians fared the best at 6.6 percent. The highest rate of disconnection, however, was among Native Americans, of whom nearly a quarter—23.9 percent—were out of school and out of work.

Disconnected young women are often young moms.
Young men were somewhat more likely to be disconnected than young women (11.8 percent versus 11.1 percent, respectively). Disconnected young women, however, were disproportionately likely to be moms, compared to their connected sisters. Measure of America found that more than one in four disconnected young women—26.7 percent—were also mothers in 2017, compared to only 6.3 percent of connected young women ages sixteen to twenty-four. The high rates of parenthood imply that unplanned pregnancy might be a leading cause of disconnection for young women (more on this in chapter 7). Parenthood, in turn, perpetuates disconnection if there's insufficient access to child care or jobs that allow a young mom to balance both her family and work obligations.

Disconnected young people are less likely
to have parental support.
A hallmark of disconnected young people is that they often don't have parents or family to fall back on or to support them through their transition to independence, as so many wealthier young people do. They are, for instance, much less likely to live with their parents than are their connected peers. Measure of America finds that nearly a quarter of disconnected teens as young as sixteen and seventeen don't live at home with their parents. Instead, many disconnected young people—as is the case with Trevor—are

homeless, and a troublingly large share of them are institutionalized. Among disconnected black men and boys, for example, nearly
as many as one in five were in prison, detention, a mental health
facility, or a group home in 2017.[17]

How the Threads of Connection Get Severed

How is it that so many young people arrive at adulthood without a
clear path to a job or to higher education?

The next part of this book attempts to explain how, with a focus
on the systemic failures that either lead young people off track or
fail to provide an on-ramp back to opportunity. In particular, I look
at the principal ways that could lead a young person to disconnection: (1) by growing up in a rural or urban "opportunity desert"
where access to both jobs and higher education is sparse; (2) by
missing out on early opportunities for work and career exploration;
(3) by growing up in foster care; and (4) by becoming involved in
the criminal justice system.

In each instance, policy failures push young people away from
opportunities and toward disengagement. The foster care and criminal justice systems, for instance, both fail miserably in their efforts
to transition young people out of their systems and into independence. Meanwhile, a surprisingly large number of Americans live
in areas with no college or community college within ready com-
muting distance and no broadband internet. Others are trapped in
highly segregated neighborhoods with few jobs and no infrastructure to get to where jobs are available. Many high schools fail to
prepare young people for the world of work and its demands—a
failure that's compounded by the disappearance of summer jobs
and work experience for teens. Teen and young-adult unemployment is in fact at crisis levels globally, including in the United
States, with major potential implications both economically and
socially. Compounding all of these problems is unplanned parenthood. Despite enormous progress on teen pregnancy rates, public
policies still don't do enough to help young women avoid getting
pregnant before they are ready to support a family. As we learned

in this chapter, early motherhood is highly correlated to the likelihood of disconnection from school and work.

Each of these challenges, however, is solvable. Even if we cannot commit as a nation to investing in each young person to the level he or she deserves, we can at least stop public policy from sabotaging their lives.

PART II

Drifting:
Avenues to Disconnection

3

Marooned: Place and Opportunity

Hop on the internet, and you can virtually visit anywhere in the world at any time. From the comfort of your desk, you can tour the great museums of Florence, trek the Amazon, or follow the Instagram journeys of hipsters leading the #vanlife from a vintage Volkswagen minibus. Google Earth will take you into space. And you can do it all inside of five minutes.

Because the virtual world has no geographic boundaries, it's easy to believe that the real world too presents an equivalently generous bounty of possibilities. For young people with the right resources, that may be right. In truth, the scope of a young person's opportunities and aspirations is often defined by the physical constraints of where they live.

At the foothills of the Appalachian Mountains in northwestern Pennsylvania is the Allegheny National Forest, a pristine reserve of more than 500,000 acres of hardwood forest.[1] With its stands of four-hundred-year-old white pines, hidden waterfalls, and two wild scenic rivers winding through miles of unbroken greenery, the forest offers a tantalizing glimpse of a bygone America, before superhighways, rush hour, and the internet.

But as idyllic as this corner of the country seems to be, many of its towns are dying.

The vastness of the Allegheny National Forest covers four

counties, including Forest and Warren Counties in the southern half of the forest. Forest County, according to the Census Bureau, had roughly 7,300 people in 2017, down about 500 since the 2010 Census.[2] Nearly a quarter of households live in poverty, and only 8 percent of residents have bachelor's degrees (compared to 33 percent nationally).[3] Warren County has more people—nearly 40,000 in 2017—but it too has lost about 5 percent of its population since 2010.

"Everything is bright green here, and it's definitely a beautiful area to live in," says lifelong resident Tesla Rae Moore, who lives in the borough of Kane, nestled at the edge of the forest. "But it's very rural. There's not a lot." Even the Walmart, says Moore, is a forty-five-minute drive. "The biggest thing we have is a Dollar General, and that was a huge thing to have come here," she comments.

Despite their beauty, places like Kane and Forest County are hard to be in if you're a young adult. For one thing, jobs are scarce. Moore, a single mom in her late twenties with two young children, commutes about forty miles each way to her job at Northwest Bank in the town of Warren. The biggest local employers are the state prison in Marienville, which houses roughly 2,400 inmates, and a juvenile detention center.[4]

According to the Social Science Research Council's Measure of America project, 72.9 percent of the young people in Forest County ages sixteen to twenty-four were "disconnected" in 2017—that is, they were not in school, nor were they working.[5] In fact, Forest County is the second-most disconnected county in America, just ahead of East Carroll Parish, Louisiana, where the youth disconnection rate is 75.1 percent. But just about every rural county in America has a youth disconnection rate in the double digits—a national epidemic of disconnection that is yet another symptom of the growing divide between the places racing ahead and the places falling behind, and the diverging fortunes of the young people in these areas.

Throughout the second half of the nineteenth century, northwestern Pennsylvania was dotted by logging boomtowns, while the state's vast forests fed the nation's growing appetite for lumber

FIGURE 3.1: Ten Most Disconnected Counties, 2017

State	County	Youth Disconnection Rate (%)	County Classification
Louisiana	East Carroll Parish	75.1	rural
Pennsylvania	Forest County	72.9*	rural
Georgia	Hancock County	71.0*	town
Georgia	Stewart County	70.2*	rural
Texas	Childress County	59.5*	rural
Texas	Madison County	57.5	rural
Arkansas	Lincoln County	56.6	small city
Georgia	Wheeler County	56.3	rural
Florida	Hamilton County	55.3	rural
Mississippi	Tallahatchie County	54.0	rural

Measure of America, Social Science Research Council. Custom tabulations from US Census Bureau American Community Survey, 2013–2017. *Asterisk denotes counties with a youth population under 1,000. Note that all of these counties have relatively small overall populations as well.*

through the Industrial Revolution. By the 1920s, however, the forests were almost entirely gone, and photos from the era show immense clear-cut patches of naked land.[6] The forests have since returned, after decades of conservation and restoration efforts, and the state is once again the nation's top producer of hardwood lumber, producing 1 billion board feet of lumber every year, according to Pennsylvania State University.[7]

The logging industry has not, however, been a boon for the young people of Forest County. While all this wood creates thousands of jobs in the cities where it's ultimately destined, logging itself employs surprisingly few people. That's because, as with farming and so much else with today's economy, machines are doing the work. The U.S. Bureau of Labor Statistics (BLS) reports that there were just 55,300 logging workers in the entire country in 2016, the vast majority of whom are logging equipment operators.[8] The BLS projects that Pennsylvania will employ 800 logging equipment operators through 2026, as well as about 150 "graders," people whose job it is to inspect and measure the logs harvested. Logging is difficult and dangerous—the BLS reports "a high rate of fatal occupational injuries," most of them happening "through contact with a machine or an object, such as a log." It's also not highly paid—logging workers made a median salary of $38,830 in 2017—and it's not year-round work.

As a consequence, many young people end up leaving Forest County to seek their fortunes elsewhere. Those who succeed stay away. "The ones with the four-year degrees rarely come back," says Amanda Hetrick, who is superintendent of the Forest County school district, a tiny district with just 450 students spread out over more than 400 square miles. Most, however, do return. "About 60 percent of our students who go off to college come back home without a degree," says Hetrick. Many, she remarks, are first-generation students for whom life at college comes as a shock. "A lot of our students are uncomfortable in those kinds of settings," she says. "They're exposed to things they haven't seen before—the drug abuse, the music, the clothing. They feel a little backward."

These young people resort to doing what they can to survive. "They end up with two or three part-time jobs, maybe the gas station two days a week, at the Subway, the hardware store," says Hetrick. "They piece together a living, but there are very few options as far as full-time jobs."

"Superstar Cities" Versus Everywhere Else

Scholarly attention has increasingly focused on "regional inequality"—the vast and seemingly worsening differences in people's income, wealth, and well-being depending on where they live. These disparities have drawn an even brighter spotlight since the 2016 election, when the election of President Donald Trump exposed the anxieties of the rural white working class and the ugly racial, cultural, and social divisions that have been brewing under the surface of our politics.

In his 2008 book of the same name, journalist Bill Bishop

popularized the phrase "the big sort" to describe Americans' increasing preference for living with people just like them.[9] Bishop's work primarily focuses on the growing cultural and political homogeneity of communities and the polarization that has resulted—a phenomenon that gerrymandering has fully exploited. Now research shows that this clustering extends to economic factors as well. Not only are Americans increasingly surrounding themselves with people who think like them, they are choosing neighbors—and spouses—with the same education, income, and wealth. Moreover, this sorting out is happening at both the institutional and individual levels. Universities, businesses, schools, and other infrastructure are also increasingly clustered in particular parts of the country, namely in big cities and on the coasts, while large swathes of the nation remain relatively deprived.

Scholars such as Joseph Gyourko, Christopher Mayer, Todd Sinai, and Richard Florida, for instance, have noted the rise of so-called superstar cities, where the nation's wealth and brainpower are becoming increasingly concentrated. These places, writes Florida, "generate the greatest levels of innovation, control and attract the largest shares of global capital and investment, have huge concentrations of leading-edge finance, media, entertainment, and tech industries, and are home to a disproportionate share of the world's talent. They are not just the places where the most ambitious and most talented people want to be—they are where such people feel they need to be."[10] These places are where corporations feel they need to be too, which also only reinforces the commanding advantages superstar metro areas are amassing for themselves. One obvious recent example is Amazon, which after months of deliberation decided to split its second headquarters between Crystal City, Virginia, just outside Washington, D.C., and Long Island City, New York (that is, before local opposition in New York prompted Amazon to pull out of its planned Long Island beachhead). In its official bid for Amazon "HQ2," Virginia promised the company would be "globally connected and surrounded by top talent, tremendous infrastructure, and a spectacular quality of life," as well as one of the best-educated populations in the country.[11]

FIGURE 3.2: Youth Disconnection Rates by County

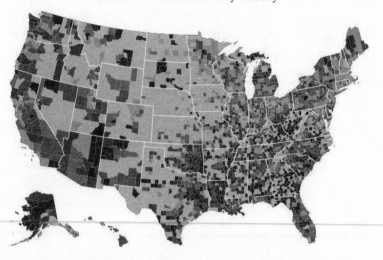

Measure of America, http://www.measureofamerica.org/Dyinteractive.

FIGURE 3.3: Distressed Communities Index by County

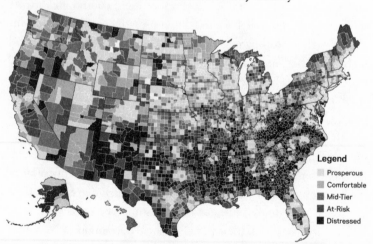

Economic Innovation Group, Distressed Communities Index,
https://eig.org/dci/2018-dci-map-national-counties-map.

FIGURE 3.4: Social Capital Index by County

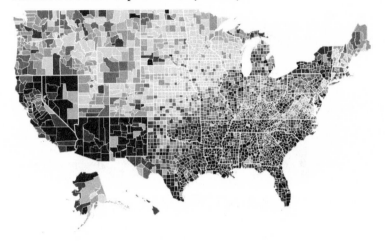

Social Capital Project, https://www.lee.senate
.gov/public/index.cfm/scp-index.

Several recent efforts have mapped this unequal distribution of economic prosperity, as well as the components correlated with these worsening geographical disparities. The Economic Innovation Group, for instance, has created a Distressed Communities Index, which rates communities based on such factors as the share of the population without a high school diploma, workforce participation, poverty rates, job growth, and median income.[12] The Social Capital Project, sponsored by Sen. Mike Lee (R-Utah), maps communities by social and demographic indicators such as the rate of unwed childbearing and marriage, along with civic engagement measures such as churchgoing, volunteering, and voting.[13] A third initiative, the Equality of Opportunity Project, spearheaded by Harvard University's Raj Chetty, charts intergenerational mobility—the likelihood that a child will do better than his or her parents.

Each of the maps generated by these efforts is strikingly similar; scramble the labels and you might not be able to tell which is which. What's also striking is the high correlation between rates of youth disconnection (as reported by Measure of America) and the places where the ingredients of opportunity are most lacking.

Take, for instance, the southern parts of the country that show up as dark gray or black on Figures 3.2, 3.3, and 3.4. These are the places, according to Measure of America, where the rates of youth disconnection are the highest. These are also the places, according to the Social Capital Project, where rates of unwed childbearing are high and of civic participation are low. They are also where, according to the Distressed Communities Index, the residents are more likely to be living in poverty or working low-wage jobs, if they are working at all. Not surprisingly, young people also face the greatest difficulties in connecting to education and employment because the pipelines to opportunity simply aren't there. Chetty's research finds that these same parts of the country are where the odds of downward mobility are the highest. Chetty finds, for instance, that in large swathes of the South, including in cities such as Charlotte, North Carolina, and Atlanta, Georgia, the average young man with parents earning $25,000 or less is unlikely to out-earn his parents.[14]

Another striking similarity among all the maps is the prevalence of distress throughout the country. One in six Americans lives in a distressed community as measured by EIG, for instance, while the Social Capital Index finds that just 9 percent of Americans live in the top fifth of states with the highest social capital.[15] What this indicates is that the constriction of avenues open to young people is only a symptom of a broader malaise afflicting the state of opportunity in America.

In both rural and urban areas, young people are trapped in places where jobs are scarce, social capital is low, and access to the means for getting ahead is limited. While each place has its own story, a recurring thread is that of economic disruption, coupled with a paucity of resources to generate new avenues for mobility. In many places, there's yet another layer—of segregation and structural racism—that further stifles young people's options.

A Rural Opportunity Desert

In the hamlet of South Boston, in rural southwestern Virginia, you'll find Sweet Cee's Gifts and Kids' Consignment, an airy boutique owned by Candace Baskervill right on Main Street, across from the town hall. On a warm spring afternoon, Baskervill, an energetic blonde in her thirties, has left the double doors of her shop wide open and put out a sandwich board advertising her current sales. Inside are a couple racks of like-new children's clothing, a table of handmade soaps, and a shelf display of aprons silkscreened with the town's logo. Baskervill makes these aprons herself; she started a business silk-screening T-shirts at her house before opening the store downtown. She still makes all the T-shirts for South Boston's baseball, soccer, and other sports teams. There's plenty of traffic whizzing by on Main Street—it's also State Route 501 and the principal thoroughfare through town—but no one on the sidewalks. When I buy one of her handmade lavender soaps for $12, she tells me it's the only sale she's made that day. "Last week over three days I did $6," she says.

Baskervill opened Sweet Cee's in 2017, after winning a $10,000 grant from the town as part of a "Shark Tank"–style competition for would-be entrepreneurs to help revitalize South Boston's downtown.[16] When we speak in the spring of 2018, however, she is funding her business out of savings. "I want to be optimistic, but there are some days when I say, 'Lord, let me make it to one year,'" she says.

It wasn't always this way in South Boston. As recently as twenty years ago, the town was a thriving blue-collar, middle-class community, with a nearby Burlington Industries textile plant and a Russell Stover candy factory.[17] Tobacco was a mainstay too—South Boston was a hub for buyers and growers and the inaugural site of the National Tobacco Festival, a three-day celebration that drew thousands of visitors in its heyday.[18] "There were plenty of jobs, and people were working," says Debra Crowder, who grew up in a neighboring town and now runs the local Workforce Investment Board. "We used to come to South Boston to shop because it was the bigger town. It had dress shops and shoe stores, and every storefront was full with retail business."

Then the plants started shutting down. The Russell Stover factory closed in 2002, the same year textile manufacturer Burlington

Industries went bankrupt and closed its facility. Textile maker JP Stevens shuttered its South Boston plant shortly thereafter. Meanwhile, the region's once prosperous tobacco farmers found themselves in losing fights against both China's burgeoning tobacco industry and the U.S. government's efforts to reduce smoking. Over just a four-year period, estimates current town manager Tom Raab, South Boston lost maybe $100 million in payroll. "Why we're still here I don't know," Raab says.

For the area's young people, the town's collapse was a double gut punch. Not only were they seeing their parents lose their jobs, but their own path to a job out of school was suddenly cut short as well. "It changed kids' quality of life when their parents had to cut way back," says Crowder. "A lot of the workers went back and got retrained for something else, but they never overcame the difference in pay."

Raab and other local leaders have been working hard to reinvent and revitalize South Boston, such as through the entrepreneurship grants competition Baskervill won. The town has also won grants from the Virginia Tobacco Region Revitalization Commission, which was created in 1998 to disburse the state's share of the $200 billion nationwide settlement between attorneys general and the country's largest tobacco companies.[19] Most recently, it became a state-designated "Opportunity Zone" under the federal tax legislation passed in 2017, making it eligible for tax-preferred investments.[20] Among the town's projects is the renovation of a downtown motel, which has stood empty for twenty years. You can still see a vertical neon sign reading "Motor Inn." "It'll have a good restaurant and a rooftop bar, and the view from up there is unbelievable," says Raab. He's also hoping developers will tackle some of the vast empty tobacco warehouses that dot downtown and convert them into retail space or loft apartments, some of which is already happening. Tourism is part of the town's new strategy, but Raab is flexible. "We would like good-paying jobs, but we're not always going to get those," he says. "We're open to anything and everything. We're not going to turn down anybody that wants to bring some jobs."

South Boston's young people, however, may not be willing to wait for that revival.

"Most of them want to get away fast," says one high school counselor who works in South Boston. "The ones that do stay, they're still working to get away, maybe to Richmond, Greensboro—not necessarily far, but a city with more opportunities." Since 2010, according to the Census Bureau, South Boston has lost 5.9 percent of its population, as has Halifax County, where it's located.[21] "There are not that many jobs for young professionals," says store owner Baskervill, who was twenty-nine when her husband got the teaching job that brought her to South Boston. "I have degrees in human resources and business, and I would never in a million years [have] thought I would be running a kids' consignment and gift store. You have to take your young professional label and tweak it."

Among the better places to work is Berry Hill, a nearby former plantation turned conference center whose history mirrors the boom, bust, and ongoing reinvention of South Boston itself. Handed down through generations of prominent Virginia families, including founding father and Virginia governor Benjamin Harrison (whose descendants include Presidents William Henry Harrison and Benjamin Harrison), the property became a corporate retreat center for the global insurance and financial services company AXA in the 1990s, according to local officials. Executives visited from around the world. AXA, however, was among the principal insurers of the World Trade Center, destroyed during the September 11 attacks in 2001.[22] The company and its subsidiaries reportedly lost more than €650 million on claims and ultimately ended up selling Berry Hill.[23] The property has changed hands several times since then and was the site of the short-lived for-profit Founders College, which the *Chronicle of Higher Education* described as "a sort of Great Books college for devotees of Ayn Rand."[24] Locals called it "Floundering College." Today, it's once again a resort. With its majestic tree-lined avenue and white-columned plantation house that evokes *Gone with the Wind*'s Tara, it's a favored wedding venue for area couples. During the week, however, it's quiet. When I was there, the spa was closed, and the restaurant had limited hours. My gigantic room, with a four-poster bed and spectacular views of the property's 650 acres, cost $119—or less than what you'd spend for a Holiday Inn near a big-city airport with nothing but views of tarmac.

Two young men were manning the front desk on my visit. One was taking a break from classes at Danville Community College, about half an hour away; the other was home for a semester from college in Oregon. Both of them told me they couldn't wait to leave the area, once they'd saved up enough money.

Higher Education Deserts

A lack of good jobs is not the only reason young people are leaving South Boston. Until very recently (see chapter 13), the town had no options for post-secondary education. Aside from Danville Community College, the only four-year public institution in the region was Longwood University, about sixty miles away.

So long as the town's manufacturing and agricultural economy stayed strong, the relative lack of college options wasn't crippling. The textile mills hired generations of workers straight out of high school, and people made great wages. Today, however, things are different.

For one thing, the lack of a skilled workforce makes it harder for town officials like Raab to attract new businesses. While 80 percent of South Boston has a high school diploma, only about a fifth has a bachelor's degree or more. In Halifax County more broadly, just 16 percent of residents have a four-year degree—half the rate of the nation as a whole.[25]

South Boston is not alone in its lack of options for higher education. In fact, according to the Urban Institute, nearly one in five American adults—as many as 41 million people—live twenty-five miles or more from the nearest college or university, or in areas where a single community college is the only source of broad-access public higher education within that distance.[26] Three million of these Americans, say scholars Victoria Rosenboom and Kristin Blagg, lack broadband internet in addition to physical proximity to a higher education institution.[27]

Living in a higher education desert is one reason rural students are less likely to go to college than their urban and suburban peers and less likely to earn a degree. In 2016, for instance, 61 percent of rural public school seniors went on to college the following year, according to the National Student Clearinghouse, compared to 67 percent for suburban students.[28] And while the share of young adults between the ages of twenty-five and thirty-four with bachelor's degrees has grown to 38 percent in urban areas, only 20 percent of rural young adults have four-year degrees, says the USDA's Economic Research Service.[29]

Lower educational attainment is one reason why rural areas often face higher unemployment, greater poverty, and lower wages than the college-rich metro areas now benefiting the most from the nation's recent prosperity.[30] Fully 50 percent of adults in the nation's top 10 percent of zip codes have a bachelor's degree or better, according to the Economic Innovation Group, compared to just 13 percent in the bottom decile.[31] And while 66 percent of the richest zip codes are urban or suburban, 72 percent of the poorest zip codes are rural.

One county over from South Boston, Mecklenburg County superintendent Paul Nichols is trying to change these trends. Nichols is a native of the area who spent his summers as a teenager working in the tobacco fields. "You pull tobacco all day for $20," he says. "But I earned enough in two years to buy my first car—a used Ford Pinto for $1,200 in 1974." After several decades working in higher education and the nonprofit and private sectors in North Carolina and Virginia, Nichols wants to bring more opportunities to the roughly 4,000 students in his district, about three-fourths of whom, he says, qualify for free or reduced lunch.

Nichols has big plans. Since arriving in 2015, he's reorganized the district's curriculum into six different "career clusters," such as STEM, advanced technology, law and leadership, and international business, that students start exploring as early as elementary school. "We're not trying to determine when a child is fourteen years old what they're going to do with the rest of their life, but we do want them to get a sense of long-term planning and completing their goals," he says. Nichols has also commissioned proprietary software so that each student has a "digital backpack" that keeps track of how the classes they're taking match up with the various career clusters and their own career plans as they develop. "Our goal is to have a 'career GPS' for each student," says Nichols.

Lately, a lot of students have been interested in computers and IT, in part because of a new Microsoft data center near Boydton, a tiny town of about four hundred that is also the county seat.[32] The data center is a complex of gigantic, windowless concrete bunkers in the middle of nowhere, surrounded by razor wire. When we drove out to take a look in Nichols's truck in the spring of 2018, it was also undergoing expansion—bulldozers had dug out a giant pit, where more concrete buildings housing thousands of servers would eventually stand.

As part of its presence here, Microsoft gave the district a grant under its Technology Education and Literacy in Schools (TEALS) initiative to launch Advanced Placement computer science classes in its two high schools.[33] One of these classes was in session at Bluestone High, where about two dozen students were studying to earn their Microsoft Word certification in a couple weeks. A few students, taking advantage of the distraction afforded by visitors, were stealthily playing video games on the computers at their desks. "A majority of these students are ninth graders," says their teacher, Amanda Bowen, who also grew up in the area. "They get certified in Word and PowerPoint in one semester, and it's a national certification—adults take it." The students are also getting college credit for their work and could potentially graduate with an associate's degree in computer science under the school's dual-enrollment program to give students a head start on college.

Nichols is, however, up against some obstacles in his quest for reform. The first is funding. Like so many rural counties, Mecklenburg County is shrinking, and the local tax rate is already low—half the state average, according to Nichols. As part of his plans, Nichols wants to consolidate the two high schools to save money, which will require a bond issue to raise the funds. Nichols can barely afford to maintain his schools as they are. Second, changing attitudes around college attendance is slow going. Although the majority of his students now make plans for post-secondary education, only about 30 percent of graduates are headed to four-year schools, Nichols says. Moreover, many of his students are battling the challenges that come with poverty and rural isolation. Gangs, for instance, are a surprisingly persistent problem. Nichols says he shut down the basketball program at Parkview High School for a year after the players got into a fight with another team. In 2017–18, he's canceled both football and basketball games. "In one basketball game, we had to have only the players play and no spectators because of threats related to gang activity outside of school," Nichols says. "It comes with poverty and when parents get engaged with drugs and families break up and kids are looking for something to belong to."

But the biggest obstacle Nichols is up against might be the local economy and whether there will be jobs for his students to go to after they graduate. Despite the benefits the Boydton data center will bring, its impact as an employer is unlikely to match the factories that were once the mainstay of the area. "It's a boon to the area just in taxes, and I do know some people who work there," says the local Workforce Investment Board's Debra Crowder. "They do hire local people—it's just not a huge number."

4

An Urban Opportunity Desert

In places like South Boston, Virginia, and Forest County, Pennsylvania, the physical isolation of residents is more obvious, and it's easy to see how young people can end up literally distanced from schools, jobs, and opportunity.

But opportunity deserts aren't limited to rural areas. Like the proverbial sailor marooned in the ocean, surrounded by water but with not a drop to drink, many young people are trapped in urban opportunity deserts, even in the "superstar cities" noted in the previous chapter, surrounded by a plethora of opportunities but with no means to access them. Here, the separation is less about physical distance and long miles to travel than it is about the economic and social isolation that come with high poverty, poor schools, and stagnant job prospects.

Consider, for instance, Baltimore, Maryland, a city that despite its gritty reputation is in the midst of a long-running—but uneven—economic revival that is leaving many of its most vulnerable young people behind even as it has become a growing hub of economic growth.

By many measures, Baltimore is prospering, home to world-renowned Johns Hopkins University as well as to such major corporate employers as Walmart, Northrup Grumman, and sportswear juggernaut Under Armour.[1] The Baltimore metro area accounts for 50 percent of the state's total economic output, according to city economic development officials, and its unemployment rate in early 2019 was among the lowest in the country for cities of its size. As of the end of 2018, sales-tax revenues were rising, as were home values—the average home in the Baltimore area cost $358,196 in the third quarter of 2018, compared to the national average of $298,000.[2]

Yet in the midst of this prosperity and optimism is the community of Sandtown—whose residents' plight is an open rebuke to city boosters' claims of Baltimore as a "premiere place to live, work and play."[3]

Formally known as Sandtown-Winchester/Harlem Heights, Sandtown is a roughly seventy-two-block neighborhood in West Baltimore that might be best known as the home of twenty-five-year-old Freddie Gray, whose death at the hands of six Baltimore police officers unleashed a wave of unrest in the city and drew national attention to the problem of police brutality.[4]

Once, it was a mecca for the city's black middle class. In the 1950s and 1960s, reports the *New York Times*, Sandtown was known as "Baltimore's Harlem" and hosted such luminary performers as Billie Holiday and Diana Ross.[5] The late Supreme Court justice Thurgood Marshall hailed from this neighborhood, as did jazz great Cab Calloway, NAACP leader Kweisi Mfume, and Clarence H. Du Burns, the city's first black mayor. All of them were graduates of the neighborhood's Frederick Douglass High School.[6]

Like the Columbia Heights neighborhood in Washington, D.C., Sandtown's decline was precipitated by the riots that consumed the city in 1968, leaving six dead, seven hundred injured, and more than one thousand businesses destroyed.[7] Unlike Columbia Heights, there has been no revitalization here since. If anything, the deterioration has only continued. In 2013, according to a Johns Hopkins University analysis, three out of five residents over age sixteen were unemployed, nearly a third of the houses were vacant, and the incarceration rate among residents was the highest in the city.[8] A 2017 study of the neighborhood by the Baltimore City Health Department piles on even bleaker numbers. About 87 percent of the neighborhood's children were living in single-parent households, and median household income was a scant $24,374 in 2017, compared to the city-wide median of $41,819.[9] Fully 50 percent of households were living in poverty. The number of liquor and tobacco stores per 1,000 residents was also about double what it was in the rest of the city, and 60 percent of the neighborhood was considered a "food desert," without ready access to a supermarket. The area had double the number of rat complaints as the rest of Baltimore and more than triple the rate of lead-paint violations. Just 5.5 percent of neighborhood residents had a bachelor's degree, compared to 29 percent for the city as a whole, and only 44 percent of eighth graders tested as "proficient" in reading, while nearly half of high school seniors missed more than twenty days of school a year. Sandtown was also one of the deadliest places in the state, if not the country. Violence was one reason—the homicide rate was more than double the rate city-wide—but residents also suffered from higher rates of heart disease, cancer, and drug or alcohol–related deaths than other Baltimore residents. Life expectancy was just 70, compared to 73.6 for Baltimore City and 78.6 nationally.[10]

Drive down Lafayette Avenue, and you'll see block after block of abandoned, boarded-up rowhouses and an occasional bodega or takeout place fortified by metal grates. Knots of men sit on stoops or stand on corners, though it's noon in the middle of the week. You'll also see on Lafayette Avenue a large faded brick building that houses Youth Opportunities (YO) Baltimore, one of the neighborhood's few bulwarks against the poverty and isolation here.

In 2000, YO Baltimore was one of thirty-six sites funded under the U.S. Department of Labor's Youth Opportunity Initiative, part of the federal government's episodic efforts to reconnect out of school and out of work young people to education and jobs.[11] Over five years, Baltimore received $43 million in federal money to set up five "youth opportunity community centers" offering comprehensive services such as mentoring, job-readiness training, internships and subsidized jobs, GED preparation, and skills training. The results were good—the Baltimore program reached more than 4,300 young people, filled more than 2,000 jobs, and helped more than 1,600 participants earn a GED, high school diploma, or other credential. In addition, female participants were 25 percent less likely to have a child than a comparison group, and participants eighteen and over experienced one-third fewer arrests.[12]

The Department of Labor did not, however, continue the initiative after those first five years. Today, Baltimore is down to two YO centers from five and is wholly funded by the city. The Westside center—the one on Lafayette Avenue—has a budget of $2 million and is still trying to do what it did before but on a fraction of the budget, something that program manager Kerry Owings concedes is difficult.

"You make sure you manage your resources as best as you can," he says.

For example, the program can't afford to provide as much help with transportation as it did before, so that young people can get to their internships, jobs, or even to the YO Baltimore center. Transportation is, in fact, one of the biggest barriers for young people in the area. Because there are few good jobs in the neighborhood, young people must commute to other parts of the city to work. Few people, however, can afford cars, and public transit is unreliable, expensive, and slow. Back in the days of the grant, the program provided all participants with bus fare; today they only have a limited number of tokens to hand out in emergencies. One thing the center still manages to do is set aside a little money every year for a field trip to Six Flags. "At the end of the summer, we do a Six Flags trip for everybody who meets a certain attendance level," says Owings. "We take them there for a day. We can even give them a meal voucher."

The center—with all of its diminished resources—is not only trying to help its clients tackle such day-to-day challenges as affording bus fare; it's also trying to overcome a lifetime of accumulated disadvantages resulting from poverty, the lack of good jobs, struggling schools, and persistent segregation. It's a challenge that others—with much greater resources—have tried to overcome and failed. In the 1990s, James Rouse, founder of the Enterprise Foundation, raised $130 million to invest in a comprehensive strategy aimed at turning around Sandtown with affordable housing,

education reform, and job training. The Sandtown-Winchester
Neighborhood Transformation Initiative (NTI) became, at the
time, one of the nation's most ambitious and most-watched revitalization efforts.[13] Former president Jimmy Carter, for instance,
announced a pledge on behalf of Habitat for Humanity to renovate
one hundred vacant homes, while the Rockefeller Foundation, the
Surdna Foundation, and an assortment of nonprofits carried out
innovative efforts in school reform and job creation. Twenty years
later, researchers Peter Rosenblatt and Stefanie DeLuca concluded
that "[i]n the long-term, the NTI had no impact on neighborhood
poverty" and that "local schools did not show sustained improvement."[14] Despite the massive investment of money, hard work, and
good intentions, the project could not overcome the broader coun-
tervailing forces at play. "In the period during and following the
NTI, Sandtown was plagued by active drug markets and the violent crime that comes with them," wrote Rosenblatt and DeLuca.
"Baltimore's economy did not become more hospitable for workers with less than a college degree, making it difficult for any of
the residents to secure long-term employment with livable wages."
Nor could this effort uproot decades of oppression and structural
disadvantage.

The condition of urban central Baltimore today is the result of
a century of blatantly racist policies aimed at maintaining segregation. According to a chronicle compiled by Maxine Wood of the
Pathways from Poverty Consortium, the city's legal commitment
to apartheid began with the passage of an ordinance in 1910 "par-
titioning Baltimore City into black blocks and white blocks," after
African American lawyer W. Ashbie Hawkins moved into a row-
house in a prestigious white neighborhood.[15] In 1925, a cabal of
Baltimore neighborhood associations urged homeowners to bind
their properties with "restrictive covenants" forbidding sales to
blacks—which a city-sponsored "Committee on Segregation" en-
forced. In later decades, segregationist policies became more sub-
tle, through redlining and discriminatory lending practices. By the
mid-1930s, Wood finds, "89% of the black population was confined

to an area surrounding the downtown central district"—including what's now Sandtown. It's a situation that has only been somewhat ameliorated today.

In Baltimore, this long legacy of poverty and structural racism has taken a toll on the neighborhood's young people. At Frederick Douglass High School, for instance, a shockingly low 2.5 percent of students were rated "proficient" in math in state achievement tests, and only 47 percent of ninth graders were considered on track for graduation. The school's report card from the state ranks it in the eighth percentile among all Maryland schools.[16] In suburban Towson, by contrast, outside the city limits in Baltimore County, 79 percent of students were rated proficient in math at Towson High School, while 95 percent of ninth graders were on track for on-time graduation.[17] Ernest Dorsey, assistant director of the Mayor's Office of Employment Development, says the average YO Baltimore client—aged twenty—comes in at a fifth-grade reading level. "Ninety-five percent of them are in survival mode," he says. "A lot of our young people are disconnected from parents. Or they're living at home but their parent is living out on the streets. A number of our people are taking care of their parents."

There is an overwhelming correlation between concentrated poverty and the problems in school that lead to dropout and disconnection, says Johns Hopkins' Robert Balfanz, who is perhaps best known for his work on "dropout factories"—the mostly high-poverty schools where graduation is the exception, not the norm.[18] Poverty, for instance, affects attendance. "It matters to be in school every day, but poverty creates all kinds of circumstances—sibling care, elder care, child care, work," he says. As one example, older children are often tasked with getting younger siblings off to school, but if they run late as a consequence, schools are often unsympathetic. "So the kid figures it's better to be 'sick' than late," says Balfanz. "Over time, there's disengagement. Kids feel they can get by on the four-day plan." Poverty can also mean the lack of a safe place to do school work, as well as a lack of internet access. "It's hard to write a paper on a cell phone," as Balfanz says. And many young people feel the stress of having responsibility for their entire families. "There are tons of avenues to get food to kids in school, but the problem is that kids know their parents are not eating," says Balfanz. "Kids are worried about their parents getting food to eat."

Many schools in high-poverty areas don't respond to these kinds of needs the right way. Not only do they not provide the supports students need, they also don't give students facing extraordinary financial pressures a reason to stay in school. "They need to see a pathway," Balfanz says. "They don't have time for the long arc of high school, college, and by twenty-seven you find a real job. The time they have is much shorter—if you don't get a foothold soon, you won't get a foothold later."

Among the former students who didn't see that relevance was YO Baltimore client Shanaye Freeman, twenty-seven, who left high school at age sixteen and has three children, ages eight, six, and two. "School was boring," she says. "They were putting thirty kids in one class, and nobody was getting one-on-one time. So I said forget it, I'm just going to stay home."

Freeman is technically too old to be coming to the center, but she has been an off-and-on attendee for the better part of ten years and is one math test away from getting her GED. There are four sections to the GED—math, language arts, social studies, and science—which students can take separately. Freeman has already taken and failed the math section twice. This time, she's determined to pass. "What made me commit this time is that I'm pushing thirty and I have these three kids and now my daughter is like, 'You didn't finish school so why do we have to go to school?'" she says. "I gotta clean it up. If I was really thinking, I wouldn't have dropped out of high school. This is a lot harder than high school."

Recruiting young people to the program and keeping them engaged are the YO Baltimore staff's biggest challenges. Every Wednesday at 10 a.m. is orientation, when young people can come in to learn about the program and sign up for GED classes or employment help, if they already have a diploma. One Wednesday when I was there, there were three young men, one of whom was returning after a four-month break while he was in detention. "I don't want to keep doing what I'm doing," said one of the young men, Timothy Toland. "I'm here to finish school and make something of my life."

Many students, however, don't end up finishing, overwhelmed by the environment outside the center's doors. "You want to prepare them for life, but you're fighting a system where they are embedded in all these wrong concepts, with money being the main focus," says Anthony McFarlane, who teaches the center's GED classes. "They do what they have to do, sell cigarettes, sell drugs, things of that nature to get money and survive. Some get killed. Some are incarcerated. We don't see them for two, three, four, or five months and they come back into the program, and we do the same thing again."

On that day, Toland and the other two young men filled out paperwork and then took a "locator" test to assess their reading and math skills. If they return for classes next week, they'll be assigned an advocate, who will work with them to figure out what services they need and what barriers stand in their way.

One of these advocates is Sharon Leeds, who says she has about ninety students on her caseload. At the moment, she is preparing for an interview with a young man who attended last week's orientation. His paperwork is in a manila folder on her desk, one of dozens piled around her cubicle. "I try my best to 'pre-look' at the forms before we meet," she says. "So on this one, I look at his life events for trauma, and he's been assaulted with a weapon. He's also been in a serious accident and has been in a natural disaster. That gives me insights about what he's been through." Another sheet asks about career interests and about the young man's living situation. This young man is not homeless and not a parent.

Getting young people to open up about their needs is an art, Leeds says, because so many are distrustful of the systems they've been in. "I always try to focus on where they are and find out what's going on or not going on," she says. "Sometimes I let them talk and get it out. One young lady said a parent died, and she just shut down. She was in that space for a while. And then another parent died and she was concerned about what they died of. . . .

Sometimes they need to get a diploma, but they have other needs that have to be met before that can be successfully accomplished."

Often, however, these other needs get in the way of their education or the path to better jobs. "They are trapped between getting a high school diploma and employment," says McFarlane. McFarlane is from Trinidad-Tobago, and his lilting voice booms over the students working quietly at their computers. He has about half a dozen students in his classroom, including Shanaye. Later, he tells me that getting his students to come consistently is one of the toughest parts of his job. "They know the importance of a diploma, but they need immediate money, so they much prefer to work at McDonald's or Walmart for next to nothing even though they qualify to take the GED test," he says.

Very frequently, the overriding priority of these students is taking care of their own children. Parenthood is, in fact, a common reason why young people become derailed from finishing their education. Pregnancy and motherhood account for one-third of high school dropouts among teen girls, according to the nonprofit Power to Decide.[19] Moreover, only about half of teen moms ultimately finish high school and are far less likely than their non-parenting peers to go to college or get a degree. As a consequence, they are more likely to be working in lower-wage jobs and living in poverty. In 2014, according to the Urban Institute, 36 percent of young parents ages eighteen to twenty-four had earnings below the poverty line.[20] Six in ten young parents also reported being jobless at some point during the prior year—many of them due to lack of child care—and many were reliant on public benefits. More than 40 percent, for instance, were on SNAP (formerly food stamps).[21]

McFarlane says he often loses students once they become pregnant. "I have about five young ladies who delivered [babies] over the last six months, and you have to be constantly begging and making phone calls and trying your best to get them to come. They say, 'You don't understand. The kids' Christmas is coming up; I've got to get a job.'"

Obtaining affordable quality child care is a perennial problem for all parents, but for these poor women and men, it's an obstacle that's practically impossible to overcome. More than one in four U.S. families spends more than 10 percent of their income on child care, according to a study by the University of New Hampshire. Poor families, however, spend an average of 19.8 percent of their household income on child care, leaving little room for other basic expenses.[22] Government-provided child care subsidies do little to ease this burden. In March 2018, Congress increased funding for the Child Care and Development Block Grant, the principal source of federal funding for child care subsidies, by $2.4 billion. This brought total federal assistance for child care to $8.1 billion in fiscal 2018, which the nonprofit Center for Law and Social Policy (CLASP) calculates would help serve an additional 151,000 children nationwide.[23] This increase, however, only partially reverses a decline in funding over the last decade—the Center on Budget and Policy Priorities estimates that only about one in six families eligible for child care subsidies actually receives help.[24] Among young parents, the share receiving subsidies is even lower—just 5 percent of young parents ages sixteen to twenty-four got help in 2013, according to the Urban Institute.[25]

States put up additional barriers to getting child care help. In Maryland, for example, mothers applying for child care subsidies aren't eligible unless they're also pursuing child support enforcement from the fathers of their children.[26] YO Baltimore staff say that young moms are often reluctant to identify the fathers of their kids, especially if they are fleeing from domestic violence or if the father is incarcerated.

As extreme as Sandtown's problems seem, it is unfortunately not alone in its status as an urban "opportunity desert," where young people face long odds against economic independence. The Johns Hopkins University researchers who studied Sandtown in 2013 also surveyed the country to discover just how many other "Sandtowns" there might be nationally, with similar levels of poverty, unemployment, crime, single parenthood, and other indicators of community dysfunction. As Figure 4.1 shows, their analysis found 177 Sandtowns across the country in twenty-five states, many of them concentrated in the dying industrial Midwest. The study also found

3,570 neighborhoods nationwide with a concentration of poverty of 40 percent or more.[27] "The double burden of concentrated poverty is real," says Robert Balfanz of Johns Hopkins. "When you live in a neighborhood where 20 to 40 percent are poor, you're impacted by your own level of income and that of your neighbors," he says.

Though these places might make up the minority of neighborhoods nationally, they are numerous enough to prompt urgent concerns about the deeply rooted systemic disadvantages that hold back communities and sabotage young people's prospects.

Strikingly, the young people in Sandtown are far more optimistic about their chances of success than many outsiders would be—which is reason alone to tackle anew the challenges of places like it.

Back at the YO Baltimore Center, Krishawn McCullough, twenty-two, is also, like Shanaye Freeman, only one test away from his GED. He takes two buses to get to the center in the mornings and also works full time at a poultry distributor elsewhere in the city. "I come to class 10 a.m. to 1:30 or 2 p.m., and I start work at four o'clock until midnight," he says. "It's not too bad." McCullough also notes that he's been coming to the center for five years now—since he was seventeen. But because he hasn't given

FIGURE 4.1: "Sandtowns" by State

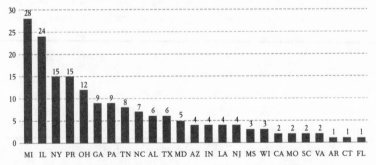

Daniel Princiotta, "How Many 'Sandtowns' Are There Nationwide,"
Johns Hopkins University Center for Social Organization of
Schools, available at https://new.every1graduates.org/wp-content
/uploads/2015/11/How-Many-Sandtowns-are-there-Nationwide.pdf.

up hope, neither have his instructors. Today, McCullough is trying on secondhand suits donated to the center, in preparation for job interviews he is someday hoping to land. He comes out of a storage closet doing double duty as a fitting room, wearing a crisp white shirt and a gray suit that looks just a little bit worn but passable. He stands up straight and looks in the mirror set up in the room where the center's staff have laid out racks of used suits on wire hangers.

McCullough's aspirations are big. "I want my own radio show," he says. "I want to go to college and major in African American history." Then he turns and leaves the room to change back into his street clothes. His suit is in a plastic bag that he'll take to class. Then, he'll head out the center's doors into his life in Sandtown.

5

When Work Disappears

No matter how established you become in your career, you never forget your first job. It might have been flipping burgers, scooping ice cream, or baking pizzas; mowing lawns or shoveling snow; waiting tables or answering phones. If you were lucky, you got to lifeguard at the neighborhood pool. The pay was probably paltry, but the salary was beside the point.

Many middle-class parents insist on a summer job for their teenagers, not just for the money but for the experience that holding down a job provides. You learn to show up on time, call in if you're late, cooperate with co-workers, and manage a boss. With the money you earn, you learn to budget and save. Importantly, you'll have the chops to get a better-paying job next summer with "work experience" on your résumé.

First jobs are a crucial anchor point for the web of connections that a person builds throughout their career. Bosses can become references and mentors. Colleagues can become connectors to other, better opportunities. Exposure to one career path can also help a young person decide if a field is right for them, which could prevent false starts and save time and money in schooling.

For a growing number of young people, however, that all-important first job—or even any job—has become increasingly elusive. As one result, the share of young adults who work has fallen precipitously in the past few decades. If young people are disconnected from the labor force, one reason is that they never get the chance to connect at all.

Despite officially rosy economic data over the last couple years, many young people who want jobs can't find them. While the recovery might have created plenty of jobs for older, better-skilled adults, a shortage of jobs for young people is driving their disconnection from the labor force, especially among those who are minorities or have fewer qualifications. The cumulative result is lifelong damage to the future earnings and career prospects of these young people—a generation of lost potential.[1] "We saw from the recession that for people who have to delay their careers, it's hard to make up ground," says Chauncy Lennon of the Lumina Foundation. "If you can't get into the workforce until you're twenty-eight, and you have to start at the bottom, you're not making up that lost decade."

The Myth of "Full Employment"

Quentin, twenty, knows firsthand the difficulties of landing a good job. A high school graduate and part-time college student, Quentin lives in southeast Washington, D.C., with his mom and sister but commutes to northwest D.C. almost daily. He works fifteen hours a week at a local Starbucks when he's not in classes at the University of the District of Columbia. It's a job that took him months to get.

"Retail jobs, average Joe jobs, store jobs, fast food jobs, I applied to a lot," he says. "All the shoe stores—I think I applied to Target, Whole Foods, Safeway, Giant."

"I know for a fact that it's hard for a person my age to get a job," he continues. "There's good jobs, but they're not going to give up the opportunity to someone like me."

On the day we meet, Quentin is dressed for class in a gray Bel Air Academy hoodie (a nod to the Fresh Prince), his dreads pulled up into a topknot. He looks exactly like the kind of hip barista you'd expect to be whipping up your latte. He speculates that the jobs he was after were getting snapped up by older applicants. "They hire twenty-five and up, that's who they hire," he says. "If you're in school, they know you're not going to be there for a long time."

Beginning in 2018 and well into 2019, speculation began over whether the economy was at or approaching "full employment"— when everyone who wants a job has one without sparking fears of inflation.[2] By the summer of 2018, the official jobless rate had dipped to below 4 percent, the lowest it had been since the expansion of the late 1990s, while corporate profits were also reaching record levels.[3] But stories like Quentin's are a warning sign of the seemingly robust recovery's soft underbelly.

For one thing, the unemployment rate does not tell the whole story of what's going on in the U.S. job market. That's because the official rate includes only those people who say they are looking for work but don't have jobs, not the share of the total population that's unemployed. For example, "discouraged" workers who've quit looking for work aren't counted toward the calculation of the unemployment rate.

This means the true extent of unemployment ends up undercounted. Say, for instance, that there are one hundred people in the economy, but only eighty of them are looking for jobs. If four of those eighty are unemployed, the unemployment rate would be just 5 percent (4 divided by 80), even though a total of twenty-four people are jobless. While the unemployment rate might seem to signal "full employment," the share of Americans actually working might still be much lower than it could or should be.

A better measure of the prevalence of work is the percentage of the total population working or looking for work—the "labor force participation rate"—or, alternatively, the number of people working as a share of the total population—the "employment-to-population ratio." Through these broader measures, we get a better sense of how much untapped labor is in the economy as well as the severity of people's absence from the job market. Including these non-workers also potentially forces examination of the reasons why people aren't participating in the economy.

Under any measure, young people are in trouble.

Unemployment among young adults is consistently much higher than it is for the overall workforce, even when times are as good as they have been the past few years. In April 2019, for instance, when overall unemployment was at a then-record low of 3.6 percent,[4] the unemployment rate among young people ages sixteen to twenty-four was more than twice as high at 8.3 percent.[5] Though this figure represents a huge decline since the Great Recession, when the unemployment rate among young people reached a whopping 19.5 percent in 2010, young people's fortunes in the job market are far from robust.[6]

First, the Great Recession took an exceptionally heavy toll on young workers. Among teenagers ages sixteen to nineteen, for example, researcher Andrew Sum and colleagues find that employment rates dropped dramatically, from 44 percent in 2000 to 24 percent in 2011. "Only about half of high school graduates not enrolled in post-secondary education and less than 30 percent of high school dropouts worked in a given month in 2011," Sum finds.[7]

Young people have also been much slower to benefit from the recovery. Many, in fact, seem to have given up trying to find work altogether. While numerous economists have noted that overall workforce participation is lower than it was before the recession, the loss of young people from the labor market has been especially persistent and severe. As the following chart from the Federal Reserve shows (Figure 5.1), the share of eighteen- to nineteen-year-olds in the labor force in 2016 was 8.9 percentage points lower than it was in 2006, before the recession, while the share of twenty- to twenty-four-year-olds was still down by 3.3 percentage points. Among thirty-five- to forty-four-year-olds, in contrast, the net decline in workforce participation from 2006 to 2016 was just 1.2 percent.

The declines in workforce participation among young adults are even more pronounced the further back in time you go. In April 2019, for instance, overall labor force participation among young people not in school was 80.7 percent, compared to 83.1 percent in April 2000.[8] This figure, however, masks particularly severe declines among certain subgroups, especially those with less education. Among young people not in school and with less than a high

FIGURE 5.1: Labor Force Statistics from the Current Population Survey, August 2016

Age	Unemployment Rate (Percent)	Unemployment Rate Change (Aug. 2006–Aug. 2016) (Percentage Points)	Labor Force (Percent)	Labor Force Participation Change (Aug. 2006–Aug. 2016) (Percentage Points)
18 to 19 years	15.2	+1.8	58.2	−8.9
20 to 24 years	9.4	+1.0	74.4	−3.3
25 to 34 years	5.3	+0.2	82.9	−2.2
35 to 44 years	4.0	+0.2	83.8	−1.2
45 to 54 years	3.6	+0.2	81.4	−1.8
55 years and over	3.2	No change	37.6	−2.2

Source: Bureau of Labor Statistics.

U.S. Bureau of Labor Statistics, https://www.federalreserve.gov /econresdata/2016-survey-young-workers-introduction.htm.

FIGURE 5.2: Employment-to-Population Ratio, Age 16–19 Years and 16–24 Years, 1950–2010

U.S. Bureau of Labor Statistics, https://www.federalreserve.gov /econresdata/2016-survey-young-workers-introduction.htm.

school diploma, for example, the decline is greater than 10 percentage points. Just 59.6 percent were in the workforce in the first quarter of 2019, down from 71.9 percent in 2000.[9]

These declines, moreover, are part of an even longer-term historical trend toward declining labor force engagement among young adults. If you look at the broadest measure of work, the employment-to-population ratio, the share of working young adults has been dropping since the early 1990s.[10]

The Racial Job Gap

While some young people may be out of the job market because they're in school, the biggest drops in workforce participation have been among young people who are not in school and who are the least educated. The young people most likely to find work and to have early work experience—such as through an internship—are college educated. Middle-class young adults and their parents are well aware of the benefits of work experience—whether an internship or paid work—and research shows it can help young people find full-time jobs later on.[11] Aside from money in their pocket and a line on their résumés, work experience helps young people develop professional contacts as well as the "soft skills" they will need later in their careers, as noted earlier.[12]

Black young adults in particular have borne the brunt of this continuing deterioration in jobs and work. In April 2019, for example, barely half of black young adults ages sixteen to twenty-four—50.9 percent—were in the labor force, while the unemployment rate among this group was 13.3 percent.[13] In contrast, the unemployment rate among white young adults was 6.3 percent, and 55.6 percent were in the labor force.[14]

As discussed in the preceding chapters, some areas are particular epicenters of a crisis in black youth unemployment. In Chicago, for instance, the Great Cities Institute found that black young people ages twenty to twenty-four were much more likely to be jobless than to be employed. In 2015, 60 percent of black youth were not working, compared to 24 percent of whites.[15]

FIGURE 5.3: The Racial Job Gap

	Unemployment Rate (April 2019)	Labor Force Participation (April 2019)
Black (ages 16–24)	13.3%	50.9%
White (ages 16–24)	6.3%	55.6%

Source: Bureau of Labor Statistics.

Some of these disparities are the result of a lingering hangover from the Great Recession, which also disproportionately affected blacks. Researchers Margaret Simms and Marla McDaniel note that in September 2010, at the height of the crisis, only one in three black young adults had a job.[16]

Even before the recession, however, black young adults had more trouble finding jobs than their white peers. Simms and McDaniel find, for instance, that it's considerably easier for a white high school dropout to find a full-time job than it is for a black high school graduate:

> [B]lack high school graduates took 16 months on average to start full-time work while white dropouts took about a year. So, a white dropout turning 18 on, say, Labor Day 2005 would have begun a spell of steady full-time work by Labor Day 2006. A black high school graduate born in the same month may not have begun earning a steady paycheck until the following New Year's Eve (2006) or even later.[17]

Black young adults are also less likely to get early work experience than whites, which can handicap their ability to compete for jobs later on. In a 2016 survey of young workers, the Federal Reserve found that just 50 percent of black young people had worked in high school, versus 62 percent of whites. Whites were also more likely to work while in college.[18]

Many reasons potentially explain this disparity—black youth are more likely to live in places where jobs are scarce or transportation to jobs is inaccessible. Black young people might also be more likely to go to lower-quality schools that are not adequately preparing them with the skills they need in the workforce. There's also out-and-out discrimination. "You've got to be lucky enough to have someone give you an opportunity," says Franklin Peralta, a staff member at the Latin American Youth Center (and whom we'll meet at greater length in chapter 10). "Especially kids who apply to retail. As soon as they see you, they're like—'Unh unh—I don't think this person is a good image for the store.' . . . It doesn't even matter if you're wearing a suit and tie. They just see the way you talk. You're being judged the minute you walk in the door."

Quentin, the UDC student, says many of his friends give up after a steady stream of these kinds of rejections. "If you keep up applying for three months straight and keep getting the same thing—'Thank you for your interest,' 'I'll call you,' or 'He's not here right now, we'll talk to you tomorrow'—they keep giving you the runaround, pretty soon you're like 'Forget it, I'm going to stop applying,'" he says.

Jobs, but Not Good Jobs

For the young people lucky enough to have jobs, their connection to the workforce is still often tenuous, and the quality of the jobs often subpar.

Keisha, twenty, lives in the Bronx and has held a string of low-wage retail jobs since leaving high school at age seventeen without her diploma. "It's hard to find jobs when you don't have experience and you're not out there in the professional world," she says. She also wishes now that she had finished high school. "I should have stayed in school," she says. "If I had my GED, I'd be working at way good places making better money." Keisha says her first job was at a McDonald's franchise owned by her aunt. "I didn't have to do an interview or suit up—I was given that job," she says. But after her aunt sold the store, she found herself looking for work. "I've worked at IKEA, Chipotle, Burlington. I worked in a school as an assistant para[professional]. I worked downtown in Hale and Hearty—that's a soup place." At the moment, she is back part-time at Burlington on the sales floor. "I've been at this job going on ten months, and I started seasonal there," she says. "Most of the jobs I started seasonal and they kept me. It's all about how you perform."

In Quentin's case, he's managed to land one full-time job in his brief career so far. When he was seventeen, he got a summer job at a Six Flags amusement park in suburban Maryland. "I was in the kitchen, and it was horrible," he says. "They had me in there all day slaving, literally slaving. I was on the register and in the back on the food." On ninety-degree summer days, he shares, the heat in the kitchen could be unbearable. He also had to commute an hour and a half each way from southeast D.C. to the park. "They had me working from 10 in the morning, and I didn't leave until 11," he says. He took both the Metro and then the bus to get to his job and was frequently not home until after midnight. He was up again at dawn to make the commute back the next morning. Nevertheless, he calls the experience "a good job" because it was a chance for steady work. "At the time, I think I got paid $10 an hour—it's not bad," he says.

According to the Federal Reserve's 2016 survey of young workers, a significant number of young people are in situations where they are not working as much as they would like, where they are overqualified for the jobs they have or assigned to schedules that make balancing work and life a challenge. Roughly half of young people working part-time say they are "underemployed" or working part-time when they'd prefer to have a full-time job. "More specifically, 42 percent of part-time employees could only find part-time work, and 17 percent had employers cut their hours," the survey found.[19] Many young workers also have unpredictable schedules. The survey found that as many as one-fourth of full-time workers and more than 40 percent of part-time workers have "nontraditional" work hours. More than half of part-time workers and nearly a third of full-timers also have schedules that change "daily, weekly, or monthly."[20]

The Federal Reserve also found that many young workers were in jobs that didn't match their skills or interests. For example,

25 percent of young people described themselves as "overqualified for their job," and even among permanent workers, less than half (49 percent) said they were in jobs "closely related to their education and training."[21]

In terms of salary and benefits, while a majority of young workers say they're "satisfied" with what their employers provide, 18 percent in 2016 did not have health insurance, and less than two-thirds had access to paid sick leave or holidays. Moreover, only 73 percent said they could "meet their monthly expenses with their household income." Many relied on public benefits to supplement their income, while others said they got regular help (including housing) from parents or family.[22]

Because of their relative inexperience, young workers obviously can't expect to make as much as their older peers. Nevertheless, young workers as a group don't make a living wage, even when they're working full time. In the first quarter of 2019, full-time workers ages sixteen to twenty-four earned 64 cents on the dollar compared to all workers as a whole.[23] They made a median of $579 a week—or $30,108 a year (assuming year-round work with no breaks).[24]

Contrary to stereotypes about young workers valuing their freedom and flexibility, the Federal Reserve's research discovered that most young people want a traditional full-time job, with standard hours, decent pay, and benefits. "Today's young adults are generally not job hoppers, unless there is an opportunity for advancement," the Fed concluded.[25]

Where Have All the Good Jobs Gone?

What's happened to young people in the job market is linked to the broader economic upheaval being wrought by automation, globalization, and technological change.

In Chicago, for instance, the death of manufacturing has decimated work opportunities for young people in the city's urban core who were once able to count on steady, well-paid work after their high school graduation.

Visit Chicago today, with its gleaming skyline and cosmopolitan sensibilities, and you would be hard pressed to believe that it was once one of the nation's largest producers of steel, defined more by its smokestacks than by its skyscrapers. Beginning in the late nineteenth century, foundries and steel mills began lining the city's southeast side on the shores of Lake Michigan and the mouth of the Calumet River, down to the Indiana border and beyond. While today the waterways are more about leisure and tourism, their purpose back then was strictly utilitarian, as a principal thoroughfare for shipping out millions of tons of finished steel and rails. Chicago-made steel was the backbone of the Industrial Revolution and then the post–World War II boom, supplying at one point as much as one-third of the nation's output of steel rails.[26]

Among the companies that established themselves in the area were Republic Steel, Acme Steel, Wisconsin Steel, Youngstown Sheet & Tube, Interlake Iron, and the behemoth U.S. Steel, whose South Works plant was one of the company's largest.[27] The mills provided an entrée to the middle class for generations of workers, beginning with immigrants from eastern Europe and then, increasingly, African American and Latino men. By the 1970s, according to the Chicago Historical Society, the United Steelworkers of America counted 130,000 members in the Chicago area, many of them Mexican and African American.[28]

Steel wasn't the only heavy industry in Chicago. In 1924, the Ford Motor Company opened a factory that started out producing Model Ts and would eventually build Thunderbirds, Torinos, and LTDs, among other models. The southeast side was also home to shipyards and a General Mills plant that produced Gold Medal flour, Betty Crocker cake mixes, Cocoa Puffs, and Bisquick.[29]

All of this industry began to die in the 1970s and 1980s. Wisconsin Steel shut down in 1980; LTV Steel (formerly Republic) went bankrupt in 1982; U.S. Steel's South Works plant closed in 1992;[30] the General Mills facility closed in 1995.[31] Between 1979 and 1986, says the Chicago Historical Society, 16,000 steelworkers lost their jobs, while the total number of Chicago's manufacturing jobs, according to Great Cities Institute researchers Teresa

Cordova and Matthew Wilson, dwindled from 657,000 in the late 1940s to fewer than 100,000 today.

Communities died along with these livelihoods. "South Chicago, South Deering and East Side were once neighborhoods where families laid down roots and stayed to build legacies," recounted former resident Roxann Lopez in the *Chicago Tribune*. "Churches thrived. Schools were good. People cared. Now, they are transient areas. No one comes to stay because there is no reason to do so. There are empty lots where the houses of friends and family once stood."[32]

But unlike in South Boston, Virginia, jobs haven't generally left Chicago. Rather, the composition and location of work has shifted in ways that have left large swathes of the population—including especially young people of color—behind. Today, Chicago's economy is centered on the so-called Loop, the downtown business district that is reputedly the nation's second-largest commercial center after Manhattan.[33] The dozens of gigantic companies headquartered there include Hyatt Hotels, United Continental Holdings (the parent company for United Airlines), Blue Cross Blue Shield, and the insurance company CNA. The jobs generated by these companies—in financial services, accounting, law, and technology—are largely professional ones that require much more than a high school diploma.

Great Cities Institute researchers Cordova and Wilson mapped the number of jobs accessible from each of seventy-seven Chicago neighborhoods within a half-hour commute by public transit and found huge disparities in both the location and the type of jobs available to different communities. "If you live in the Loop, you have access to over 700,000 jobs via public transit, while there are some communities on the South Side that have access to less than 10,000," says Wilson. The researchers also found that the highest-paid, professional jobs in the Loop were disproportionately held by whites, while retail and custodial jobs were disproportionately held by blacks and Latinos. Despite its prosperity, Chicago, like Baltimore, has its own opportunity deserts within its city limits.

Popular perception might portray the fifty-five-year-old former factory worker as the archetypal victim of globalization and the shifting nature of work, but young people face particular disadvantages in today's changing economy.

First, they are competing against older workers with experience, and they are caught in the catch-22 of not being able to get jobs to gain experience because they don't have the experience to get the job. Second, for young workers who have not yet completed their education, there are many fewer jobs available to them at the educational level they do have, especially after the Great Recession.

According to Georgetown University's Center on Education and the Workforce, the recession permanently eliminated as many as 6 million jobs from the U.S. economy, with the biggest hits to jobs requiring a high school diploma or less. While jobs for these lesser-educated workers would have declined anyway, Anthony Carnevale and his colleagues find that the recession enormously accelerated this trend. Carnevale also finds that while workers with higher levels of education have not suffered the same net losses in the number of jobs, job creation has not made up for the recession's impact. As of 2015, he writes, "there are still 2 million fewer jobs for workers with some college or an Associate's degree than there would have been if the recession had not occurred" and 1 million fewer jobs for college graduates.[34]

The most significant disadvantage young workers are facing, however, is that their schools are not adequately preparing them for careers in the new economy.

The Missing Links Between School and Career

Though education matters more than ever to the success of young people in the workforce, the nation's educational institutions are currently failing to help young people connect to jobs. In a 2012 survey by Civic Enterprises and the America's Promise Alliance that asked young people the top obstacles they faced in getting a job, 51 percent of young people said that "no jobs are available where they live." But 50 percent also said they "don't have enough work experience (50 percent) or education (47 percent) to get the job they want," and nearly one-third (32 percent) said that "they do

not know how to prepare a resume or how to interview."[35] Another
survey, by Gallup and Strada Education Network in 2017, found
similar concerns even among college students. In this survey, just
34 percent of students believed "they will graduate with the skills
and knowledge they need to be successful in the job market," while
just 53 percent believed "their major will lead to a good job."[36]
These perceptions point to very specific gaps in what students
aren't getting from school about their potential careers.

Missing Link #1: Career Information

The first missing piece is as simple as basic information about
career options. While forward-thinking educators such as Superintendent Paul Nichols of Mecklenburg County, Virginia, are
teaching elementary and middle school kids about their potential
future paths, not enough schools are following his lead. According
to the Federal Reserve's survey of young workers, more than a third
of young people said they did not get "information about jobs and
careers" during high school and college.[37]

Though research shows that career exploration should begin
as early as middle school—when students first start disengaging
from school and potentially put themselves on the path to dropping
out—learning about potential careers is not a part of most eighth
graders' curriculum. This lack of knowledge can translate to bigger problems down the line. "Middle school students may . . . have
unrealistic career plans, and know little about the demands of the
work-place or how their education choices relate to future careers,"
says a report from the Association for Career and Technical Education (ACTE). "Girls, minorities and at-risk students are more
likely to begin to limit their career aspirations after being exposed
to stereotypes about which jobs are appropriate for whom."[38]

One potential reason career exploration isn't on the table for
middle schoolers is the focus on academic achievement, as measured by standardized testing. While testing may have improved
schools' accountability to their students, schools focused on getting
their students to pass state standards aren't likely to make other
concerns a top priority. Another reason career learning gets short

shrift early on in students' careers is that there's very little funding to support it. Middle schools are generally underfunded—schools serving grades six to eight got just $2.5 billion in federal funding in fiscal 2015, compared to $31.1 billion for post-secondary education and $26 billion for early childhood and elementary education.[39] And to the extent schools offer "career and technical education" (CTE), the lion's share of it occurs in high school, when it may be too little too late.

Missing Link #2: Relevant Job Skills

This leads to the second missing link between schools and jobs, which is the lack of curriculum aimed at providing students with skills relevant to the jobs they might want in the future. According to the Fed's survey of young workers, only 41 percent of young people believe "they have the level of education and training needed for the type of job that they would like to hold in the next five years."[40]

One specific deficit is the lack of funding and availability of career and technical education, which could give students the specific skills they need to qualify for a job while at the same time keeping them engaged in school. According to the nonprofit Advance CTE, the graduation rate among CTE students is significantly higher than for non-CTE students, in part because students see the coursework as more "relevant" to them in providing real-world skills.[41]

In the bad old days, so-called vocational education earned a bad rap—and deservedly so—for tracking lower-income and minority students away from higher education and toward lesser-skilled, second-tier jobs. In the early twentieth century, for instance, vocational education was a blatant mechanism for maintaining segregation, and educators made no effort to hide their biases. Among the influential voices at this time was the famed psychologist G. Stanley Hall, who invented the study of adolescent development at the turn of the twentieth century. Scholar Deberae Culpepper notes that in a 1905 study purportedly researching "Negro intelligence," Hall concluded that "[the] Negro's education should be practical, domestic, agricultural, chiefly if not entirely industrial . . . no provisions for even a few exceptional Negroes," while an earlier work opined that "the Aryan race entered school with more developed organs that connected vision with knowledge."[42]

More enlightened views on students' capabilities, along with a greater emphasis on college preparation and expanded course requirements in many states, helped push vocational education out of favor beginning in the 1980s.[43] Recent years, however, have led to a revival of interest in career and technical education, particularly as a growing number of employers have complained of "skills gaps" leading to jobs they cannot fill. Many of these jobs, moreover, are so-called middle-skill jobs that require some sort of specialized training or education beyond a high school diploma but not a four-year degree. According to the National Skills Coalition, as many as 53 percent of jobs in 2015 fit into this category.[44] Examples of these kinds of jobs include office administrators, computer technicians, nursing assistants, machinists, welders, and truck drivers.

In July 2018, President Donald Trump signed legislation reauthorizing the principal source of federal funding for career and technical education in schools, the Carl D. Perkins Career and Technical Education Act. Among other things, the Strengthening Career and Technical Education for the 21st Century Act increased authorized funding levels by more than 10 percent, to $1.38 billion a year, by fiscal 2024.[45] This is only the first step, however, in reversing a decades-long decline in access to CTE. According to the National Center for Education Statistics, the average number of CTE credits earned by high schoolers dropped from 4.2 in 1990 to 3.6 in 2009.[46]

Missing Link #3: A Diploma
The third missing piece between a young person's schooling and their entry into the job market is, all too often, the credential itself—too many students are dropping out, either out of high school or out of college.

Among these young people is Keisha, the young woman from the Bronx who was working at a Burlington Coat Factory. She stopped going to her high school after her older brother died. "I was distracted for a very long time," she says. "I felt like education didn't matter. I really didn't care at that moment." She notes that her teachers also never reached out to her to bring her back or to get her the support she needed.

In 2004, Johns Hopkins University researchers Robert Balfanz and Nettie Legters first shone a spotlight on so-called dropout factories—high schools where the graduation rate is less than 60 percent.[47] In their landmark report, they found more than 2,000 high schools—or 18 percent of schools nationwide—that fit this description. They also discovered that the vast majority of these schools serve mostly minority students and are concentrated in a subset of about fifteen states. Moreover, they found that nearly half of all African American students and 40 percent of Latino students were enrolled in dropout factories, compared to just 11 percent of whites.

Balfanz and Legters's research led to a national campaign to reduce the dropout crisis, which has made remarkable progress in just a decade. In 2016, the national high school graduation rate was at 84.1 percent, up from just 71 percent in 2001.[48] And while Balfanz's updated research identified roughly 2,400 "low-performing schools," the goalposts have also shifted to define these schools as those with graduation rates of less than 67 percent. These gains, however, have been uneven.

"Progress is happening, and we should recognize that," says Balfanz. "The challenging news is that [in] 2018 . . . more than 1 in 5 low income and minority youth are not getting a diploma." In 2016, according to Balfanz's research, "76.4 percent of Black students and 79.3 percent of Hispanic students graduated on time, compared to 88.3 percent of white students."[49] Similarly, 77.6 percent of low-income students graduated on time, compared to about 90 percent of students who were not low-income.

These graduation rates are, however, better than the current completion rates for post-secondary education. Just 50 percent of students attain a post-secondary credential six years after enrollment, according to the Department of Education.[50] Thirty-five percent have dropped out by that point, while another 15 percent are "persisting"—remaining enrolled but without a credential. Sub-baccalaureate students have the lowest completion rates; only 39 percent earn a credential within six years of enrollment. By comparison, 67 percent of bachelor's students manage to complete their degrees.[51]

These numbers should be especially troubling given the rising expense of higher education and the debt burdens that students are accumulating. In 2017–18, the average cost of one year's in-state tuition, room, and board at a public four-year university was $18,432.[52]

Obstacles like this aren't on Keisha's mind, however, when she talks about her ambitions. "I have friends who went away to college," she says. "I want to experience that. Having that dorm experience, you know? I feel like when you go away, doors open. Even if college doesn't work out for me, doors will open for me if I try and meet other people." Ultimately, Keisha wants to get a bachelor's degree in education so she can teach special ed. But first, she needs her GED. "I'm close," she says. "I feel like I can taste it."

6

Abandoned by the State: "Aging Out"

Government failures loom large in the slide into disconnection for many young people. In the case of young adults living in opportunity deserts, both rural and urban, these governmental failures are predominantly the result of inaction—whether neglect, inattention, or indifference. But there are other instances in which government itself is the instrument of disconnection.

There is no perfect substitute for the support of parents and family as a young person approaches maturity. But there are also times when the state is forced to step in and take on the role of a parent. One such case is to protect a child from abuse or neglect by her caretakers or if a child has lost her family through some tragedy. In that instance, it's the obligation of the child welfare system to ensure the child's safety and to find a loving foster or adoptive family or guardian who will raise the child to and through adulthood. Ideally, the system should leave its young charges in better circumstances than how they found them. Unfortunately, that all too often isn't the case. As it turns out, the state is a terrible parent.

In the top-floor conference room of a boutique hotel in downtown Baltimore one June evening, about two dozen twenty-somethings from around the country are gathered over barbecue, corn bread, and a mile-high strawberry cake.

Each of them is extraordinarily accomplished—many have graduate degrees and work in positions of responsibility beyond their years. One is a social worker, another is hoping to break into public policy. They are charismatic, bright, and outspoken. As everyone moves through the buffet, chatting, you can hear the laughter from down the hall.

Each of them is also a veteran of the foster care system and stayed in long enough to "age out." Instead of parents and family to usher them into adulthood, they'd had courts, caseworkers, state agencies, and, if they were lucky, caring foster parents. Now as young adults, they meet several times a year under the auspices of the Jim Casey Youth Opportunity Initiative, part of the Annie E. Casey Foundation, headquartered in Baltimore.

Their success has been in spite of the system that raised them, not because of it. Their mission now, as advocates, is to fix it.

One young man speaks about the separate bathroom his foster family forced him to use while the family's biological children used a nicer bathroom upstairs. "We had to stay in the basement and clean up in the sink," he says. The biological kids could also take showers when they wanted and raid the fridge when they were hungry, while he and his foster siblings could not. His voice still boils with indignation as he shares this memory. "What were we—dirty?" he asks. Almost everyone here has piled up tens of thousands of dollars in school debts because they had no family to help pay for college and little counseling about financial aid. "I picked up $13,000 in debt to stay on campus because I had nowhere else to live," says one young woman.

Every year, more than 650,000 children are confirmed by child welfare authorities to be victims of abuse or neglect, and many are removed from their homes. As of September 2016 (the latest date for which data are available), about 437,000 children were living in foster care.[1]

"Government takes [these children] away from the care of their parents under the presumption that government can and should do better," write scholars Mark Courtney and Darcy Hughes Heuring.[2]

But for the roughly 21,000 young adults who "age out" of foster care every year, it's tough to see how that's the case.[3] As things currently stand, the nation's child welfare system is a passport to disconnection for the young adults in its care.

Bleak Futures

In the current terminology of the child welfare system, young people who become too old to remain in care are "emancipated" from the system. In many ways, the better word might be "abandoned." So long as a young person remains in the custody of the state, all of her basic needs are, in theory, taken care of—she has a place to stay, food to eat, and clothes to wear. There are social workers, judges, and guardians ad litem whose job it is to represent her interests. But the day she turns twenty-one—or as early as eighteen in some states—all of those supports and that small army of people abruptly disappear, like a faucet with the spigot turned off.

"I won't have a social worker anymore. I won't get paid for taking care of myself anymore. All the resources that I have, I won't have those resources anymore . . . they just kind of shut down," says Mykell in *The Day I Aged Out*, a web-based documentary about two young people who grew up in Seattle's foster care system. On the day the filmmakers caught her, Mykell was on the eve of her twenty-first birthday, May 13, 2016. Born to a drug-abusing mother, she was raised in ten different foster homes over the course of her childhood. On camera, she looks exactly like the college student she is aspiring to be, with glasses, long braids, and a gap between her two front teeth. She seems dazed by what she is about to lose. "Since I'm turning twenty-one . . . it's all gone," she says.

Mykell is one of the lucky ones too. The documentary reveals that she's enrolled in community college and living with her uncle while she looks for an apartment with the Section 8 housing voucher the city provides to former foster youth. But many young people don't have any sort of net below them. These young people fall hard and fall fast, with little or no connections to a job or school to keep them afloat or provide a path to a better future.

"Independent Living"

In 1985, the *New York Times* told the story of Reggie Brown, who was thirteen when he entered foster care in New York City and was discharged from a group home five years later, one week after his eighteenth birthday. "All he was given," the article says, "was cab fare and directions to the men's shelter."[4]

The following year, child welfare advocates helped ten former foster youth sue New York City for its failure to provide transitional help as they left the system. Six of the ten had become homeless and were, according to court documents, "forced to seek shelter in tenement buildings, subways and public parks."[5] One plaintiff, according to a piece by Mary Lee Allen and Robin Nixon, ultimately "returned to the state prison system where he was born."[6] The New York state court found that the city's child welfare agency had failed its statutory obligations to prepare young people for discharge and didn't follow up with them after their departure. In fact, it didn't even have a system in place for doing so.[7]

Today, under federal law, states must work with every young person in foster care to develop a transition plan whose contents are dictated by statute.[8] Oregon, for instance, has a forty-one-page "youth transitions procedure" with painstaking instructions on how to prepare a "comprehensive transition plan," along with numerous checklists, forms, and other paperwork.[9]

Requirements like these are the result of several waves of federal legislation passed by Congress after stories like Reggie Brown's and a spate of public attention brought light to the fate of former foster youth. Several mechanisms currently provide federal support to young adults in the foster care system beyond age eighteen to help them prepare for adulthood on their own. Chief among these is the Chafee Foster Care Independence Program, passed by Congress in 1999, which provides up to $140 million to states every year to help fund "independent living services" for older youth in foster care until age twenty-one. These services can include housing assistance, help finding a job or going to college, mentorship programs, financial coaching, and other support.[10]

Separately, Congress sets aside about $45 million a year for "edu-
cation and training vouchers" to help fund post-secondary education for former foster care youth until age twenty-three.[11] Another
source of federal support is Title IV-E of the Social Security Act,
which reimburses states for part of the cost of providing care to
low-income children in foster care. In 2008, Congress passed the
Fostering Connections to Success and Increasing Adoptions Act,
which gave states the option to claim reimbursement for foster
care kids up to age twenty-one, an option that about half of states
and the District of Columbia have exercised.[12] More recently, Congress acted to extend Medicaid coverage to foster youth as part of
the Affordable Care Act passed in 2010. At the same time that
the law allowed all young adults to stay on their parents' insurance
plan to age twenty-six, the law gave former foster youth access to
Medicaid until age twenty-six as well.[13]

But in some ways, things have not changed since Reggie Brown
was handed cab fare and directions to the shelter. Despite the dozens of pages of forms and detailed policy manuals, many young
people leave foster care without such practical skills as how to pay
their bills, find an apartment, or put together a résumé. An extensive ten-year-long evaluation of the first generation of independent
living programs variously found little or no impacts on the young
people getting help. One such program, a five-week classroom-
based "life skills training" for foster youth in Los Angeles County,
was found to have "no significant impacts" on education, employment, or earnings.[14] Similarly, a program in Kern County, California, that provided job search help and other employment services
showed "no significant differences" in whether foster youth were
able to find jobs.[15]

On FosterClub.com, a site for alumni of the foster care system, a
young man named Isaiah posted this entry in 2009 as he prepared
to meet the world after aging out:[16]

Hey everybody,
So i am transiting out of foster care in 26 more days. I am
very excited but in a way i am very scared due to that fact i

dont know what to do since everything was taken care of for the last 8-9 years. Then Yeah that is really about it. I dont think i have all the skills i need to be successful at this point of time. I think Independent Living failed for me in some departments like getting medical insurance, telling me what to do in case of an emergency since i probably after a while. cause i am getting old and want to experience things on my own but i am not ready. Why cant the system extend your say until you exit college or something have a good job. I think i have a feeling i am going to struggle and i dont want to struggle. I struggled for almost all of my life, and i dont want to anymore. I want to be successful but i dont have a chance i grew up to early like most youth they have time and in my life i didn't have time to bee a kid. it from being a youngster to being an adult and caring on my own. But i have to make the best of everything wish me luck and pray for me

Very few former foster youth end up earning a college degree, and many don't make it past high school. Only a little more than half have earned a GED or high school diploma by age nineteen, according to the federal National Youth in Transition Database, and just a quarter are enrolled in post-secondary vocational training or college.[17] These young people, moreover, don't catch up as they get older. A 2011 survey of former foster youth in Illinois, Wisconsin, and Iowa by Courtney and his colleagues at Chapin Hall found that only 8 percent of these young people had a two-year or four-year degree by age twenty-six.[18] By comparison, 46 percent of Americans age twenty-five to thirty-four now have a two-year degree or more.[19]

Employment among former foster youth is little better. The Chapin Hall research found that fewer than half of twenty-six-year-old former foster youth had jobs, and the average income for the past year was a scant $13,989. Not surprisingly, given this kind of crushing poverty, these young people reported severe levels of economic hardship—more than a quarter said they couldn't pay their rent, and 10 percent had been evicted. One in six said they were hungry but couldn't afford food, and about one-fourth had visited a food pantry. Nearly a third said they had been homeless.

These high levels of disconnection from school and work lead to yet other bleak outcomes as well. Federal data, for instance, find that more than a third of nineteen-year-old former foster youth say they've been jailed, while more than a quarter of seventeen-year-olds have been referred for substance abuse assessment or treatment.[20] By age twenty-six, according to Chapin Hall's research, a majority of the young women have been arrested, as have 80 percent of the young men.[21] Nearly 80 percent of women also reported having been pregnant. Distressingly, 8 percent of the children born to these young women were themselves already in foster care.

"A Disruptive System"

Though the extreme specificity of the statutorily mandated transition plan is intended to protect kids from being neglected by the state up to and through the day they age out, child welfare staff can end up "checking boxes and moving people through the system," as one young woman at the Baltimore convening, the social worker, describes it.

Many young people leave the foster care system without a caring adult committed to their future success—whether they find a job or go to college. When I ask the young adults at the Baltimore convening if they feel they'd had an adult mentor who'd helped them through their transition out of the system, no one raises a hand.

Some experienced a merry-go-round of staff. "I wish I had one person instead of having a case worker, then an independent living worker, then being twenty-one and told 'have a nice life' or whatever," says another young man at the Casey gathering. "It would have been nice to have the consistency of one person instead of having to tell your life story over and over."

Perhaps it's no surprise bureaucracies make terrible parents. Teaching anyone—and teenagers in particular—how to be autonomous and self-reliant is a difficult enough task for parents. It is extraordinarily difficult for government. The inherent nature of the state is to control and to regulate, and the child welfare system is the epitome of state control. All of the players involved—birth parents, foster parents, and the children removed to the state's custody—are, in theory, strictly monitored by both caseworkers and the courts. In fact, in its annual report to Congress on the performance of the nation's child welfare systems, the Administration for Children and Families provides detailed statistics on the percentage of children in foster care receiving monthly visits from their caseworkers.[22] Adulthood, however, is about the opposite of bureaucratic control; it's about independent decision making and personal responsibility. Regulatory structures are fundamentally at odds with that kind of freedom.

Bureaucracies are also intended to create standardized, one-size-fits-all processes. This works fine for providing human services such as Social Security benefits. Once the system gets the inputs it needs—namely, a worker's wages and work history—a formula spits out the appropriate benefit amount, and a check goes in the mail. The virtue of bureaucracy is its fairness and consistency; everyone with the same wage and work history gets the same money. While there is no customization of benefits to people's individual needs, there's also much less room for arbitrary decision making by officials or for bias.

Young adults, however, are a different matter. Each one brings to the table a different set of needs, strengths, and weaknesses. And here is where states' multipage transition manuals, worksheets, and checklists morph from comprehensiveness to rigidity. The absence of a trusted adult means no one to go to for emotional support or sound advice. It also means young people have no one to advocate for them when the system doesn't see their individual needs. One young woman, for instance, says that when she was having trouble in school, her caseworkers automatically tried to push her into special education; it turned out, however, that she belonged in the gifted classroom and had simply been bored by the regular material. "It seemed like I wasn't paying attention or whatnot, but it was because I wasn't getting services catered to my strengths," she says.

(This young woman is also now pursuing a Ph.D.) Another young man says erroneous expectations cut in the other direction as well. "A lot of times the case workers will be so worried about the numbers, the statistics or whatever, that they push a young person to get post-secondary education when it may not be the best thing for that person," he says.

The emotional hardship of being in foster care was another burden that young people felt they had to take on by themselves. "One thing all youth need is to hear that trauma isn't their responsibility," says one young woman. "It was years later that someone told me that."

One problem is that older foster kids have trouble finding permanent, stable homes, either through reunification with their own parents or through adoptive or foster parents, extended family, or a guardianship, even though this goal is one of the child welfare system's core functions. In 2015, while nearly 90 percent of all children in foster care exited to a permanent placement—either back home with their parents, to an adoptive family, or to a legal guardianship with an adult who agrees to be legally responsible for the child—the permanent placement rate was just 66 percent for children older than twelve.

The government cites several reasons for this disparity, including a shortage of foster parents willing to provide permanent homes for older kids, as well as "agency practices that may act as barriers to permanency for older youth." In particular, says the government, child welfare agencies may "lack the commitment needed" to find permanent homes for older kids or prefer to focus on "providing independent living services to youth rather than finding permanency options," although it's unclear that's the better option for most kids.[23] Worst of all, the government concedes, child welfare agencies may simply give up on older kids and "believe these individuals are unadoptable." It's a characterization that young people hotly dispute. "A lot of time there's this implicit bias that they're just bad or poorly behaved kids and they are disruptive youth," says one young man. "But in fact it's a disruptive system."

In the absence of stable placements, many young people in

foster care end up in group homes or institutions, where it's often even tougher to find adult mentors and where the setting, paradoxically, contributes to their sense of aloneness. Group homes tend to be staffed by "relatively young shift workers who tend not to stay in their jobs very long," in the words of researcher Mark Courtney.[24] Life in a group home can also be both rigid and impersonal—with "too much structure, too little love," as writer and foster parent Cris Beam puts it in her book on the foster care system, *To the End of June*. "Imagine living in day care," says one young man at the Jim Casey convening, describing his group-home experience. "You get your meals, you go to bed, this is your life now. It desensitizes you. It changes your personality. You're not going to be the person your family saw as a child."

"Nobody to Teach Me How to Grocery Shop" or "The Only Option Is Us"

The lack of emotional support and mentorship is a chief reason why so many young people are leaving foster care without the basic skills they need to live on their own, let alone pursue an education or find a job.

"I had nobody to teach me how to grocery shop, cook, or balance a checkbook," writes Shawn Denise Semelsberger at FosterClub .com.[25]

Services also end too early. While the majority of states now extend foster care services beyond age eighteen, federal support for former foster youth (except for Medicaid) ends at twenty-one—an age that is arguably too young for most young people to be financially and emotionally independent, let alone those who've had to face the severe challenges of being raised in the child welfare system. "We have to have some sort of support," says one young man at the Jim Casey convening. "We need people who can help us even after childhood and in our early adult years. We're still developing."

Among the crucial skills many young people leaving foster care lack is financial literacy, along with savings of their own to draw on in the case of an emergency or to help them get started in life. One study of nineteen-year-old former foster youths, for instance, found that these young people had median assets of just $100 and that only 30 percent owned a car.[26] Studies also find that only about half of former foster youth have a bank account by age twenty-one and that they rely heavily instead on check cashers and other predatory "alternative" financial providers. Many even develop what some researchers call "a culture of fear in regards to banking."[27]

A potential strategy for teaching young people financial skills while helping them save is through the creation of Individual Development Accounts (IDAs), or matched savings accounts, which have proven effective in other contexts to help low-income people save. So far, however, Washington State has been the only place to pass legislation creating these accounts for foster youth, and, unfortunately, according to the National Conference of State Legislatures, this program was eliminated in 2010 as a result of budget cuts.[28] A growing number of communities, however, have adopted Opportunity Passports, an IDA program sponsored by the Jim Casey Youth Opportunity Initiative.

Many former foster youth also get insufficient help with housing and paying for college, which as we saw earlier are two of the most significant financial benefits middle-class young people get from their parents in early adulthood. The lack of these supports is an enormous barrier to foster youths' ability to finish their schooling and find a job.

Because they have no parents to draw on, former foster youth who make it to college have no choice but to borrow for their education, often substantially. The education and training vouchers available under the Chafee program are grossly inadequate, providing just $5,000 per year per young person when the average cost of one year's in-state tuition, room, and board at a four-year public university was $18,432 in 2017–18.[29] While twenty-eight states waive tuition at state schools for former foster youth, these waivers tend to be age-limited (often only to age twenty-one) and cover just tuition, not books, room, or board.[30] These programs are also unavailable to young people coming from states that don't offer this kind of help.

Housing is an even greater need, given the high rates of homelessness among former foster youth. Existing programs for former foster youth are small, scattershot, and generally offer only short-term help. Young people ages eighteen to twenty-one are, for instance, eligible for housing vouchers under the federal government's Family Unification Program (FUP), the only program dedicated to providing housing for youth involved with the child welfare system. There are, however, only about 20,000 vouchers circulating nationwide, and they expire after eighteen months.[31] And while states are allowed to spend up to 30 percent of their Chafee funding on room and board for young people in transition, that support also ends at age twenty-one. Meanwhile, the lion's share of federal funding on homelessness more broadly is targeted toward adults. Though the Department of Housing and Urban Development spent $2.38 billion on homelessness assistance in 2016, just $134 million went to youth-specific services and shelters.[32]

A consequence of this imbalance is that shelters like the LAYC's drop-in center for homeless young adults are becoming increasingly burdened. On one of my visits there, center director John Van Zandt, whom we met in a previous chapter, interrupts our conversation to take an urgent call. He returns a few minutes later, shaking his head. "I just got a call from child welfare," he says. "I have a client who's aging out in ten days, and she's coming by this week. It can't be and shouldn't be that the only option is us."

Van Zandt is right. Unfortunately, however, young people leaving the foster care system are all too often swept up into another system that does yet more damage to their prospects of connecting to a stable future: criminal justice.

7

"Justice"

In 2017, New York City police arrested 449,386 people—a number equal to slightly more than the total population of Salem, Oregon, and twice the population of Burlington, Vermont.[1] It's an average of 675 people per day. Among those caught in the city's massive justice system was Carlos, a twenty-three-year-old African American young man from the Bronx. Like the plurality of offenses now adjudicated in the justice system nationally, Carlos's offense was drug-related.[2] Though he doesn't get into the details, he's upfront about how he got into trouble. "I [saw] my brothers and friends and their friends not having successful jobs but selling drugs and buying cars—always having the girls, fast money always gained, watches and clothes, buying cars every week," he says. "That's what I was always seeing. I wanted to be like that. I always had a lot of friends who had a lot of money."

Nevertheless, Carlos is hardly a "super predator"—the term made infamous in the mid-1990s that catalyzed the "tough on crime" policies that have come to prove so destructive.[3] Rather, Carlos is soft-spoken to the point where it is difficult to hear his words. Like Rochelle, the young woman from the introduction of this book, he is a client of the New York–based nonprofit Center for Alternative Sentencing and Employment Services (CASES), which offers educational and job training services as an alternative to incarceration. At CASES, Carlos is working on his GED as part of a plan to leave his former life behind. "I want to get my diploma," he says. "After that, I want to find a trade and just continue pushing forward."

Carlos's assignment to CASES, mandated by the court, also allowed him to avoid jail time. That makes him one of the lucky ones. On any given day, there are roughly 9,100 people in New York City's jails, and as in the rest of the country, the city's jail and prison population skews disproportionately young and black.[4] The Justice Policy Institute reports that while about 8 percent of the city's population is between the ages of eighteen and twenty-four, young adults make up nearly 22 percent of the city's jail population.[5] The institute further estimates that there are about 400,000 eighteen-to twenty-four-year-olds in prisons and jails nationwide—roughly half of whom are young people of color.[6] Young people also account for nearly a quarter of all arrests; the FBI reports that in 2016, police made nearly 2.1 million arrests of people aged eighteen to twenty-four.[7]

Shocking as these figures are, they are still a major improvement compared to even just a decade ago—thanks to the dogged activism of criminal justice reform advocates shedding light on the travesties of discriminatory policing and mass incarceration. At the end of 2016, U.S. jails and prisons held 6,613,500 inmates—a number that while still astonishingly high is down by 726,200 since 2007.[8] Nevertheless, youth incarceration remains a major driver of disconnection, both in the moment for young people behind bars and in its aftermath as young people struggle to regain their lives with a blemished record and years of lost time and opportunity.

The majority of people in U.S. jails are technically innocent. The Pretrial Justice Institute reports that as many as six out of ten inmates are in jail not because they've been convicted of a crime but because they are awaiting trial.[9] Most of them are there because they can't afford to free themselves with bail. The evidence shows that unnecessary incarceration causes many more problems than it purports to solve. People who go to jail risk losing their jobs and housing, thereby robbing them of economic self-sufficiency and increasing the likelihood they end up on public assistance;

they are also more likely to be rearrested and for more serious crimes, thereby raising the risk to public safety.[10] Jailing people is also expensive. In New York City, for instance, each inmate costs $264 a day—or $96,233 a year.[11]

For young people, incarceration poses exceptionally dire risks— especially for sixteen- and seventeen-year-olds being tried as adults and thrown into adult jails and prisons. These young people, for instance, are much more likely to suffer violence from both staff and fellow inmates.[12] They are also more likely to become violent themselves. The Centers for Disease Control, for instance, finds that experience in the adult criminal justice system "is associated with subsequent violence among juvenile participants" while having no effect on deterring crime, either specifically among the young people treated so harshly or in the general population.[13] The Campaign for Youth Justice likewise argues that putting young people in adult jails "can increase exposure to criminogenic surroundings, thereby offering youth opportunities to gain criminal 'training' from incarcerated adults."[14] "Taking a young person and putting them into the adult system is basically ensuring that you're going to turn them into an adult criminal learning from the people around them," says Thaddeus Ferber, vice president for policy at the Forum for Youth Investment.

At the same time, many adult jails fail to provide any sort of educational or job-training services, which puts young adults at an even greater disadvantage when they are ultimately released. According to the Justice Policy Institute, "nearly 40 percent of adult jails do not provide any education services, and only seven percent provide services to help train young people for a job."[15] Moreover, as Kisha Bird of the Center for Law and Social Policy (CLASP) points out, federal law currently forbids incarcerated individuals from accessing Pell grants for higher education, a ban that was included in the now roundly vilified 1994 crime bill.[16] These deficits, when compounded by the difficulty that a criminal conviction already poses to someone looking for a job, virtually guarantees a young person's long-term disconnection.

Juvenile detention is little better. Though it theoretically carries fewer physical risks than an adult prison, a 2010 Bureau of Justice Statistics survey of youth in detention centers found that as many as 12 percent of detainees had been sexually victimized by staff or other youth.[17] Damage to mental and physical well-being is also common. The Justice Policy Institute reports that "for one-third of incarcerated youth diagnosed with depression, the onset of the depression occurred after they began their incarceration."[18]

Juvenile incarceration is ineffective as well as dangerous. According to the Justice Policy Institute, young people in detention are "more likely to reoffend than youth who are not detained, physical and mental health conditions often worsen during detention, and detained youth can face significant challenges reconnecting to school, getting a job, and staying employed."[19] In fact, some research finds that incarceration is a greater predictor of recidivism than carrying a weapon or belonging to a gang.[20] One study, by the Annie E. Casey Foundation, reports that 70 to 80 percent of incarcerated youth are rearrested within two or three years.[21]

Incarceration as a young adult can have lifelong impacts on earnings and employment, even for those who avoid further entanglement with the justice system. When researcher Stephen Raphael at the University of California, Berkeley, looked at data from the National Longitudinal Survey of Youth covering the years 1979 to 1996, he found that young men who served any length of time were less likely to be married and more likely to work less and earn less.[22] Another study, by the National Bureau of Economic Research, found that incarcerating young people between ages sixteen and twenty-five "reduced work time over the next decade by 25 to 30 percent."[23]

Fortunately, with the help of justice reform advocates, states are beginning to understand the folly of sending children into adult jails and prisons. "Raise the Age" campaigns in numerous states, for instance, have successfully led many states to eliminate laws automatically sending sixteen- and seventeen-year-olds into the adult criminal justice system. In New York, for example, sixteen-year-olds will no longer be tried automatically as adults after October 2018, while the same will be true of seventeen-year-olds in

2019. Since 2007, according to the Vera Institute for Justice, Illinois, Louisiana, Massachusetts, Mississippi, New Hampshire, and South Carolina have all passed similar laws, while Connecticut and Vermont have gone one step further to raise the presumed age of "criminal responsibility"—i.e., the age at which an offender is no longer eligible for juvenile court—all the way to twenty-one.[24]

In the meantime, fewer young people are ending up in juvenile detention as well. Scholar Cara Drinan, author of the 2016 book *The War on Kids*, finds that "[o]ver the past 15 years, the number of young people incarcerated annually by juvenile justice systems nationwide has been cut by half," along with reduction in juvenile arrests and felony petitions.[25] Among the most significant reforms that led to this change is the Juvenile Detention Alternatives Initiative, which was launched by the Annie E. Casey Foundation in 2013 and now involves more than 250 localities in 30 states plus the District of Columbia. Under this initiative, jurisdictions are encouraged to use day and evening reporting centers, home confinement, and shelter care as alternatives to juvenile detention, and to provide services such as mental health treatment and other services to help a young person stay connected to school and community.[26] And in places like New Orleans, young people who commit minor offenses, such as littering or marijuana possession, will face warnings or summonses, instead of arrest.[27]

There is, however, much to be done before the justice system is no longer a pipeline to disconnection for young people.

Transfer Laws

Even as states are raising the age at which young offenders are automatically sent into the adult system, every state still has "transfer" laws that allow minors—in some cases as young as ten—to be tried as adults. There are several separate mechanisms under which this can happen. Forty-five states, for instance, allow for a "judicial waiver," where a juvenile court judge can decide whether to remand a defendant to an adult court. In this instance, there is a waiver hearing, and the prosecution bears the burden of showing why an adult court is more appropriate. In fifteen states, according to Drinan, the decision to put a child into adult court is a question purely for prosecutorial discretion. Under these so-called direct file statutes, "there is no evidentiary hearing, no record of the prosecutor's decision, and no basis upon which the juvenile defendant can challenge the judgment."[28] Finally, twenty-nine states automatically transfer a juvenile to adult court depending on the nature of the offense. While murder is the most common offense that results in automatic transfer, some states also allow it for robbery, assault, and even drug offenses.[29]

One result of these transfer laws is that there are still too many kids in prison, most of whom are awaiting trial and have not been convicted of any crime. As Drinan writes, "[O]n any given day in America, 10,000 kids are housed in adult jails and prisons. Over the course of a year, close to 100,000 youth will spend time in adult facilities."[30]

Racial Disparities

Young people in jail are disproportionately black. If, as Michelle Alexander brilliantly argues in *The New Jim Crow*, mass incarceration has replaced Jim Crow as a mechanism for social control, nowhere is that more true than for young adults.

In 2010, according to ChildTrends, as many as 8 percent of young black men ages twenty to twenty-four were incarcerated, compared to 3.3 percent of Hispanics and just 1.3 percent of whites.[31] And the transfer laws just discussed have a disproportionate impact on black youth. The Campaign for Youth Justice finds that black young adults are "substantially more likely than their white counterparts to be tried as adults."[32]

Public outcry over mass incarceration may have benefited whites more than blacks, and in some cases worsened disparities in the justice system. A study by the Sentencing Project, for example, finds that while placements in juvenile detention facilities dropped by 54 percent between 2001 and 2015: "white youth placements have declined faster than black youth placements. Overall, the

racial disparity between black and white youth in custody increased 22 percent since 2001." Black youth, moreover, "were more
than five times as likely to be detained or committed compared to
white youth," and in six states—New Jersey, Wisconsin, Montana,
Delaware, Connecticut, and Massachusetts—African American
youth were ten times more likely to be held than white youth.[33]

School to Jail

Closely linked to these inequities is the disproportional suspension and expulsion of black students from K–12 public schools
that feeds the so-called school-to-jail pipeline. In their 2015 landmark report, scholars Edward Smith and Shaun Harper found
that 1.2 million black students were suspended from school in the
2011–12 school year, with 55 percent of these suspensions taking
place in just thirteen states in the South. In 743 of these districts,
black students were 50 percent of the suspended students, while
in 181 districts, fully 100 percent of the students suspended were
black.[34]

As Smith and Harper document, suspensions and expulsions
are linked to a host of negative consequences for young students,
including a greater risk of dropout and the greater likelihood of
being held back a grade. Suspensions are also "strongly associated
with subsequent participation in juvenile and criminal justice
systems. . . . The overrepresentation of Blacks among students impacted by discipline policies and practices has incontestably helped
sustain the school-to-prison pipeline," Smith and Harper write.[35]

In December 2018, Congress and President Trump passed the
bipartisan First Step Act, a landmark effort to undo the "tough
on crime" federal sentencing laws that propelled the mass incarceration phenomenon.[36] Among other things, the legislation gave
judges more discretion to avoid the "mandatory minimums" re-
quired under prior law, which should lead to shorter sentences for
more prisoners. It also included several mechanisms to provide for
the earlier release of inmates with good behavior or who participate

in education or vocational programs. As the name implies, the law was a first step—albeit an important one—in the overall project of criminal justice reform. What it didn't do, and what the next step should, is address the particular burdens of incarceration on young people, who bear the brunt of the system's flaws, are the most vulnerable to its abuses, and have the most to lose in terms of their lifelong prospects after they re-enter society.

In the meantime, organizations like CASES are working hard to divert as many young people from the pain and consequences of incarceration as possible. Currently, the organization serves roughly 4,000 clients a year.[37] "You have to give people a chance," says Joel Copperman, CASES's CEO. "It's in everyone's best interests if our clients succeeds. It's better for everybody if they're not in jail, not on any kind of public assistance, and [are] successful in life."

Among these clients is Nazir, a twenty-one-year-old who immigrated from Bangladesh as a child. Short and slightly built, Nazir defies all stereotypes of someone who spent most of his youth on the streets. "I grew up around a lot of drugs and guns, shooting and violence and stuff," he says. His father was deported when Nazir was about six years old, and he grew up with his stepmother, four stepbrothers, and five stepsisters, only one of whom he is in touch with today. Money was tight, his family was in constant turmoil, and it wasn't long before he fell in with the wrong crowd. "I was around eleven when everything shifted off," he says. "I became rebellious hanging out with the wrong guys in the street," he adds. "I found my own ways of being a man and being who I wanted to be." He dropped out of school in tenth grade and ultimately ended up arrested. "I was incarcerated . . . it was hard going through it," he says.

Nazir was ordered to come to CASES three years ago as part of his sentence but has since been coming back voluntarily to work toward his GED. "I love CASES," he says. "Every time I come to CASES, there's a hand out to help you, even if you're not willing to appreciate it sometimes."

For Nazir, CASES has become a substitute family. "Every time something bad happens, every time to get my mind off of that,

I come to CASES," he says. "I used to have one-on-one therapy, and I always used to talk to the therapist about everything, and it would ease my mind off." In addition to helping him with his mental health, CASES helped him renew his passport and replace his citizenship papers and birth certificate, documents his family refused to give him when he left home. "I had so many family issues in my life it paused my whole life at one point—the things they were doing to me and stuff like that," he says.

Today, he feels his life is more on track. "I'm just maintaining, trying to get myself together," he says. He makes money delivering food for Uber Eats and Caviar. He records his own music and has dreams of college. "I want to study to be an EMT," he shares. "Probably do a little bit of business management and open my own business one day." He's grateful for the second chance and the opportunity to dream.

"Without this organization, I would probably be in a more messed up place than I was before," he says. "This program changed my mindset around and influenced me to do better each day. . . . You have to learn from your mistakes to proceed through life."

PART III

Anchored: Paths to Reconnection

8

Throwing Lifelines

America is suffering from a crisis of opportunity among its young adults. Despite a seemingly robust economy and record low levels of unemployment as of this writing, millions of young people who should be launching their careers are instead on the sidelines, disconnected from both work and school. As with so many other debates involving poverty and social policy, it might be tempting to dismiss the misfortunes of these young people as products of poor choices and poor parenting, fostered by a dysfunctional "culture of poverty." And certainly, choices play a role. Some young people turn their backs on the opportunities presented to them or are so imprisoned by their short-term desires that they ignore the counsel of their parents, teachers, and other adults around them.

But as we saw in previous chapters, the primary drivers of disconnection in many young people's lives are vast structural forces that few individuals can overcome on their own—low-quality schools, deep poverty, geographic and social isolation, the uncaring machinery of the criminal justice or foster care system. For young people in these circumstances, the threads of connection to a better future are often tenuous and fragile, if they exist at all, and far too easily severed. Moreover, government is all too often the instrument of that severance—either directly, as in the case of foster youth unceremoniously "aged out" of care, or indirectly, through policymakers' failure to invest in interventions that could help more young people stay on track.

Recall Keisha, the young woman in the Bronx from chapter 5 who has been mired in a cycle of low-wage retail jobs since dropping out of high school. For her, losing the parent who was her biggest motivator and coach was what propelled her toward her currently precarious path. "I lost my father," she says. "He used to be always on me waking me up at six in the morning. My mother, she would sleep past the time I was supposed to go to school, like I was in one of those homes that wasn't stern about going to school." Keisha was also among the oldest in a houseful of siblings, which made it even easier to slip under the radar at home. "It's overwhelming for parents that have more than four kids," she says. "My mom had nine kids, and she raised all of us by herself, no help, alone."

Today, Keisha is in danger of repeating the cycle she grew up in. When I meet her in September of 2018, she is three months pregnant. "I'm going to raise my baby to be the best," she says. "I'm going to instill into my baby school is very important. Don't let anybody tell you it's not, because when you stop going, you realize there's opportunities where you need school." Despite her determination, however, she lacks the practical resources to ensure she can afford a better future for her child. She hasn't yet thought about child care, how she is going to finish her GED, or whether her part-time job as a sales clerk at Burlington will allow her to afford the things she and her baby will need. She is out of touch with the baby's father. She doesn't have her own place and is instead doubling up with members of her extended family or "couch surfing" with friends.

It's easy to imagine the potential trajectory Keisha's future could take. She could lose her job at the Burlington store if she can't find reliable, affordable child care. She might lose her housing if her friends or relatives decide they don't have the space or want the disruption of a squalling infant and sleepless mom. Certainly her aspiration to earn a GED could be derailed, and with it her hopes of a better job. If she's lucky, she might secure a scarce spot in public housing; if she's not, she's headed for the instability and hardships of life in a shelter. In either case, she's likely to be dependent on public benefits rather than her own earnings.

But this future is only inevitable if we let it be—as we have for far too many young people already. Reweaving the threads of connection for young adults is by no means an easy task, but it is not impossible. In fact, an emerging body of research over the last twenty years tells us the kinds of approaches that work best to help young people reboot their lives and reconnect to the opportunities that should have been theirs from the start. As I illustrated earlier in this book, the paths to disconnection are varied, as is the degree of disconnection. In some instances, a young person might have the skills and education they need to start a career and just need help finding the right opportunity. In other cases, a young person might need help going back to school or getting occupational training before they can join the labor force productively. Still others might need housing, substance abuse or mental health treatment, or other services before they are ready to reconnect to school or work. In each instance, a dedicated and growing corps of youth-oriented nonprofits is developing innovative models and best practices to ensure that young people in need of help get the right combination of supports.

In Keisha's case, what might work best for her and her new baby is a "transitional living" program like the one I describe in the following chapter for homeless young moms. In these intensive programs, Keisha would have a place to stay, help finishing her GED and then finding a job, assistance in getting child care, Medicaid, and other benefits to supplement her wages, plus the company of other young mothers facing similar struggles and the support of a caring staff.

It's unlikely, however, that she'll get the chance to benefit from this kind of intervention. According to the U.S. Department of Health and Human Services, the federal government only spends just over $45 million a year in grants to support this type of program and funds just 236 such programs nationwide. In fiscal 2016, transitional living programs reached just 5,000 youth [1]—a bare fraction of the 3.5 *million* young adults who experience homelessness over a twelve-month period, according to Chapin Hall.[2]

In general, the federal government badly underinvests in preventing or combating disconnection among America's young people. This includes severe underinvestment in programs that could help young people connect to school and jobs, such as second-chance adult education for high school dropouts, education and training support for former foster youth, and national service programs such as AmeriCorps that can help young people secure a foothold in the job market through work experience and job training. In fiscal 2015, for instance, what the federal government spent all told to combat youth disconnection was 0.4 percent of what it spent on defense ($582 billion), 0.2 percent of what it spent on Social Security ($882 billion), and an infinitesimally small fraction of the total federal budget of $3.7 trillion.[3] The government in fact spent nearly one hundred times more to pay interest on the national debt ($224 billion) than it did to create opportunities for young people.[4] As one result, the Forum for Youth Investment finds that federal programs reached just 339,719 "opportunity youth" in 2015—or just 7 percent of the then 4.9 million young people out of school and out of work.

The numbers have improved a little bit since then, thanks to a hard-fought drive by the Reconnecting Youth Campaign, a coalition of youth advocacy organizations and nonprofits aiming to increase funding for youth programs. In fiscal 2019, the federal government will spend a total of about $2.53 billion on programs aimed at reconnecting youth—an increase of $122 million over 2017 levels.[5] Nevertheless, this figure is still about $4 billion a year shy of what's needed to reach 1 million young people each year.[6]

The bulk of this funding, moreover—about $1.7 billion—in fact will go to just one legacy government jobs program, Job Corps, which unfortunately delivers mixed results (as will be discussed in a later chapter).[7] Meanwhile, only about $39 million will go to adult education, $42 million to training and education vouchers for former foster youth, and barely $200 million will go to high-impact initiatives such as YouthBuild and National Guard ChalleNGe, two programs that have demonstrated the best results among the "comprehensive" education and employment programs currently federally funded (which will be profiled in the next chapter).[8]

And while some programs—such as child welfare—appear to be much bigger line items in the federal budget, very little is spent on older youth and their transition out of foster care. In fiscal 2014, for example, states spent a total of $29.1 billion in federal, state, and local funds on child welfare services, according to ChildTrends, but only 2 percent of federal dollars and 2 percent of state and local dollars were spent on services for older youth.[9] The bulk of the money—about two-thirds—went to pay for foster care, adoption, and guardianship assistance, while another 30 percent went toward child protective services (investigating claims of neglect and abuse, for example) and in-home services to prevent abuse, neglect, and the removal of kids into foster care.[10] As writer Cris Beam has pointed out, child welfare agencies are principally geared toward protecting the safety of very young children, not the development of teens and young adults.[11] As a consequence, the funding of services to help young people transition out of care gets short shrift, and the odds of their future success diminish accordingly.

It Pays to Invest in What Works

This pattern of persistent underinvestment in young people is both shortsighted and costly. The greatest tragedy of disconnection is the loss of individual human potential—not only the energy, talent, and ideas that each young person can bring to the table, but also the positive economic contributions a young person can make as a working, taxpaying citizen. "We don't know what we will have lost, the dreams and visions those kids have that we'll never get back," says Judith Dittman, executive director of the nonprofit youth organization Second Story, which will be profiled in the next chapter. Disconnection spells the loss of these benefits while creating significant costs society must ultimately bear.

In a 2012 study for Civic Enterprises, scholars Clive R. Belfield and Henry M. Levin estimated that taxpayers lose $13,890 per young person per year in direct fiscal costs for every year of disconnection between ages sixteen and twenty-four, leading to lifetime costs per person of $235,680 (in 2012 dollars).[12] These costs include not just lower tax collections as a result of lost wages but also higher government expenditures for incarceration, Medicaid, and welfare. Belfield and Levin further calculate that if the broader social costs of higher poverty and crime are considered, the total burdens imposed by each young person who is out of school and out of work is even higher—as much as $704,020 in lifetime costs.

In truth, the costs of disconnection are likely difficult to quantify precisely, but it's hard to dispute that society bears the price when a disconnected young person later becomes an unproductive adult. On the flip side, when a young person does successfully connect to the labor force, pays taxes, and contributes to his or her community, the societal benefits are just as great, if not greater. The Reconnecting Youth Campaign, for instance, argues that every $1 spent on youth programs could potentially return between $2 and $5 in taxpayer money saved on public benefits, incarceration costs, or other expenses and $3.50 in net tax revenue from wages earned. In the aggregate, the campaign argues, the $4 billion in additional funding for youth programs needed—to reach 1 million young people a year—could help save taxpayers as much as $65 billion in long-term expenditures and net as much as $105 billion in new tax revenues.[13]

Without doubt, any call to spend more federal dollars on any effort will be met with consternation from deficit hawks concerned about the nation's future fiscal health. These critics are right that the government's finances are in dire straits. But the consequences of not investing in young people are more severe still, and the rewards of even a modest investment in America's youth will be more than repaid in full.

The next few chapters describe some of the most promising types of programs where these investments should be made and the ways in which these initiatives are transforming the lives of young people who would otherwise forever be shut out of the mainstream of opportunity. While these efforts cannot fully undo the impacts of broadening inequalities in the circumstances of young adults, they can still give lower-income young people a better shot at catching up to their more affluent peers—or at least erasing some of the disadvantages imposed upon them. What these programs also have in common is the foundational belief that all young people with the desire to remake their lives can build the capacity to do so. And as the following chapters show, young people are in fact seizing that opportunity.

9

Intensive Care

Carla is an energetic, ambitious young Latina woman with sleek, chin-length brown hair and an open, confident manner. We meet in the summer of 2018 over bubble teas at a Korean coffee shop off a busy street in Reston, Virginia, not too far from the defense contracting firm where she works full-time. Though just twenty-five years old, she is already managing multimillion-dollar projects for her firm as a procurement specialist—her bosses had quickly promoted her from the entry-level clerical job where she'd started out. She is also a homeowner as well as a mom, the proud owner of a small condo she shares with her boyfriend and two young sons.

But it was only a few short years ago that Carla was homeless, pregnant, and struggling to stay in school. She'd run away from home after getting pregnant at age seventeen, fearing that her parents would force her to get an abortion, as they did when she was pregnant the first time, at fifteen. "I literally ran into the woods," she says, recalling the night she left home. After that, she spent two years "couch surfing" with friends and relatives while trying to graduate from high school and holding down a part-time job at a Wegman's grocery store to support herself. "I was living in a lot of different places," she says. "I was living at my sister's house, my son's father's sister's place, then my boyfriend's friend's place sometimes." At one point, she stayed with her then-boyfriend's mother, who was renting out space in her house for extra cash. She slept on the floor with at least a dozen other people, all of them adults, scattered throughout the house. "I had bedbug bites everywhere," she says. Knowing she needed to continue her schooling, she enrolled at the Northern Virginia Community College in Fairfax County but failed all her classes. "My son was really little," she says, "and I was going through too much." She had not reconciled with her parents, and her son's father had become increasingly abusive. He was eventually deported after committing assault.

What ultimately salvaged Carla's prospects was the help of an innovative local nonprofit called Second Story, which she'd heard about through a friend. Over the course of about four years, the organization gave her a place to stay, along with the support she needed to finish school and find a job. Second Story even set up a savings account to help her put aside $19,000, which became the down payment for her condo. Residents are required to sign over 45 percent of their net earnings to the program, which keeps the money in escrow until the women graduate. Counseling services helped Carla reunite with her family.

Aiding Carla was Second Story's "transitional living" program, a model that offers homeless young people—such as runaways like Carla or youth aging out of foster care or leaving the justice system—a temporary place to stay as well as intensive services to put them on the path to self-sufficiency. Her journey is proof positive that with the right kind of help, young people even in the direst of circumstances can get their lives back on track. Her story also raises the question: how many other Carlas could we be helping that we are not? Unfortunately, there are far too few nonprofits like Second Story and far too many young women like Carla.

Almost Home

Middle-class kids and parents often take for granted the value of structure and stability in a child's home life. In fact, middle-class parents of toddlers and young children often bemoan the tyranny of the schedule that rules their lives—naptimes that if missed lead to early-evening meltdowns; the daily march of snacks, meals, baths, and bedtimes; playdates and structured activities; and, over it all, the exhaustion of unending vigilance that comes with keeping a young child out of mischief. But parents also instinctively realize the benefit of routine in helping build a child's sense of security and self-confidence. Routine is the invisible scaffolding that keeps a healthy household together. Kids in typical households don't question whether they will have a place to sleep or if they will be fed. Rules about appropriate behavior not only help keep them safe ("Don't play with matches!") but also impart the importance of self-management. And as much as children test the boundaries of the rules parents set (along with their parents' patience), these explorations are also intended in part to test how much a parent cares about their well-being. ("Is mom going to notice if I go play in traffic?")

The importance of this structure and stability becomes all the more apparent when it's not there. For young women like Carla, for instance, their disconnection from school and work is a direct consequence of their underlying estrangement from their families. Organizations like Second Story fill the void—at least temporarily—and provide the support that connected young people take for granted in their homes but the highest-need young people don't have or never had. In many instances, having that refuge can make the difference in whether a young person can arrest their slide into permanent disconnection and regain their footing.

Often, this begins with something as basic as a place to stay.

In the case of Second Story, the organization maintains an emergency shelter for homeless teens in a split-level house on a commercial street in Tysons Corner, Virginia, sandwiched between an apartment complex and an office park. Fairfax County, where Tysons Corner is located, just outside D.C., is among the most affluent counties in the country. In 2016, the median household income was an impressive $114,329, and the median home was worth $516,800.[1] Even so, there's plenty of diversity and significant pockets of poverty and homelessness—according to the county, more than 2,300 homeless children were enrolled in the Fairfax County public schools in 2017–18.[2] "People are always surprised there's homelessness here," says Judith Dittman, Second Story's executive director.

Moms like Carla live in one of three townhouses Second Story maintains for its transitional living program. One of these is in a complex in Fairfax, Virginia, and is home to two young moms and their children. There are three bus stops nearby and a Metro station within walking distance so the women have ready access to transportation.

The townhouse is sparsely furnished but comfortable. On the main level is the living room with a desk and a computer, a playpen, and baby seats. Toward the back is a small kitchen and a dining room with a wooden kitchen table and four chairs. There's a washer and dryer in the basement, and upstairs are two bathrooms, along with two small bedrooms and nurseries for the kids. All of the furniture has been donated or bought secondhand. None of it is stylish; all of it is serviceable. There are also plenty of strings attached—something that's crucial to the theory behind the program. In exchange for a place to stay, program participants must work, go to school, and use the time they have to prepare for a life without the organization's support.

For instance, when clients move in, their first priority is learning how to maintain their new home and keep it clean. This task is a key component of the structure the program provides. By giving clients the responsibility of maintaining their living space, they learn self-efficacy, time management, and accountability. Conceptually, it's no different from a parent's demands that kids clean up their rooms.

"The first thirty days are focused on learning about the house," says Megan Huebner, director of Second Story's residential services. "How do you operate the washer and dryer? What do you do if there's water coming out of the shower and you can't turn it off?" Many of the young women, Huebner says, have never kept up their own place. The housing also comes with many other conditions—there are rules and rules and rules. Curfew is at 9 p.m. each night, and visitors are not allowed without permission. The staff comes in for "chore check" to make sure the place is clean, and there are random checks at odd hours to ensure that people are where they are supposed to be and people who aren't supposed to be there are not. "You have to call in by nine on the voicemail every night," says Carla. "You say, 'Carla calling in for curfew, then hang up.'" The first month is a probationary period, and if all goes well, you earn a weekend pass away. The young women also earn points for house-keeping, which they can turn in for pizza, gift cards, or a curfew extension.

While the rules might sound draconian to some, they impose the structure and routine that many of these young people have never experienced before. "It made me really responsible for my-self," says Carla. Even the curfews were helpful, she says, by keep-ing her away from the people in her life who were destructive, such as her abusive boyfriend. "What helped me was forcing me to be independent and isolated from people who gave me anxiety," she shares. "It forced me to just focus on myself and my son."

The rules at Second Story also include mandatory attendance at therapy, weekly meetings with a case manager, and group ses-sions on Monday and Tuesday nights focused on basic life skills: parenting, budgeting, how to read a lease. The women learn about the right way to discipline their kids, how to introduce their ba-bies to new foods, and milestones in development. They also learn about the "soft skills" they need to get and hold a job. "Once, this neuroscientist came and talked to us about emotional intelligence," says Carla. "It was the first time I'd heard of it, and it was really eye opening."

Over the course of just a couple years, Second Story essentially provided Carla with the lifetime of support that middle-class par-ents give to their children. In addition to learning the skills they need to run a household and be good moms, the women are re-quired to spend at least thirty hours a week at work or in school or training. Each young woman works with her case manager on a "service plan"—a written plan with goals for their physical and mental health, parenting and life skills, and career and education. "My case manager, Angel, was amazing," says Carla. "She worked around the clock."

In Carla's case, Angel connected her with a local workforce program called Training Futures, which put her into an internship, where she worked in office administration from 9 a.m. to 2 p.m. every day, learned Microsoft Word and other skills, and earned a certificate.[3] That internship helped her land her first job, as a facilities assistant at a defense contracting agency in the area. "It was easier to find a job after I completed that program," she says. It was there that she met the person who would help her get her current job at the defense contracting firm—a connection that she likely would never have made without the help of Second Story.

"Scooping Out the Bad Stuff"

Structure is also a major component of other effective high-intensity programs such as National Guard Youth ChalleNGe and YouthBuild and is the secret of their success. These models have also proven effective in helping young people with even the highest needs reconnect successfully with school and work.

ChalleNGe, for instance, is a seventeen-month residential program run by the U.S. Department of Defense through the National Guard Bureau for young people between the ages of sixteen and eighteen who have either dropped out or been kicked out of high school. Begun as a pilot project in 1993, it was made permanent by Congress in 1998 and is now available at thirty-nine sites around the country.[4] If programs like Second Story are a metaphorical boot camp in parenting and life skills for young moms, ChalleNGe is a literal boot camp. For five months of the program, young people—the cadets—live in barracks on a military base, get haircuts, wear uniforms, and have a strictly regimented schedule with military-style discipline and no access to cell phones. Adult "cadres" supervise and serve as mentors while the cadets work toward their GEDs as well as on physical fitness, job skills, leadership, and life skills.

Program founder Hugh Price (who is also known for his role as the longtime president of the National Urban League) says the program is intended to be all-consuming. He worked with Daniel Donohue of the Center for Strategic and International Studies in the late 1980s to devise the curriculum. "Dan said to me, 'We're going to get these kids onto a military base for five months and what we do is freeze dry their brains, scoop out the bad stuff, and systematically inject the good stuff,'" Price says. "That's an indication of how intense the experience is." It's an approach that works.

One of the program's now more than 155,000 alumni is Victor Ehienulo, whom I met at the program's twenty-fifth anniversary celebration in 2018 at one of the sparkling new hotels in D.C.'s Wharf District, on the banks of the Potomac. In a room filled with cadets in fatigues and military brass in full dress uniform, Victor stood out in a bright blue embroidered tunic evoking his native Nigeria. "Eight years ago, I was in the streets," he said. Victor said he was often in fights (he showed me scars on his neck to prove it) and was expelled from three different high schools before enrolling in a ChalleNGe program in Virginia Beach, Virginia, when he was seventeen.

There, he met the mentor he had never had before. "I would go up to a cadre to play checkers and talk about life and get guidance," he said. "I wasn't doing it consciously, but I formed a relationship, and I was like, 'Man, I'm learning so much from this guy.' He spent his time talking to me. That's where the impact starts." Victor earned his GED while on base, then went on to community college and then to Howard University. After that, he landed a job at Microsoft and is now living in California, hoping to launch a tech start-up.

"You asked where I would be without ChalleNGe—I don't know," he said. "Some of my friends are dead already. But I turned my life around. I changed everything about myself. I can't believe I did this. I finished school. I'm living in California. I'm meeting new people. That's the reason for ChalleNGe, to show you the different opportunities out there that you can explore."

Victor also mentioned the importance of a sense of belonging and loyalty when he was in ChalleNGe—to his squad, to his cadre, and to the program as a whole.

This sense of belonging, which is something that many disconnected young people don't get with their own families, is also what defines another "high-touch" program, YouthBuild.

On its surface, YouthBuild—a national program first launched in the 1970s and which serves about 10,000 young people a year—looks simply to be an education and job training program for kids in trouble. Its participants are ages sixteen to twenty-four, 90 percent are high school dropouts, all of them are low income, and many are also involved with the justice system, aging out of foster care, have disabilities, or are children of incarcerated parents.[5] Over twelve months, participants work toward their GEDs, learn construction skills by helping to build affordable housing in their communities, and get opportunities for leadership development. Unlike ChalleNGe, YouthBuild participants don't live together, but the program in many ways is as intense as ChalleNGe. And like ChalleNGe, the program also seeks to develop something more than skills, which is a sense of community and belonging. "I must have heard a thousand times, I came to YouthBuild looking for a GED but found a family," says Dorothy Stoneman, YouthBuild's founder.

One signature component of the program is a one- to two-week "Mental Toughness Orientation," designed to teach life skills such as collaboration and self-discipline as well as soft skills such as punctuality. Team-building exercises are also a big part of the curriculum. Stoneman says that "MTO" was developed by one of her construction managers in Boston in the 1980s. "He said, 'I have to build houses on schedule and they have to be correctly built. But people have internalized so much hopelessness and bad habits that they're not producing the way I need them to. We need hard work and determination, and they've given up.'" MTO is not, however, punitive. Rather, it's the opposite. "I tell the staff that your job is to surprise the young people by how much you care and to do things they would never expect a grown-up to do," says Stoneman. "Love coupled with self-discipline, leading to opportunity and success. What comes from that is gratitude and a desire to give back."

National evaluations show promising results for both National Guard ChalleNGe and YouthBuild. A 2011 study of 1,200 ChalleNGe alumni found, for instance, that graduates were much more likely than a control group to have earned a GED and college credits and more likely to be employed. On average, their earnings were also about 20 percent higher than their control-group peers.[6] And beyond tangible outcomes on jobs and education, interviews of National Guard ChalleNGe participants showed that the program "was successful in changing their attitudes and bolstering their self-confidence." Likewise, a study of seventy-five YouthBuild programs found that participants were more likely to earn a GED and enroll in college or vocational training. They were also more likely to be employed and to earn higher wages the first year after graduation. YouthBuild alums were also more civically engaged, including by being more likely to volunteer.[7]

Transitional living programs like the one Second Story offers are relatively new by comparison. According to HHS, a large-scale evaluation is in the works but will not be completed until at least 2019.[8] A 2016 evaluation of the Youth Villages transitional living program in Tennessee, however, found some promising early impacts for participants, who were primarily involved in the foster care and justice systems, including modest increases in employment and housing stability.[9] Anecdotally, transitional living programs like Second Story are meeting with impressive results. While Carla seems to be one of Second Story's more spectacular successes, the list of Second Story's successes is in fact a long one. Residential services director Huebner says the program has graduated more than one hundred young moms in its fifteen years and consistently has an average of thirty young mothers on its wait list. Many of the alumnae stay in touch. "There's one mom who's twenty-seven years old, and she calls to check up on me," says Huebner. These successes are all the more remarkable given the depth of the challenges young women are facing when they arrive on Second Story's doorstep.

The typical Second Story client, for instance, is a low-income young mom whose education is inadequate and whose background is scarred by trauma. "Eighty percent of our moms were daughters of young moms," says Second Story executive director Judith Dittman. "We also see a huge level of violence that's present in the families. Kids aren't leaving home because it's a fun thing to do.

They're forced out or they've taken up risky behaviors because of whatever situation."

Second Story former client Carla says many of her fellow program participants came from abusive situations. "There was one girl, her baby was born premature, so her baby had a disability," she says. "She told us it was because her boyfriend threw her out of the car when it was moving and she went into labor." In her own case, her parents were inattentive, as well as volatile. "I was drinking when I was thirteen," she shares. "I was drinking a lot until I had my son, like by myself in my room. I was probably really depressed but didn't know."

Getting to Escape Velocity

Initiatives like YouthBuild, National Guard ChalleNGe, and the transitional housing program Second Story provides, show that all young people have potential, no matter how dire their situations seem to be. For Carla, Second Story gave her a chance to relaunch her life. "You have to be willing to sacrifice a lot," she says. "You have to be very determined. There were a lot of times I would take a long shower and cry. But it worked."

Programs like these, however, touch only a fraction of the young people who need help and are a prime example of how underinvestment in young people is allowing too many to fall through the cracks. Transitional living programs, for instance, were first authorized by Congress in 1988, yet, as noted above, there are fewer than 250 of these programs nationwide.[10] Moreover, Second Story executive director Dittman is constantly scrabbling for dollars from a variety of federal, state, and local sources as well as from private philanthropy. Dittman says that Second Story is the only surviving homeless shelter for youth in Fairfax County—five others have closed over the years for lack of funding. Federal funding also only allows the programs to last eighteen months, which Dittman argues is too short. "It's unrealistic and unreasonable to expect a young person who is a parent to enter a program and eighteen months later have completed their education, found a job, learned

to be a parent, and make enough money to afford market-rate housing," she says.

A Second Story for Everyone

Despite their effectiveness, high-touch initiatives like these are no
panacea for disconnection. Not every young person disconnected
from school or work needs the intensity of the services provided
by programs like Second Story. Moreover, these programs, despite
their successes, cannot solve the structural obstacles young people
need to overcome for lifetime self-sufficiency.

In a high-cost area like Fairfax County, for instance, achieving financial self-sufficiency can be very difficult. Most of Second
Story's participants, for example, are high school graduates, but
that credential will not get you far in the D.C. Metro area. "If you
work at McDonald's forty hours a week at minimum wage it's very
difficult to support yourself here," says Second Story residential
services director Huebner. However, low-wage service jobs make
up the bulk of the kinds of jobs the young women are able to get.
"It's a lot of retail, food service, not so much apparel, but restaurants, Michael's, Safeway," says Huebner. A few, like Carla, are able
to land office jobs or to work in allied health fields such as being
a dental technician or a certified nursing assistant, but typically
only after they've gotten some schooling under their belt. Affording
child care and transportation are also often obstacles. Carla, for
instance, recalls that because she didn't have a car, it took her at
least two hours every morning and multiple buses to get her son to
day care and then herself to work.

High-intensity programs also can't provide that intensity for the
extended length of time many young people might need—they can
provide a home for a while, but not a home forever. The MDRC
evaluation of National Guard ChalleNGe, for example, found that
some of the immediate gains participants enjoyed from the program
tended to diminish over time, after young people went back to the
destructive environments they came from. "The data . . . suggest
that it is difficult for many young people to maintain momentum

afterward in a society and labor market that offer few opportunities for young people who have limited family support and do not follow a linear pattern from high school to college," the evaluation concluded.[11] Results like these show that while these programs might be necessary to rescue some young people from disconnection and deserve much greater investment than they are currently getting, they are still not sufficient by themselves to ensure a young adult's long-term economic success.

These programs should, however, play an important role in the panoply of options available to young people who become disconnected or are at risk of disconnection. The purpose of high-intensity programs is to pick up the pieces after a young person has already hit bottom, dropping out of school, becoming homeless or involved with the criminal justice system, or engaging in risky or destructive behaviors. Equally important are efforts to preserve the connections a young person has and to prevent a slide into disconnection in the first place. As Second Story's Judith Dittman puts it, "It's one thing to pull the babies out of the river before they drown, but let's find out who's throwing in the babies in the first place."

The ultimate need is for a broader restructuring of access to opportunity in America, including for young people, and in the face of that challenge, every solution is at best incomplete. Nevertheless, as the next few chapters show, there's plenty we can do, even under the burden of these structural obstacles, to give more young people a shot at mainstream economic success. For many young people, all that might be needed is a single caring adult—a mentor.

10

Super Mentors

In Greek myth, the original Mentor was a relatively minor character in Homer's *Odyssey*, the appointed caretaker of Odysseus's son Telemachus while Odysseus went off to fight the Trojan War. Where Mentor gains his significance is when Athena, goddess of wisdom, assumes his identity to provide Telemachus with advice that proves crucial to the return of his father and the defense of his family's kingdom. By heeding Athena/Mentor's advice, Telemachus becomes a man in his own right as he acts to protect his family.

In the modern day, real-life mentors can play a similarly pivotal role in the lives of young people and might be all that a young person needs to stay on track through young adulthood. They are also all too often what's missing in the lives of young people at risk of disconnection.

In the middle class, young people typically enjoy the support of many adults who play key roles in guiding their lives. First and most important are parents, but most young adults in the middle class and above typically have a full roster of adults at their disposal to dispense advice, provide emotional support, and open doors when necessary: teachers, coaches, tutors, guidance counselors, pastors and rabbis, parents of friends, and friends of parents—the list goes on. Nor does the importance of mentoring end once a young person begins his or her career; if anything, it only grows in importance.

This is why so many companies have formal mentorship programs for young employees and why so many professional networks emphasize the significance of mentoring relationships. A 2016 article in *Inc.* titled "10 Reasons Why a Mentor Is a Must" cited a mentor's role as a "sounding board," a "connector," a "trusted adviser," and someone who could rescue a mentee from making mistakes.[1]

For many lower-income young people, however, the lack of mentors—either in number or in quality—contributes to their risk of disconnection. For instance, indifferent teachers in poorly performing schools are unlikely to push struggling students to achieve excellence. That's what happened to Shanaye in Baltimore, who ultimately ended up dropping out. Other young people might be in neighborhoods where positive role models are few or nonexistent. That's the story of Carlos in chapter 7, who saw his friends and brother sucked one by one into the neighborhood drug trade and ended up getting caught himself. He did not have an adult who could connect him to other (legal) job opportunities or warn him away from the disastrous consequences of his choices. Still others might have mentors who can provide love and emotional support but lack the practical skills necessary to help a young person navigate the maze of college admissions, career choices, first jobs, and other crucial milestones in the transition to young adulthood. This is one reason why first-generation college students are significantly less likely to earn a degree than fellow students whose parents are college graduates. "[F]irst-generation students cannot benefit from their parents' college-going experience—a valuable source of cultural capital that helps students navigate college (e.g., understanding the significance of the syllabus, what 'office hours' means, or how to cite sources in written assignments)," concluded a recent study by the Department of Education. "This lack of cultural capital negatively affects even those first-generation students who are academically well prepared for college."[2]

Public policy cannot replicate the embarrassment of mentors that middle-class young adults enjoy, but it can support high-quality mentoring programs of the sort described in this chapter that have transformed young people's lives.

A Web of Thread

One nonprofit that sets the bar for how mentorship programs could and should work is Thread, an organization based in Baltimore not far from the YO! Baltimore center where Shanaye from chapter 4 is working to get her GED. Thread convenes teams of up to five volunteers to work with a young person identified as struggling academically, beginning in his or her freshman year of high school. In 2018, according to the organization, more than 850 volunteers worked with more than 415 students, spending more than 30,000 total hours together.[3] Thread reports that 87 percent of the young people who stayed with the program six years ended up graduating from high school and that nearly the same number ultimately earn a two-year or four-year college degree.

To get these results, volunteers go to extraordinary lengths to help a young person succeed, such as by showing up at a student's door every morning at 7 a.m. to provide a ride to school, supplying clothes and food, and helping them find a job.[4] Students receive not just material support but also exposure to new possibilities and connections. For some students, their Thread mentors are the first people they've met with degrees and professional careers, which by itself can be transformational. "If you don't know anyone who's gone off to college and gotten a middle-class job, it isn't an option for you," says founder and president Sarah Hemminger. The value of the relationship also goes both ways. For volunteers and the community more broadly, the program seeks to break down the social isolation and segregation that has scarred the city. The goal, says Hemminger, is to "create touchpoints between people across lines of difference." More than just a mentoring program, "Thread is a tool to build relationships," she says.

Thread is not, however, a social services agency. A key piece of Thread's success, in addition to the intensity of the relationships it fosters, is the long-term commitment to each student from high school up to and even through college. The results the organization sees are the product of relationships and the trust between mentors and students that can take years to achieve.

Its volunteers, however, are not professional caseworkers or social workers, and while they can refer a young person to the services he or she needs, it's not their job to ensure that a young adult's basic needs are met or to manage the complex set of problems a young person might be facing. As effective as Thread has shown itself to be, it is still an incomplete solution for many young people who need a specialized array of services to stay connected to school and work. Nevertheless, Thread's approach is a model for how social services agencies can effectively incorporate the benefits of mentorship into the services they provide to young clients as a strategy for preventing disconnection.

In truth, the kind of long-term commitment and investment of "patient capital" that nonprofits like Thread provide is alien to the world of public policy, and the provision of social services in particular. Caseworkers typically don't stick with their clients for multiple years as they move from one system to another or from program to program. Rather, their involvement is program specific or system specific. Moreover, "mentor" is not within the traditional job description of a case manager. Rather, a caseworker's typical job is to manage a young person's participation in a program or monitor their access to a benefit, often with a strict eye toward compliance with bureaucratic requirements and processing paperwork. Recall the multistep checklists that caseworkers in the foster care system prepare as part of state-mandated transition plans for older youth about to age out of foster care. While the preparation of a plan could provide ample opportunities for mentorship, it just as easily becomes a check-the-box exercise for busy caseworkers eager to unburden themselves of a case.

One innovative nonprofit, however, is demonstrating the feasibility—and benefit—of combining the kind of long-term personal relationships offered by organizations like Thread with the professional case management traditionally offered by social service agencies. These super-mentors—called Promotores—are a potentially powerful way to ensure that young people with high needs get the benefit of a caring adult, as well as the expert supports and services that would help them grow successfully into their early adulthood. These Promotores could also be a secret weapon in the fight against youth disconnection.

The Promotores

One model example of these Promotores is Franklin Peralta, a solidly built Dominican man in his late thirties who works at the Latin American Youth Center (LAYC) in Washington, D.C. (the same organization that sponsors the drop-in center from chapter 2). Peralta has a caseload of twenty clients from ages seventeen to twenty-three, each of whom checks in with him at least once a week, depending on what's going on in their lives. A big part of being a Promotor is being on call 24/7. "They're going to have me around as long as they want me around," he says. "I can basically help them with anything. It could be homelessness, it could be going back to school, employment, reunification with family, court-related, anything they have going on, they'll have a person who can support and guide them through whatever it is." Peralta has walked the walk of many of his young clients, which makes him especially suited for his current role. He first came to LAYC as a participant when he was fifteen or sixteen and found a mentor in Alvin "Pibe" Alvarado, who later became the organization's first Promotor.

Unlike mentors at other programs who are primarily volunteers, Peralta is also a professional case manager. He can open his contacts and connect a client with an emergency shelter, a doctor or therapist, or a food pantry. He knows all the job-training programs in the city and how to help someone finish high school. This professional knowledge is a big part of what sets Promotores apart from other mentors.

"You have a lot of mentoring programs where the mentors aren't trained to handle all the issues that come up," says Shayna Scholnick, director of the Promotor program. "So if you have a youth who experiences mental health issues, they don't necessarily know how to handle that." Scholnick says Promotores need at least four years' experience working with high-need youth before they are hired and undergo extensive ongoing training.

At the same time, Promotores also develop the same kind of deep relationships with their clients that mentoring programs encourage but few caseworkers have. "A lot of case management programs work on whatever goals a youth might have, but because of the requirements of the program or the length, you don't have time to build that long-term relationship to get all that case management done," Scholnick says. "This is the best of both worlds."

The Promotores also work with the kids who need the greatest intensity of social services to stay connected to school or work. In choosing whom to assign a Promotor, LAYC looks for young people without a high school diploma or GED and who face serious issues such as homelessness, violence, substance abuse or mental health issues, or criminal justice involvement. They may also be young parents or struggling to find a job. Many are receiving public benefits such as SNAP, and a significant number are veterans of the foster care system.[5]

Among Peralta's former clients is Joseph Aria, now twenty-seven. Aria lived in the neighborhood and was only twelve when he started coming to LAYC after school. Peralta was not yet a Promotor and was running a workout program for young men aimed at gang prevention, which Aria started attending. "It was like a brotherhood," Aria says.

Aria, a towering young man, was an excellent high school basketball player, which bought him some allowances in school. But it didn't stop him from being kicked out of one high school, leaving two others, and dropping out before graduation. "I've always had trouble focusing," says Aria. "I couldn't sit in a classroom and hear people repeat the same question twenty-five different ways. I was never a bad academic student. I was never good with people giving me attitude."

Peralta helped Aria get back on track. He helped Aria find a GED program, start thinking about college, and then find a job. At the time we speak, Aria is working as a lineman for PEPCO—"It's a great job," he says—and is about to take the physical exam to become a firefighter. "I have some good options right now," he says.

Aria says this turnaround was only possible because of Peralta's long-term commitment to him, first as an LAYC staffer and then as Aria's Promotor. "Growing up, he would give me advice," says Aria of Peralta. "I wouldn't take it that moment, but later on, I'd be like, 'Maybe he's right.' I remember him and I had a conversation one time and he said, 'You know the guys you're hanging around with, right? Leave the area three months and come back and I'll bet you they'll still be there, doing nothing.' He was right."

Promotores say that the long-term relationships they develop with their clients are necessary for several reasons. As with Aria, young people need time to make mistakes and recover. It also often takes time for good advice to sink in. "He made a lot of mistakes," says Peralta of Aria. "I would tell him, 'I don't think that's good for you to do,' and he'd do it anyway. . . . He turned out to be amazing. He's very responsible. He's very intelligent. . . . But it took a while for him to realize what I saw years ago."

Many young people also need time to learn to trust an adult. "A lot of the youth we work with have been in other programs, have had other workers, and have a distrust for the system or people coming into their lives," says director Scholnick. "It takes time to get them to trust you. . . . It may take a few years before they even disclose certain information, especially trauma." It also takes a long time to get results. "These youth have gone through so many years of trauma and disconnection before we get to them, you can't expect that even in a year you're going to see a change," Scholnick continues.

Remarkably, in a field known for its high turnover, the program has so far recruited a strong cadre of Promotores willing to make this kind of long-term commitment to their clients. "It's about sticking around for these youth," says Promotor Jaime Rogers. "Because if you leave, it interrupts what we do." So far, says Rogers, all but one of the Promotores have been with the program for longer than two years, which she says "is unheard of in this profession." LAYC also does what it can to prevent burnout.

"We are encouraged to take days off, especially when we've had a hard week," says Peralta. "It can be really crazy sometimes. You're trying to deal with so much. You can get to a point where your core energy changes. You don't want your clients to see that."

At the moment, the program has twenty full-time Promotores like Peralta who are based at LAYC, plus twenty-five other Promotores who work out of the D.C. public schools. LAYC has also launched a national Promotor Network to spread the model around the country.

Super-mentors like the Promotores bring about change in young people's lives in several important ways. First, they offer emotional support that might otherwise be lacking. "We have kids who come in with parents who have completely abandoned them or parents who are drug addicts," says Promotor Jaime Rogers. "But we also have kids who have parents but who maybe don't have the skills. And some of them have great parents who try really hard but they're working three jobs because they're a single immigrant mom who's supporting four kids and is never home."

"Franklin was a brother/father figure," says Aria of Peralta. "My dad wasn't around like that, being that my mother and he were going through . . . troubles and stuff. I understand it now, but at the time, it was hard for me. I needed that presence of a father around. Franklin was there when I needed that."

Second, mentors can open young people's eyes to greater possibilities for their lives. Young people with mentors are more likely to aspire to college and to enroll, according to one 2014 analysis. They are also more than twice as likely to take on leadership roles and nearly twice as likely to volunteer.[6]

Peralta, for instance, organized a tour of college campuses for Aria and several other young men, going on an overnight trip to Virginia Commonwealth University in Richmond and to the colleges around Norfolk. "That was eye opening because some of them were thinking about going to college but didn't know exactly what to do," says Peralta. "A lot of parents are immigrants who work all the time. They never did an application for college, they just work and come here to provide. They don't have resources or knowledge. . . . For [the young people] to see it hands on and get the information, walk the campus, see the dorms, get the presentation, they were like, 'I can do this.'"

As a result of this trip, says Peralta, at least half the young men went on to college after high school, including one young man who recently graduated from Pennsylvania State University.

"Before that experience, I had no idea what college was," says Aria. "I was going by what other people were doing versus believing in myself and aiming high. I was stuck with the fact that so-and-so was doing that and thinking I could do that versus believing I could achieve greater things."

"You're in this four-block radius around here, and the only jobs available for you are working at the Potbelly or retail," says Peralta. "You don't know the way out unless someone comes and says there's opportunities here."

The third thing that the Promotores provide is advice without judgment, which Promotor Rogers says is critical to gaining their clients' trust. "That's how you lose kids fast," she says. "The minute they see you judging them, they're not going to tell you anything ever again."

It's not, however, always easy. "There are situations where it's really hard not to be judgmental," says Rogers. "They're selling their body or doing something extreme—but you still have to be like, 'This makes me worried because this is not the safest thing for you, but we're going to figure out the safest path possible until you're not doing it anymore.' But you can't say, 'Oh my god, that's horrible,' because they may not be ready to stop those behaviors yet."

So far, the Promotor "pathway" is delivering results.

A 2016 evaluation by the Urban Institute concluded that the program "serves an important role by filling a void in the lives of high-need at-risk youth."[7] The evaluation found that young people assigned a Promotor were more likely to stay in school, significantly less likely to have a child, and significantly less likely to have slept in a shelter.[8] Although the program did not seem to increase employment among young people with a Promotor compared to a control group, the evaluators also reasoned that this could have been a result of more young people staying in school rather than dropping out to work. The evaluators also found that young people were highly engaged with their Promotores, reaching out to them consistently and frequently, demonstrating the depth of their relationships.

Peralta says that while five or six of his clients have since aged out, they all still stay in touch, including especially Aria. "Even though they aged out of the program, it doesn't mean they can't see me," he says. "After you have a relationship with a person that you've been working with five or six years, it doesn't turn off in a day."

Aria is proof of that. He typically stops by the LAYC every week or so to check in and often brings Peralta a sandwich so they can eat together. Peralta's greatest impact on Aria might be the aspirations he's ingrained into his young former client.

Although Aria doesn't know where his career will ultimately take him, what he does know is that he wants to be for others, including his own three kids, the kind of mentor that Peralta was for him. He also now has bigger plans for transforming his own community. "I'm going to be a boss," he says. "I want to provide jobs for people struggling with believing in themselves."

Aria's desire to give back might ultimately be the biggest benefit of mentorship programs like the Promotores. By providing the initial thread of connection that Aria needed, the program is in turn prompting Aria to weave a stronger fabric of connection and opportunity for his children and in his community. And if Aria succeeds in his ambition to create jobs, the opportunities he can provide for work and work experience could permanently end the cycle of disconnection in which the young people around him might otherwise be trapped. A chance to work, in fact, might be the best protection from disconnection.

11

The Apprentice and the Intern

It's 6:45 a.m. during the height of summer construction season, and the asphalt plant at Cedar Mountain Stone Corporation in Mitchells, Virginia, has been buzzing with activity since before dawn. Thousands of pounds of crushed rock are moving along conveyor belts to be mixed with hot liquid asphalt in a gigantic drum, while trucks line up under a massive chute to take the finished asphalt away.

The company's nearby quarry has been running 24/7, mining eight thousand tons a day of the high-quality granite for which this part of central Virginia is known. Some of this rock will end up cut and polished for people's kitchen countertops, or lining streams and roadbeds, but much of it will end up in Cedar Mountain Stone's asphalt plant, processed into blacktop for the thousands of miles of roads and highways that crisscross the state.

Making that asphalt is the job of Allen Miller, one of eleven apprentices at Cedar Mountain Stone. Like any good brew, good asphalt is hard to make. "We have to have certain gradations of stone, the right amount of dust, and not too much asphalt binder in it," says Ed Dalrymple, Miller's boss and the fourth-generation owner of Cedar Mountain Stone. "If we have all of that in the right proportions, the road's going to last."

In many ways, Miller's apprenticeship is exactly what young people need to ensure their lifelong connection to mainstream opportunity. Through his apprenticeship, Miller is getting both schooling and valuable work experience, along with professional connections, mentorship, and, importantly, a living wage.

Every day, Miller works from 6 a.m. to 6 p.m. or later and then goes to night school at Germanna Community College in nearby Fredericksburg for specialized classes in asphalt technology that are part of his training. "It makes for some very long days," he says. But if he sticks it out, Miller will finish his apprenticeship with a journeyman's license in industrial maintenance; multiple certifications in asphalt technology from the Virginia Asphalt Association, which will help him land jobs anywhere in the industry; and four years of work experience.

Under the tutelage of a mentor at the company, Miller is learning how to operate, fix, and maintain the asphalt plant that is the lifeblood of the company; how to formulate asphalt so that it can withstand twenty years of freezes, thaws, and the weight of thousands of tractor-trailers every day; and how to test it so that the quality of the state's roadways passes the standards of the Virginia Department of Transportation (VDOT). On any given day, Miller is out drilling core samples from freshly laid road beds, watching the computerized control panels monitoring the moisture levels of asphalt being mixed at the plant, or taking twenty-pound samples of asphalt to the company's on-site laboratory for analysis. Though he makes just $35,000 a year as an apprentice, his salary could jump to near six figures thanks to the highly specialized skills he's acquiring.[1]

Much More Than a TV Show

Well-run apprenticeship programs are a boon for both apprentices and the companies that hire them. Miller, for instance, will have no school debt once he finishes his apprenticeship. Cedar Mountain Stone is paying for the cost of Miller's coursework at Germanna Community College with the help of a state grant program that helps pay for non-college-credit occupational credentials. Meanwhile, Cedar Mountain Stone's Dalrymple is getting workers exactly trained to his needs. Dalrymple created the apprenticeship program at his company in partnership with Germanna Community College, which has developed similar programs for other local firms. Dalrymple is also looking to his eleven apprentices to become the next generation of workers at his business. Miller's mentor at the asphalt plant is in his seventies, as is Cedar Mountain Stone's current master electrician, who is mentoring another of the company's apprentices, Alex Campbell.

Through their apprenticeships, both Miller and Campbell have found a lifeline out of the near-disconnection that threatened them both. Both Miller and Campbell credit their apprenticeships with giving them the direction and job security they hadn't had before. Miller, for example, says he "floated" for several years out of high school before connecting with Cedar Mountain Stone. "I did a little bit of construction work, I worked on a farm, I worked in a sales position at a video game store, I worked in a couple of restaurants. A few of them were really just jobs to make ends meet," he says.

Campbell likewise says his experience after high school was mostly a series of odd jobs. Now, at twenty-five years old, he is about a month or two away from his journeyman's electrical license, which requires eight thousand hours of on-the-job training under a master tradesman. He too is taking classes at Germanna Community College, and in addition to his job at Cedar Mountain Stone, he works side jobs on weekends doing electrical and plumbing work in homes. "Right now, I'm making decent money, more than most people I know," he says. "When I started working for Ed, I was able to move out of mom and dad's house, I have a nice reliable truck, and have some money to put aside. It's been great for me because I've been able to seize the opportunity."

America Is Not Germany

Despite increasing efforts to grow apprenticeship programs and the obvious benefits of such programs in promoting connection and preventing disconnection, apprenticeship opportunities are still relatively rare in the United States.

In 2016, the Obama administration announced $50.5 million in new funding for states to expand their apprenticeship programs, and the Trump administration has also embraced apprenticeships as a way to help businesses meet their needs for skilled workers.[2] In July 2018, President Donald Trump issued an executive order creating a Council for the American Worker aimed at expanding apprenticeship opportunities, in addition to other job-training programs.[3]

This growing interest has had some impact. Since just 2013, the number of apprenticeships registered with the Department of Labor has grown by more than 40 percent; in 2017, the DOL reported that 533,607 people were enrolled in apprenticeship programs nationwide.[4] Nevertheless, fewer than 5 percent of young workers are training in apprenticeship programs, according to workforce development expert Tamar Jacoby, while in places like Germany, the share of young people enrolled in apprenticeships is closer to 60 percent.[5] As one benefit of this system, Germany's youth unemployment rate in 2014 was just 7.4 percent, compared to 23.7 percent for the Eurozone more broadly.[6]

A variety of reasons explain why the number of American apprentices is so low and why apprenticeships may never have the same level of prominence in the United States as they do in countries like Germany. First, Germany is much more accepting of "tracking" young people into vocations at a very early age, something that Americans eschew with good reason. In the bad old days of "voc ed," the students most likely to be tracked into the vocational, non-college track were minorities. Voc ed was essentially a mechanism for institutional racism.

Second, Germany's vocational education system is highly regulated and requires a much higher level of cooperation between government and business than American companies are accustomed to seeing. Under Germany's so-called dual-training system, trainees spend part of each week at a vocational school and the rest at a company closely aligned with the school that is also likely to become that student's employer.

A third reason is the decline of labor unions in the United

States, which were a principal provider of apprenticeship opportunities in the past. Just 6.7 percent of private-sector workers were unionized in 2015, according to the Department of Labor, about half the rate in 1983.[7] Apprenticeships are also lengthy and expensive and require a level of commitment from both workers and companies that neither party may be willing or can afford to give. Ed Dalrymple and Cedar Mountain Stone are the exception, not the rule. For young people, an apprenticeship means a significant, multiyear commitment, which means no millennial job-hopping allowed. It can also mean hard, often physically demanding work, which weeds out candidates as well. Apprenticeship programs can also be surprisingly selective. Dalrymple, for instance, says many of the applicants for his apprenticeships didn't make the cut. Either they dropped out on their own because they didn't want the long hours that come with the work of building roads or—more tragically—they couldn't pass a drug test, a mandatory requirement in a field that involves the use of heavy machinery and explosives.

While apprenticeships might be the gold standard for the "work-based learning" that companies can provide to young people, it's unrealistic to expect apprenticeships to become a universally available experience. The right kind of internship, however, can prove just as valuable—while being more broadly available in a greater array of fields.

The Power of Internships

The headquarters of the U.S. Chamber of Commerce in downtown Washington, D.C., is an imposing stone building footsteps away from the White House. Majestic columns adorn its façade, and its hushed high-ceilinged hallways are replete with dark wood, marble, and portraits of patrician white men. The place evokes power, prestige, and established wealth.

On this November evening, the Chamber's ballroom is full of nervous but excited high school students dressed in their best and making occasional forays to an extravagant but teen-friendly buffet of chicken tenders and other finger foods. Most of them are African

American students from D.C. high schools, and they are the latest class of interns with the Urban Alliance, a national nonprofit that runs a ten-month-long internship program for young people at risk of disconnection. Typically, about a quarter of the program's participants have no working adults in their households, and fewer than a third have two parents at home. The overwhelming majority live in highly segregated neighborhoods, and about half come from places where the poverty rate is higher than 25 percent.[8]

Many of these young people have never been at a reception like this one, which is why it's part of the program experience. The Urban Alliance aims to ensure that by the end of the year, every intern will be comfortable in a professional environment and equipped with both the practical and "soft" skills that can help them land a well-paying future opportunity. Perhaps most important, the Alliance wants to expand the realm of what the students believe is possible for themselves. By holding this event in the Chamber's ballroom to kick off this year's program, the message to students is clear: You belong here too.

For many middle-class young adults, internships are less a privilege than a right. Every summer in D.C., for example, thousands of interns descend on Capitol Hill to sort mail, run Capitol tours, and answer phones. Despite the drudgery, internships are valuable experience. According to the Federal Reserve's survey of young workers, 26 percent of young adults who held an internship during college said it led to a paid job, while more than half said the experience "improved their skills."[9]

Access to internships, however, often requires two things: money and connections. As mentioned in chapter 1, the vast majority of internships are unpaid or poorly paid, which means that parents must typically subsidize these opportunities, such as by paying for housing. Second, many young people get their internships through the networks they or their families belong to. Many elite colleges, for instance, run "summer in D.C." programs for their students. Other opportunities might come about through the professional connections of parents, teachers, and family friends.

These hurdles mean that a good internship is out of reach for many lower-income students, though it may be the one boost they need to get ahead. While young people facing the biggest challenges might need intensive interventions like the ones described in earlier chapters to get them back on track, many others simply need better access to opportunities and skills than what their communities currently offer.

Bridging that gap is the goal of organizations like the Urban Alliance, which is one of a number of efforts, including long-standing programs such as Year Up and AmeriCorps, that aim to expand the early work opportunities available to young adults and provide the support they need to succeed in the job market.

In the case of the Urban Alliance, the organization places more than five hundred high school seniors a year at one of more than two hundred companies in D.C., Baltimore, Chicago, and northern Virginia. Participants benefit from four main components: a paid internship, formal training in job and life skills, mentors, and post-program follow-up from an "alumni services" team. A six-year-long evaluation by the Urban Institute, which involved more than one thousand students, found this formula to raise participants' comfort levels with "soft skills" while providing a head start on "hard" skills such as how to use office technology and software. The most dramatic impacts, however, have been on college attendance and persistence for young men, who were also more likely to graduate from high school if they were enrolled in the program. Researchers found that 70 percent of young men who completed the internship enrolled in college, compared to 55 percent in a control group. These young men were also 20 percentage points more likely to complete a two-year degree.

In the case of Year Up, which works in eight cities nationwide with young people ages eighteen to twenty-four (versus high schoolers), two separate studies have found that program graduates earn significantly more than a control group of their peers.[10] The most recent evaluation, from 2018, found that Year Up alums were earning as much as 53 percent more on average per quarter.[11] Like the Urban Alliance, Year Up offers participants training in both hard and soft skills, followed by a six-month-long internship at a private company, often a Fortune 500 firm. Because the program works primarily with high school graduates, it also offers occupation-specific training in fields such as IT and office administration.

For most students in these programs, the internship is their first exposure to an office environment, which is why the Urban Alliance tries hard to set them up for success. Before they even set foot in their new offices, interns undergo six weeks of "pre-work" orientation, every day after school from 2 p.m. to 5 p.m. The sessions cover everything from résumé writing to budgeting to career planning. Students who attend 80 percent of the sessions get a $250 bonus in their first paycheck, and one session features a bank representative who helps them open a savings account if they don't already have one, which is often the case. Roughly 7 percent of U.S. households were "unbanked" in 2015, including 13 percent of young people ages fifteen to twenty-four and 23 percent of people without a high school diploma. An additional 20 percent of households are "underbanked," meaning that while someone in the household has a checking or savings account, they also rely on high-cost "alternative" financial-service providers such as pawnshops, check cashers, title loan companies, and rent-to-own stores.[12]

In one session, convened at the Northern Virginia Community College in Falls Church, Virginia, instructor Chris Young is talking to the roughly two dozen students in his class about how to set long-term goals. There is a writing exercise, where the students are asked about the three to five things they'd like to achieve before they're twenty-five. One stylishly dressed student, Debra, says her goal is to open an online boutique for teenagers, an idea that the class is invited to critique. Chris Young gently probes her on the kinds of clothes she wants to sell, where she would get her inventory, and how much she would need to sell to make a living. Another young woman says that her goals are to get a Ph.D., teach English in Korea, and work at the EPA. "Those are three huge goals!" Young responds. They talk about the events that could derail someone from their ambitions, and Young confides to the class that it took him six years to graduate from college.

"I came from a low-income background, and there are certain things I did not consider," he tells his students, who are hanging on every word. "My very first year, my mother had a disease, and the doctor told her she had five years to live. I had to take some time from school to deal with that. I also changed my major. My car broke down. And I had to drop a course because I could not take a course at a certain time." Lack of finances forced him to hold down two jobs to get through school. "I worked at Walmart and then an overnight shift at Pillsbury," he says. "I hated every second, but I kept my eyes on the goal. I did what I had to do."

Today's session is also happening the day before the students are interviewing for their internships with potential employers. Young switches from guidance counselor to career coach. "Come with copies of your résumé," he says. "If you do not have access to a printer, email me, and I will print it out for you. Come with good energy. Do not come with a downtrodden disposition. Come energetic. Come excited. Make sure you speak loudly and clearly. Avoid using slang. Listen; don't interrupt. Last year, an individual came dressed in jeans, tennis shoes, and a T-shirt. Do not do that." He tells students to ask for interviewers' business cards and to email a thank-you right away. Everyone is frantically taking notes.

Internship programs like the one offered by the Urban Alliance benefit students in multiple ways. Perhaps most important is the pay. "Eighty percent of our young people are contributing to their family's income," says Nathaniel Cole, who served as executive director of the Urban Alliance's D.C. office for five years. "This isn't like young people coming in, having a field day, and blowing their income at Chipotle and the movies. They have to contribute to their households."

Supported internships like these also lower the risks for students entering into what is for many an alien environment and play an important role in equalizing the odds for lower-income young adults versus more affluent ones.

First, young adults acquire the skills they need to compete against their more affluent peers. "I'm shy, so communicating with a bunch of different people and networking was good for me," says Nia, a recent graduate of D.C.'s Dunbar High School whose Urban Alliance placement was with the Washington office of 20th Century Fox. "I learned to use Excel. I learned what to wear, what to do, and what not to do." She says her internship was good experience to put on her college applications, and she was accepted into six different schools. Her top choice was Morgan State University in Baltimore, where she planned to enroll in the fall of 2018.

Second, these internships broaden the professional and social networks of students in ways that otherwise wouldn't happen. Sometimes, it's as simple as exposure to cultural diversity. Kevohn McCormick, for instance, interned with the World Bank as his Urban Alliance placement. "I got to meet lots of folks from different places around the United States and the world," he says. "And I got to eat the amazing food in the cafeteria," he adds. More significant is the ability of young people to build "social capital" by meeting and working with people they otherwise wouldn't meet in their schools or neighborhoods and who have the potential to become future colleagues, supervisors, or mentors.

Recall the study by sociologist Mark Granovetter that found that someone's "weak" ties—the loose relationships and acquaintances developed with colleagues and professional networks[13]—are more effective than "strong" ties—the bonds people have with family and close friends[14]—in helping to find jobs. That's because you can access a broader network outside of your usual circle, which also means better access to information about potential opportunities. (Think, for instance, of all the people you "know" on LinkedIn, if you have a profile on that platform.) In his research, Granovetter also found some workers were more likely to have broad networks of helpful "weak" ties than others. In particular, he discovered that "professional, technical, and managerial workers were more likely to hear about new jobs through weak ties (27.8 percent) than through strong ones (16.7 percent)," while less educated workers were more likely to rely on strong ties in their job searches.[15] This imbalance is one of the deficits programs like Urban Alliance are striving to overcome by helping young people develop networks that will be valuable later in life.

A big part of this network is with other young people. For instance, another of the speakers at the Urban Alliance's kick-off event is program alum Marie D., who interned at the World Bank and the Boston Consulting Group and is now a sophomore at George Washington University. "Being surrounded by other youth who wanted to make something of themselves and create change in their communities really encouraged me to want to do the same thing and to focus on my career goals and my educational goals," she says. Before then, she says, "I was really lost about what I wanted to do with my life and after high school . . . I lacked self-confidence and continuously doubted myself."

Interns also sometimes find a professional mentor who ends up changing their lives.

The Jedi Master

Michael Akin is president of LINK Strategic Partners, a D.C.-based public affairs firm that has hired Urban Alliance interns for the past six years. Young, fast-talking, and energetic, Akin runs a company that's a dream job for millennials. The firm's offices, located inside the National Urban League's historic headquarters, include an open bullpen with snacks, a lounge area, whiteboards, and squadrons of hipsterish young people, all with the same enthusiasm and energy as Akin. Propped up against the walls are sample public service announcements for one of the firm's ongoing campaigns, to promote safe sex among young people in D.C. (Their client is the city's Department of Health.) The firm does most of its work for nonprofits, social service agencies, and charities, which is why its involvement in the Urban Alliance made sense, says Akin. "Businesses across the board like to speak a really good game about their community engagement, but this is a direct opportunity to live up to that in a real way."

Interns, he says, are treated as "full members of the team." "They're given business cards, they represent us at events, they go to client meetings . . . they're fully set up to do work here," he says. High school senior Sorcha, for instance, one of this year's interns, audited the firm's Twitter account and wrote a report for her boss and mentor, Caroline Potolicchio, about the kinds of posts that get the most interaction. "Most people like organic posts rather than [preprogrammed ones from] Constant Calendar," Sorcha says. She's also pitched press releases to the media and will take notes later today at a brainstorm meeting for another of their clients. "They do a lot of marketing and branding and stuff that I didn't know about before," she says. "This is helping me out, exploring new things."

But as much as Sorcha is learning from the Urban Alliance, LINK is benefiting as well. Two of its former interns, Chauncey Johnson and Tray McGhaney, are now associates with the firm, working full time over the summers while finishing college. They also do some hourly work over spring and winter breaks to earn some extra money. During one of these stints, McGhaney accompanied the team to SXSW to set up a system for logging business cards collected at an event being run by the firm. "He built the system and logged 6,000 cards over three days," says Akin of Mc-Ghaney's work.

McGhaney says his experience at LINK has influenced the classes he's taking at George Mason University. He's angling for a full-time job at LINK after he graduates (though he hasn't been promised one) and wants to make sure his skills are in line with what the firm needs. He says he expects to graduate with a degree in web design and multimedia communications. But the biggest change he's made since his internship, McGhaney says, has been in his personality. "I was very quiet," he says. "I would not speak to anyone unless someone spoke to me. I came, did my work, and left. Working at this firm in a place that's collaborative—me opening up is the biggest change." Meeting McGhaney, who is talkative and effervescent, this is tough to believe.

"He was the single most serious person I've ever met in my life," says Akin. "He would wear a suit every day or change into one. He would always be on time. It was incredible to see that level of discipline, but then over the years we've been able to work together to watch all those other dimensions of Tray's personality come out." Since his internship, McGhaney—who holds a second-degree black belt in karate—has led two trainings in martial arts for the firm's staff. He also runs his own YouTube channel for gamers. "I still live with my mom, and she loves it that I'm doing something with my life," he says. "I'm going on a different pathway from a lot of people we know."

Akin and his firm are extraordinary employers. When McGhaney ran into trouble with his financial aid at George Mason, Akin made a call that helped straighten things out so that he wouldn't have to drop out of school. When another former intern needed $11,000 to stay in school because his financial aid fell through, LINK helped set up a GoFundMe campaign to raise the money, lobbied foundations to pitch in, and worked with his financial aid office on strategies. "His mom is a single mom trying to get him through school, but they couldn't make up an $11,000 gap," says Akin. "It was messy, it was hard, it wasn't guaranteed, but it also wasn't insurmountable." Akin had also once walked in this intern's shoes. "I went to college on a full scholarship," he says. "My mom was a high school janitor, and college was beyond comprehension for us."

Akin is also insistent, however, that his partnership with Urban Alliance is not an act of charity but one that makes good business sense. "The SXSW experience was a good one for us," says Akin. "Tray was a rock star down there, blew it out of the water, built the software, delivered it in real time, and came back with a stack of cards. That wouldn't have come without Urban Alliance having introduced us three years ago. It took that experience for us to know."

Nathaniel Cole, who served as Urban Alliance's executive director in D.C. for five years and is now at the America's Promise Alliance, says his goal was for every company to have the same revelation about the untapped potential of young people, particularly those considered "at risk." "Too often, with people coming through the public system, individuals create a story arc about them before they open their mouth," he says. "When our young people open their mouths, they're able to weave in tidbits about how they've interned at X company or X individual is their mentor. It causes folks to reexamine that local talent that's sitting across the table from them."

What's sometimes difficult, however, is persuading more companies to make that initial investment in an intern. Companies that partner with the Urban Alliance, for instance, pay a set fee per intern, most of which goes to pay their wages (which is minimum wage), but also helps subsidize the pre-work training and other supports the organization provides throughout the program. "Companies don't always see the investment because there are so many college interns who are willing to come in for little or nothing," Cole says. "For us, it's elevating the story of local talent at the high school level where they can bring in as much value or similar value as a college intern."

Fortunately, a growing number of companies are beginning to see that value. Besides LINK, the businesses that have gone on to hire Urban Alliance interns include such major firms as the Coca-Cola Company, Deloitte, the Chicago Transit Authority, JPMorgan Chase & Co., US Foods, and Marriott International.

"I want every young person in the city, brown or black, to be able to have the same opportunities to have major companies on their resume," says Cole.

If Cole gets his wish, not just in D.C. where the Urban Alliance makes its home but throughout the country, the result could be a monumental turnaround in the risk of disconnection for young adults, especially those who are otherwise less likely than their more privileged peers to gain the many benefits of early work experience. Internships not only provide young people with a chance to develop good work habits and "soft skills"; they also help young people build social and professional networks that will prove valuable throughout their careers. But increasingly, high-quality private-sector internships are the preserve of the affluent middle class, who have the means and the connections to land plum opportunities and to work for free. Programs like the Urban Alliance help to equalize the opportunities available to young people and thereby narrow the growing divergence in fortunes between have and have-not young adults. And as interns like Tray and Sorcha amply demonstrate, the dividends waiting to be reaped from the investment in their skills and potential are immense.

These programs, however, do not exist in a vacuum. As important is the role schools play in ensuring that students like Tray and Sorcha are well prepared for internships and other career opportunities and are encouraged to pursue them. Schools should, in fact, be on the front lines of preventing disconnection by facilitating seamless transitions from school to work, school to college, or, in many instances, both. The next chapter explores how one model district is achieving this goal.

12

A Texas Turnaround to Make Schools Work

Over the years, the south Texas border town of McAllen has had its share of bad press. In 2009, *New Yorker* writer Atul Gawande singled out McAllen as one of "the most expensive health care markets in the country" as well as one of the unhealthiest, with an obesity rate of 38 percent and an incidence of heavy drinking 60 percent higher than the national average.[1] In the summer of 2018, it became the epicenter of the crisis over family separations at the border and the Trump administration's "zero tolerance" policy on illegal immigration. Images of children trapped in cages made of metal fencing at a McAllen detention facility, about four miles north of the border, were beamed around the world, sparking international outrage.[2] The attention was ironic—85 percent of the town's population identifies as Hispanic.[3]

McAllen is also one of the most disconnected cities in the country for young people ages sixteen to twenty-four. In 2017, the town ranked among the ten most disconnected metro areas in the country, according to Measure of America, at 16.9 percent.[4]

But McAllen and its neighboring towns in the Rio Grande Valley are on the verge of a turnaround, twenty years in the making, to become one of the most economically vibrant areas in the state. In March 2019, the McAllen unemployment rate stood at 5.7 percent, down from nearly 29 percent in February 1990.[5] Its population is also booming, up nearly 9 percent since 2010.[6] The region has also potentially cracked the code on disconnection, with the creation of a national model that integrates schools, colleges, and local industry into a seamless school-to-job pipeline for the region's young people. Its secret ingredients are a diverse economy, a visionary school superintendent, and an upstart community college that twenty years ago did not exist but is now the best in the state. While some of the elements of this formula seem unique, what's happened in McAllen could still serve as a model for the nation.

Before and After

A scant thirty years ago, better than 60 percent of the residents in and around McAllen and its surrounding towns had no high school diploma, and poverty was endemic. "A lot of dirt streets and outdoor privies" is how south Texas native Gary Gurwitz remembers McAllen in its earlier days. Of the residents who had jobs, many worked in the citrus groves that produced Texas's famous Ruby Red grapefruit, but there wasn't much of a middle class. "You worked the fields, or you owned the fields," is one how resident puts it. Two hard freezes in the 1980s—one in 1983 and another in 1989—together destroyed more than half the Rio Grande Valley's producing trees, throwing thousands out of work.[7]

Compounding the region's economic problems was the Mexican peso crisis of 1994, when the Mexican government cut the value of the peso by half and sent that country spiraling into a recession.[8] The downturn was a huge blow to border towns like McAllen, which relied on cross-border retail trade from Mexican consumers as well as the trade enabled by the newly passed North American Free Trade Agreement (NAFTA). Keith Patridge, CEO of the McAllen Economic Development Corporation (MEDC), recalls that during the 1990s, unemployment in some parts of the Valley was up to nearly 60 percent.

The worst conditions were in the *colonias*, settlements of extreme poverty along the Texas–Mexico border where residents lived in plywood shacks without such basic services as sewer, running water, and electricity. A report by the Federal Reserve Bank of

Dallas from the 1990s found that more than 40 percent of *colonias* residents were using "cesspools" and outhouses, creating high rates of cholera, dysentery, tuberculosis, and other diseases more common to developing countries.[9]

Today, the *colonias* are still there but far diminished in their presence. Where there was once obvious poverty, there is now conspicuous prosperity. There is a gleaming new conference facility and a performing arts center, where the national tour of *Les Misérables* was playing. The luxe La Plaza Mall is the largest in the Rio Grande Valley, with more than 1.2 million square feet of retail space and every conceivable brand from Abercrombie to Victoria's Secret.[10] It draws shoppers not only from all over the region but also from over the border. Affluent Mexicans reportedly even fly in to McAllen Airport, across the street from the mall, to get in their fix of American brands.

If you start from the city's southern limits and drive north, you drive through the history of its progress and successive waves of development. On the south end of 10th Street, one of the principal thoroughfares bisecting town, you'll see check cashers, pawn shops, and other storefronts that are remnants of the town's economic distress. But as you head north, storefront taquerias give way to Chipotles, and instead of mom-and-pop appliance stores there's Best Buy and Home Depot. All of this is brand new.

On the northern outskirts of town is a massive new planned community, Tres Lagos, that locals say is a beacon of the emerging McAllen. You can buy a brand-new four-bedroom, two-bath house with two-car garage for $200,000 or a mansion for $1 million. The master plan includes a shopping center, an outdoor amphitheater, and a community pool. The development will also have its own elementary and high schools and, eventually, an outpost of Texas A&M University.[11] Theoretically, it would be possible for someone born in Tres Lagos to not leave until after graduating from college. In the summer of 2018, much of the place was still under construction. A young couple was emerging from a tour of the model home, and "Sold" signs were on many of the houses being built.

Desert to Oasis

What handicapped the Rio Grande Valley for a long time was its status as a higher education desert. While there was one university in the area—the University of Texas Pan-American (since shut down and reopened)—there was no community college in the entire region where students could acquire occupational skills. "We had PanAm, but it was relatively expensive and academic only," recalls McAllen attorney Gary Gurwitz, who first moved to McAllen in 1959. "You couldn't learn to weld or be a truck driver or HVAC or anything else." The lack of skilled talent also made it hard for the region to attract new businesses to the area. "We couldn't provide the skilled labor the companies needed, because we didn't have any way to train them," says McAllen Economic Development Corporation president Keith Patridge.

This finally changed in 1993, when local leaders persuaded then-Governor Ann Richards to open a community college in the area, what's now South Texas College (STC). "Imagine a community of 700,000 with no community college," says Shirley Reed, STC's current and founding president. "The whole region along the border had been criminally neglected not only by the state of Texas but by the federal government."

Today, the school is arguably the anchor of the Rio Grande Valley, with more than 120 course offerings, five campuses, and 31,000 students. An additional 15,000 students are high school students who are dually enrolled in STC classes, giving them the opportunity to graduate from high school with college credits and potentially even an associate's degree already under their belt. Ninety-five percent of the student body is Hispanic, and more than 70 percent are the first in their families to go to college.[12]

What has made the college so successful is its connection to local industries. Companies can essentially order up the kinds of workers they need, which also means virtually guaranteed jobs for students. On one July afternoon, the general manager of the GE Aviation facility down the street from STC's technology campus was meeting with STC faculty about the company's plans for future hiring. The plant manufactures parts for aircraft engines, including the blades you see spinning inside jet-engine turbines if you get a window seat. The manager tells me that GE has about 530 employees in McAllen but is looking to hire ten to fifteen machine operators in the short term and another fifty over the next several months. STC will help supply those workers by tailoring coursework to meet GE's needs and then sending promising graduates GE's way. It's a win for students, the company, and STC.

Mario Reyna, STC's dean for business and technology, says every course offering is intended to be a pipeline to jobs for their graduates. Inside the massive technology campus, which was once an abandoned manufacturing facility, there is a twelve-bay garage, where students taking automotive classes are working on cars donated to the school by General Motors. There's also a lab filled with diesel engines and transmissions for students to dismantle, a computer lab complete with 3D printers, and an outdoor workshop for would-be welders. "We have everything from cake decorating to welding," Reyna says.

Economic development official Patridge credits STC with helping the Rio Grande Valley rebuild its economy after the disasters of the 1980s and 1990s. Today, the area has become a hub for advanced manufacturing in sectors ranging from aeronautics and automotive to medical and food processing.[13] In 2017, according to Patridge, McAllen brought in eleven new companies that created more than two thousand new jobs and more than $55 million in payroll, while another nineteen companies expanded their footprint.[14] The town has also revitalized its trade with Mexico and considers itself a "bi-national" metro area because of its proximity and relationships with the Mexican city of Reynosa, just across the border. In fact, many of the manufacturing concerns in McAllen are cross-national operations with production in Mexico and management in the United States. McAllen has also become a major port of entry and distribution hub for Mexican produce, which is off-loaded from trucks into giant cold-storage facilities on the outskirts of the city and then reloaded for shipment throughout the United States. Nearly half of all fresh fruits and vegetables arriving from Mexico enter the United States through south Texas, according to one study, and imports through Texas have grown by more than 90 percent in the last decade. In 2016, that was about $5.1 billion worth of produce over more than 220,000 truckloads.[15] Not surprisingly, South Texas College offers certificate courses in import/export, customs processes, and logistics management to help support these operations with trained workers.[16]

The final and most important piece of the Valley's turnaround, however, was to break the cycle of disconnection and dropout among its high school students that was feeding the region's historical problems of low education and high unemployment. So long as south Texas's schools could not produce graduates ready to succeed in the programs STC was developing to build a workforce attractive to potential employers, the region's turnaround plans would come to naught. While STC was building the capacity to train skilled workers, it needed its own pipeline of incoming students eager to take advantage of new opportunities.

Disconnection to Connection

The man who solved the region's dropout crisis was Daniel King, superintendent of the Pharr-San Juan-Alamo (PSJA) Independent School District, which borders McAllen to the east. Ninety-nine percent of PSJA's students are Hispanic, and 85 percent are "economically disadvantaged," including a fair number living in the *colonias*.[17] When King took over PSJA in 2007, the district's dropout rate was close to 20 percent, double the state average, and the high schools had been labeled "dropout factories" in national reports.[18] The prior superintendent had also been indicted, along with three other school board officials, in a bribery scheme that involved $600,000 in cash, paid vacations, and other gifts in exchange for steering business involving the district to certain contractors.[19]

Today, just a decade later, thanks to King, the dropout rate is down to 1 percent, and 92 percent of students graduate on time.[20]

King, who among his accolades was named Texas Superintendent of the Year by the American Association of School Administrators in 2013, is an unlikely looking revolutionary. Rather, he looks like one of the dads you'd see at the neighborhood barbecue—not the boisterous one organizing a touch football game for the kids but the quiet one at the grill, methodically frying up burgers and dogs that everyone will soon devour without a second thought. His parents were Scotch-Irish and German, but he's deeply tan and has a slight, undefinable accent that's not the broad drawl of a ruddy white Texan. Everyone thinks he's Latino. "I've assimilated well," King jokes.

Before coming to PSJA, he had already turned around one school district, in nearby Hidalgo, where he started out as a high school teacher. As with PSJA, Hidalgo's schools were among the worst performing in the state. "The high school was poorly run, discipline was out of control, there was no advanced curriculum, no AP classes, math pretty much ended with Algebra II—there was no calculus, no physics," says King. "College was not an expectation in the homes but also among my peers, the faculty. . . . A lot of the faculty had a 'blame the kids, blame the families' sort of approach and didn't expect much of the kids.'"

These expectations were the first thing that King changed when he became the principal of Hidalgo's high school and then superintendent of the district.

"I really pushed on the idea that our students can do anything anybody else can do—that language, economic circumstances, and ethnicity should not be limiting factors," he says. "I brought in calculus and physics, and then I started insisting students challenge themselves." Among those new expectations was that every student was capable of going to college, and in 2006, Hidalgo became the first district in the country to offer "early college" to all of its students, where students take a mix of high school and college classes and earn college credits along with their diplomas. In 2007, it was named the best high school in Texas.[21]

Career Academies and Early College

In PSJA, King's formula for eradicating the dropout problem was two-fold. First, he organized a campaign, Countdown to Zero, that sent out teachers or volunteers to knock on the doors of every student who wasn't coming to school. Many times, he says, this was all it took—students just needed to know that someone noticed and cared. The second thing he did to keep kids engaged in school and re-engage dropouts was to raise the expectations of them, not lower them: he offered them college. And while it sounds counterintuitive, it worked. "I needed a reason for these students to come to school every day," he says. The chance to earn free college credit was a powerful incentive, King discovered, along with the chance to earn credentials that could land them a good job.

For students who felt compelled to leave school to work, the chance to earn a better living was a powerful inducement to come back, says Virna Bazan, principal of PSJA's Thomas Jefferson Early College High School. "Their living conditions are bad, they feel old enough to help," says Bazan. "So rather than spend eight hours at school, they'd rather get paid for it and bring money home. They felt high school wasn't providing anything for them. . . . What they understand now is that we're saving them time and money. Before, it was just about their high school credits; now it's about earning an associate's degree and getting a better job than they can get now."

King created a "career academy" for the students who had dropped out and were returning, in what was once a Walmart in downtown Pharr. At the academy, students not only pick up their diploma but also college credits, as well as industry credentials that can land them a job immediately after they graduate. In the 2017–18 school year, says principal Darcia Cuellar, there were 129 students enrolled, sixteen of whom finished the year with college certificates and thirty-four with industry certifications in fields such as phlebotomy, EMT training, and electrical, along with their GEDs. "Just giving them a high school diploma is not changing their lives at all," says Cuellar. "We have to have them walk out of here with a skill."

The PSJA career academy is modeled after a broader "career academies" approach pioneered more than forty years ago that combines academics with workforce skills training and has proven effective in keeping high-risk kids—particularly young men—in school. In a fifteen-year-long study of nine career academies around the country, research organization MDRC found that young men graduating from career academies earned an average of 17 percent more per year than their non-career academy peers. This in turn led to higher rates of financial independence and, interestingly, higher rates of marriage among young men.[22] The National Career Academy Coalition estimates there are about seven thousand career academies currently operating nationwide, many of which are developed in partnership with local employers so that the linkages between school and job are clear.[23]

At the same time King was giving students who had dropped out a second chance to finish their diploma, other students were getting a head start on their post-secondary education either through dual enrollment in college courses or "early college," under which students can graduate with an associate's degree along with their high school diploma. According to the district, 3,000 of its 32,000 students are enrolled in college courses. And unlike other school districts where early college is an option only at a few high schools, all of PSJA's high schools are "Early College High Schools." As a result, close to three-fourths of the district's graduates each year graduate with college credits, says King, while 370 of the 1,900 students who graduated in 2018 also earned associate's degrees, thereby saving themselves two years' worth of tuition.[24] The district also started offering college courses as summer school—tuition-free—and now enrolls between 1,600 and 1,800 students a summer. "Basically, we convert one of our high school campuses into a college campus for the summer," says King.

In recent years, a growing number of states have embraced enrolling high school students in college courses as a way to prepare students for higher education while also saving them money on college costs.

According to the National Alliance of Concurrent Enrollment

Partnerships (NACEP), as many as 10 percent of high school students—or 1.4 million students—were enrolled in college courses in 2010–11 (the latest year for which data are available).[25] Moreover, the share of these students has grown by 7 percent per year since 2002–3, with the fastest rates of growth among minority and rural students and among students in states that have made dual enrollment a priority. According to NACEP executive director Adam Lowe, more than half of students are graduating with at least one college course in states like New Mexico, Iowa, and Indiana, while Utah and Missouri are not far behind.

One reason states are embracing dual enrollment is its proven effectiveness in preparing students to succeed in college. A 2010 study of Oregon's dual-enrollment programs, for example, found that dually enrolled students are more likely to go to college, are less likely to drop out as freshmen, and have higher grade point averages than students who did not take college classes in high school.[26] Having experience with college-level courses can also make the transition to college easier, which could be of particular benefit for students more likely to struggle. For example, research from Columbia University found that lower-income and lower-achieving dual-enrollment students saw bigger gains in GPA than other dually enrolled students.[27] Students are also less likely to need remedial coursework. A 2014 study by the Colorado Department of Education found that students in dual enrollment were 9 percent less likely to need remedial education in college.[28]

Similar benefits accrue to students enrolled in "early college," particularly for minority and low-income students. A 2014 evaluation of early college programs, of which the Bill and Melinda Gates Foundation was an early champion, found that early college students were nearly 10 percentage points more likely to go to college and 20 percentage points more likely to earn a degree.[29] The study further found that "[a]mong minority students, Early College students were nearly 10 times more likely to obtain a college degree than comparison students (29.4 percent vs. 3.0 percent)" and that "low-income Early College students were approximately 8.5 times more likely than low-income comparison students to obtain a college degree (22.1 percent vs. 2.6 percent)."

While the bulk of dual-enrollment and early college opportunities offered nationwide are in English, math, and other general education courses—which allows students to skip those prerequisites when they get to college—roughly a third of dual enrollments are in career and technical education (CTE) programs.

In Culpeper County, Virginia, for instance, where dual enrollment is also a priority, an emphasis on CTE has given many students the benefit of early work experience in addition to its other advantages.

One such former student is Haleigh Funk Butler, who already had seven years of professional experience in nursing when she was just twenty-four years old. At seventeen, she started training at Culpeper Community Hospital in Culpeper, Virginia, while dually enrolled at her local high school and Germanna Community College in Locust Grove, Virginia. She took the LPN exam a month before her high school graduation and continued her studies at Germanna. At nineteen, she was a registered nurse and working in the medical-surgical unit at the Novant Health–UVA Health System Culpeper Medical Center.

She continued to work and study and eventually earned a bachelor's degree in nursing in 2016 from the University of Mary Washington in Fredericksburg, Virginia. "If I had gone the traditional route, I would only have been a nurse for two years or maybe three years by now," Funk Butler says. "I feel like I'm in a much more mature state than other people I know who are still struggling to find that job as a career." Best of all, Funk Butler is debt free. "I was lucky that my parents had a little bit of a college fund for me, but I didn't even really break into that at all," she says. "I have no school debt—nothing."

In Pharr-San Juan-Alamo, Superintendent King has a surfeit of similar stories. "We have students finishing Texas A&M within two years of finishing high school," he says. "We have students who are physicians' assistants at twenty, going to law school at twenty. . . . It's saving time and money, and what we're seeing is a lot of students going for post-graduate work because they finish so young and [are] more likely to be debt free or have minimal debt."

The McAllen area still has some distance to go, of course, before its turnaround is complete. In 2015, the Federal Reserve Bank of Dallas estimated that about half a million people still live in the *colonias,* including a significant number in and around the Rio Grande Valley. Of them, 60 percent live in poverty or just above the poverty line. Forty percent also rely on public assistance or SNAP. The employment rate is 50 percent, but much of it is in the "informal" economy. In 2015, the median household income was about $29,000. Fifty-five percent have less than a high school diploma. Broadband internet access is also a problem—McAllen has the lowest broadband subscription rate in the United States.[30]

Instilling a college-going culture is also taking time. "We still have parents who say, 'You don't have to go to school, it's not all that great. Look at me, I didn't go to school, and I make a good living,'" says career academy principal Cuellar. Other parents are reluctant to allow their children to leave home for school, says Thomas Jefferson principal Bazan. "I think my kids would do great things at an Ivy League or far away from here so they can learn new things and explore and discover," she says. "But it's a challenge because their parents are very much against it."

One hopeful sign, however, is that many of the young people who do go away to college are coming back home to McAllen. Among them is attorney Gary Gurwitz's son, who is now a lawyer at Gurwitz's firm, where the senior Gurwitz is managing partner. "It's a real blessing to me," he says. "We're getting more and more of our best and brightest coming home."

And as these young people returning home raise their own families, the area will see even greater progress, says PSJA superintendent King. "When parents are college educated, children are more likely to go to college," he says. "This cyclical impact is going to propel everything forward in the region."

The story of McAllen is about much more than a single extraordinary superintendent and his role in the turnaround of a struggling school district. The broader lesson is how youth disconnection is intimately correlated to a community's overall economic well-being. High rates of disconnection—which inevitably mean a less-skilled workforce—limit a region's prospects for revitalization and make it tough to attract new job-creating industries. However, investing in young people's education and career prospects can be key to an area's economic development. This means that combating disconnection and investing in youth should be central to every community's workforce and economic development strategy. Investing in youth could, in fact, be the catalyst for economic revival in struggling communities nationwide.

PART IV

A New Youth Agenda

13

The "Fierce Urgency of Now"

The problem of young people's disengagement from school and work broadly captured the attention of policymakers at the height of the Great Recession. In 2010, President Barack Obama signed an executive order creating the White House Council for Community Solutions to tackle what was then a crisis in youth unemployment, when as many as 6.7 million young people—or one in six young Americans—were disconnected.[1] But advocates such as Thaddeus Ferber of the Forum for Youth Investment and Kisha Bird, director of youth policy at the Center for Law and Social Policy (CLASP), had already been working for nearly a decade to raise the issues of youth disengagement from school and work to the forefront. In a relatively short period, they and other advocates had succeeded in increasing funding for youth-focused federal programs and worked to include young people's priorities in legislation such as the Workforce Innovation and Opportunity Act (WIOA), which substantially increased investments in programs to reconnect out of school, out of work youth.[2]

But while the number of young people disconnected from school and work has since diminished, the crisis is no less urgent. The persistence of disconnection in the midst of nearly a decade of economic recovery is troubling and speaks to deep structural inequities in the opportunities available to young Americans.

There are also broader reasons why young people deserve to be a priority.

First, the growing problem of inequality—now at a level not seen since the 1920s—cannot be solved without greater attention to the plight of young people in the economy. In 2016, the top 1 percent of households grabbed 24 percent of the nation's income and held 39 percent of the nation's wealth.[3] The returns to being born to wealthy parents have moreover grown over the last several decades. From 1975 to 2010, according to Melissa Kearney of the Brookings Institution, families in the top 5 percent saw their incomes grow by 57 percent, compared to just 3.7 percent in the bottom 20 percent of families.[4]

This extreme maldistribution isn't just a concern about fairness or social justice. Inequality also slows growth and makes economies less dynamic. Research by the Organisation for Economic Co-operation and Development (OECD), for example, finds that inequality may have depressed U.S. economic growth by as much as nine percentage points in the two decades leading up to the Great Recession, primarily by limiting people's opportunities for education and skills development.[5] There is, for instance, an extreme tilt in who has access to higher education. As important as college has become in today's economy, it is the households that already have the greatest benefits that are best positioned to pass on this privilege to their young. According to the Pell Institute and the University of Pennsylvania, students from the top 50 percent of households earned 77 percent of *all* bachelor's degrees awarded in 2014.[6]

Until now, policymakers concerned about inequality have tended to focus on either equalizing opportunities at the very front end of people's lives, such as through early childhood education and preschool, or equalizing outcomes in adulthood, such as through proposals for "universal basic income" or a higher minimum wage. Where there's been less focus, however, is what happens in-between, during a person's young-adult years when their career paths are in their most formative stages. While the idea of "free college" has gotten considerable attention, it's insufficient to solve the problem of young people's disconnection from work and education. Many young people disengage before college is even a possibility; others are not ready to succeed. Moreover, making college more affordable isn't enough to ensure that young people will have the skills they need to land a well-paying job or that jobs will be available.

Young people's fortunes are increasingly divergent, depending on where they live and their personal circumstances, and the lengthening path through adulthood is exacerbating these inequalities. While affluent young adults now have a longer runway to maturity, with more time, resources, and opportunities for self-discovery, lower-income young adults too often lack that support. Nor do they get second chances if something goes wrong. "Affluent kids fail all the time, but there are support structures that make that failure not life determining," says Johns Hopkins University's Robert Balfanz. "But in high-poverty environments, there are no nets, and a couple failures can be life determining."

The inequality of young people's experiences in these early years—in education and financial and emotional support—translates into lifelong advantages or disadvantages, with disconnection the greatest disadvantage of all. Tackling disconnection is an important way to even the field.

Disconnection is also expensive, which is another reason why youth investment should be a priority. Disconnected young adults are costly because they are likely to grow into disconnected, or weakly connected, older adults if the challenges they face are left unsolved.

Take, for instance, the problem of homelessness. "Shelter providers can tell you that some of the [homeless] adults they see now are the same people they saw as kids," says Barbara Duffield, executive director of the nonprofit advocacy group Schoolhouse Connection. In one large-scale Australian study, researchers found that youth homelessness was the largest "pathway" into adult homelessness, accounting for as much as 35 percent of homelessness among adults.[7]

Adult opiate addiction and drug abuse also often have their

genesis in the teen and young adult years. A 2015 study found that while the attention on opiates has been focused on rural areas, rates of adult drug abuse are actually higher in urban areas because of the wider variety of drugs available and because these adults were more likely to have abused drugs as children.[8]

Most distressing is that young-adult disconnection seems self-perpetuating: disconnected young adults grow up to have disconnected children of their own. Measure of America's Kristen Lewis says the strongest predictor of high disconnection rates in any specific part of the country is the rate of youth disconnection in that area ten years ago. "Disconnection could be a normative thing in these communities, where people are growing up seeing their families and neighbors that way," she says.

"You can't be what you can't see," says Teresa Cordova of the Great Cities Institute, in words that echoed what many young people have also said. In Chicago, for instance, where Cordova is based, "we're looking at multiple generations of people who haven't been in the formal labor force. We're looking at kids who don't see a father who gets up and goes to work at eight and gets back at the end of the day either with a lunch pail or a briefcase."

A third reason to prioritize young adults is because the rest of the world is already doing so. America is not alone in its problem of youth disconnection. The International Labour Organization (ILO) reports that in 2017, the global unemployment rate for young people ages fifteen to twenty-four was 13 percent, or about three times the unemployment rate for adults.[9] As many as 64 million young people worldwide are jobless, according to the ILO, while 145 million young workers are living in poverty.[10] The situation is sufficiently dire that the World Economic Forum in 2014 identified youth unemployment as one of the top risks in its annual assessment of risks to the global economy, particularly since the highest rates of joblessness are in the Middle East and North Africa, regions that tend to be politically unstable as well as economically precarious. "The extent of unemployment and underemployment risks generating social instability, especially in post-conflict settings or fragile states," the forum found.[11]

Why Have We Been Ignoring Young People?

Given the importance of young adulthood in the trajectory of people's lives and the consequences of our national failure to invest in young adults, why isn't solving the problem of disconnection already a priority?

A few explanations—some benign and some less so—come to the fore.

First, young adulthood as a distinct phase of life is still a relatively recent phenomenon. Research and policy simply haven't yet caught up to the current social and cultural reality. Moreover, this new reality is still emerging, which means the boundaries of young adulthood are still undefined and thus hard to study. Scholars don't yet agree who is a young adult and who is not. While Measure of America tracks young people ages sixteen to twenty-four, for instance, other researchers have looked at young people ages eighteen to twenty-four, while still others have focused only on young people in poverty.

Compounding the research and data challenge is the fact that disconnected young people have literally dropped out and are therefore hard to find and to study. Because they are out of school, they are not counted by school systems or colleges; because they are not working, they're off the radar of employers and governmental agencies that track wages and employment data. They are also often invisible to social service agencies. The 2017 Chapin Hall study on youth homelessness, for instance, is actually the first national attempt to define the scope of that problem. Because the federal government doesn't currently consider "couch surfing" to be homelessness, and because young people tend to avoid adult shelters as too dangerous, homeless young adults are literally not counted in government efforts to quantify the nation's homeless population.[12]

There are, however, even more pernicious reasons why the problem of young adult disconnection is not front and center. Chief among these is an emerging double standard toward young adults, depending on their race and class. We have become increasingly indulgent of the preference of affluent young adults to take their time in assuming the responsibilities of maturity. We allow them to live at home and take gap years and do our best to cushion them from their mistakes. Wealthy young adults are infantilized and in some ways deprived of agency, despite the fact that they, more than others, are best equipped by resources and education to fend for themselves.

Societal attitudes toward poor young adults, however, is far harsher. As is all too often the case when it comes to questions of poverty, race, and class, disconnected young adults are blamed for their situation, casualties of either "poor parenting" or "destructive life choices." Personal decisions matter, of course, and assuming responsibility for your actions and life course is at the heart of what it means to be an adult. And yet choices are always constrained by environment and circumstances. For young adults with access to plenty of resources and the guidance of caring adults, those constraints are relatively few. But for those without such blessings, the choices available are not really choices at all. Rather, these young people face an ever-narrowing funnel of options toward a limited set of outcomes.

One example of this implicit assignation of blame was the former tendency of researchers to describe out of school and out of work young adults as "idle," a loaded word if ever there was one— as well as untrue.[13] "They are anything but idle and hustling like crazy to survive from one day to the next," says Thaddeus Ferber, vice president for policy at the Forum for Youth Investment. Nevertheless, the label assigned a value judgment to young people's situation and implied that this "idleness" was the result of "laziness" or other self-directed behaviors, rather than the product of structural problems such as lack of jobs or a safe school environment. These value-laden descriptors reinforce negative stereotypes about young people—and "urban youth" in particular—which in turn influence public policy. Blaming young people for their disconnection also creates a convenient excuse for not wanting to know more about who they are and the nature of the systemic failures they've endured that put them on their current path.

Young people, for their part, are acutely aware of the choices they make and sometimes even tend to be tough on their peers. Take, for instance, Quentin, the young man from chapter 5 who works at Starbucks. "Me and my friend—we want to do something with our lives," he says. "We're trying so hard. We got jobs, we're trying to go to school, trying to go to university. Our other friend, he's not. He will sit in his house. He'll get up at ten and smoke all day—literally all day till midnight and do it again, seven days a week. We yell at him, come on, get a job. He gets fired in two days. . . . I don't know where he's going to end up. It's sad, but it's his fault. He gets $10, he gets weed. He chooses that over everything. That's crazy, right? But it's to that point. You can't force anybody to do anything." Quentin's remark shows that, if anything, young people might be too willing to shoulder more of the blame for their circumstances than they should rather than demanding the access to opportunity that is their due.

This reticence translates to political silence as well. Despite the media attention paid to young people as a political force, they actually do not vote. According to ChildTrends, turnout among eighteen- to twenty-four-year-olds peaked in 1972—at 50 percent—which was also the first election in which eighteen-year-olds got the right to vote.[14] Both turnout and registration have declined ever since. The closest the youth vote has come to that historic high was in 2008, with the election of President Obama, but even then turnout was only 44 percent. And in 2012, just 38 percent of young people cast a ballot. Off-year turnout is even more dismal, at only 16 percent in 2014.[15] By comparison, the overall voter turnout rate was 61.8 percent in 2012 and 61 percent in 2016.[16] (As of this writing, the voter turnout rate among eighteen- to twenty-four-year-olds in 2016 was not available—among the older cohort of eighteen- to twenty-nine-year-olds, however, turnout was 46 percent.[17]) Despite the size of the millennial and post-millennial generations, they have yet to show their force as a voting bloc that can tilt resources and policy priorities their way.

A final potential reason for disinvestment in young adults is public cynicism—to some extent deserved—in the effectiveness of government job-training programs for young adults.

Unfortunately, the largest amount of federal dollars might be going to a program that may not be as effective as it should be. In 1964, President Lyndon Johnson launched Job Corps, a two-year program that offers young people ages sixteen to twenty-four room and board in a dorm-like setting, along with education and training. The program was modeled after the successful Depression-era Civilian Conservation Corps, and Kennedy family scion Sargent Shriver was the first at its helm. Today, there are 120 Job Corps centers nationwide reaching 60,000 young people a year, according to the program's website. Administered by the U.S. Department of Labor, the program costs about $1.7 billion a year—or the majority of the funds the department spends annually on employment and training programs for young people.[18] While a 2008 evaluation found some promising results, a 2018 evaluation by the Department of Labor's inspector general concluded that "Job Corps could not demonstrate the extent to which its training programs helped participants enter meaningful jobs appropriate to their training."[19] This report followed a 2011 audit that found "Job Corps placed participants in positions unrelated to their training, placed participants in positions that required little or no training, and in general overstated the success of its job placements."[20] Job Corps is, moreover, nearly three times as expensive per participant as the programs that do work, such as YouthBuild or National Guard ChalleNGe. In fiscal 2015, for instance, Job Corps cost $30,106 per participant, versus $10,036 for YouthBuild and $13,889 for ChalleNGe.[21]

Among the inspector general's dismal findings about Job Corps:

> For example, one participant worked as a fast food cook and cashier prior to entering Job Corps, graduated after attending carpentry training for 347 days, and obtained a job working as a pizza restaurant waiter. Five years after exiting the program in 2010, this same participant was working at a convenience store earning approximately $11,000 per year. Job Corps reported this as a successful graduation and placement.

Additionally, we found four participants returned to the same employer for whom they had worked prior to entering Job Corps. For example, one participant worked as a cashier at a retail store before attending Job Corps in 2011, spent 310 days in bricklaying training, and then returned to work at the same retail store as a stock clerk after graduating. Job Corps also reported this as a successful graduation and placement. In 2016, this former participant trained in bricklaying was working for a bottling company.

If advocates for youth are to argue for greater resources, they will need to show some ruthlessness toward programs that fall short—even those with a historic vintage.

14

Seven Steps for Ending Disconnection

Young people need four things to transition into economic independence successfully. First, they need to have met their basic needs for shelter, food, and safety. Second, they need skills and knowledge adequate to secure a job that will lead them to financial security. This can be a college degree, but it could also be an occupational credential, such as a welding certificate or a commercial driver's license, with recognized industry value. Third, young people need opportunities in a growing economy where they can exercise those skills and knowledge. Ideally, this means a full-time job on the path to a meaningful career, but it could also mean an internship, an apprenticeship, or a part-time job, so long as there are opportunities for advancement. Fourth, and perhaps most important, young people need mentors and caring adults in their lives to offer guidance and support.

Government cannot fully supply each of these building blocks to connection, nor can it ever substitute for what two loving parents can offer to a child. Moreover, breaking the cycle of disconnection will ultimately mean tackling the broad chronic problems of poverty, structural racism, and educational inequality that have seemed so intractable for so long. Nevertheless, there are some very specific—and eminently doable—ways in which government policies can provide more opportunities to young people or, at the very least, stop sabotaging their prospects. The following seven steps can help dramatically reduce the ranks of disconnected young Americans and ensure that every young person has a shot at success on their own terms.

Step One: Ensure Every Young Person Counts

The first step for ensuring that young people get the attention they need from policymakers is as simple as collecting sufficient data about their economic circumstances and challenges. Government's abandonment of vulnerable young adults begins with its failure to acknowledge and account for the millions of young people slipping out of the economic mainstream.

Currently, neither the Census Bureau nor the Bureau of Labor Statistics officially tracks youth disconnection, nor do government data adequately monitor the well-being of young people. To address this gap, the federal government should create an official measure of youth "disconnection" and report at least annually on the state of young people's economic fortunes, in the same way that the Census Bureau releases annual figures on the poverty rate and the share of Americans who are uninsured. The United Kingdom, for instance, releases a quarterly statistical bulletin on young people it calls "NEET"—not in education, employment, or training.[1] (In March 2019, the share of young people who were NEET in the United Kingdom was 11.0 percent—roughly comparable to the U.S. rate.)

This should not be a heavy lift. Measure of America, for instance, derives its analyses from data already gathered by the Census Bureau's American Community Survey, which samples a subset of the U.S. population every year to supplement the decennial census.[2] The government could simply adopt Measure of America's technical definition of "disconnection"[3] or, alternatively, adopt the United Kingdom's definition of NEET.[4]

Measuring and tracking out-of-school and out-of-work young people would have numerous benefits. Most important, it would help prioritize disconnection as a policy focus and validate disconnection as a phenomenon worthy of significant attention. It would also help drive scholars' and policymakers' thinking about whom to target for help and how to measure progress so that government and private resources are spent wisely. And it would help catalyze the kind of systemic reforms we need to tackle disconnection at its roots.

Step Two: Invest More—A Lot More— in Programs That Work

As part III of this book makes clear, disconnection is not an insoluble problem—we know the approaches that work. What we're not doing, however, is investing in these solutions and bringing them to scale.

The current lack of investment means that the most effective programs are struggling to meet demand for their services. National Guard ChalleNGe, for example, is 75 percent funded by the federal government and 25 percent funded by the states. It's also supported by private money, which is raised by the nonprofit National Guard Youth Foundation. In fiscal 2016, federal funding was $145 million, according to Brig. Gen. Allyson Solomon, president of the National Guard Youth Foundation, short of what it needs to establish a program in every state. "We'd like to see 20,000 young people have the opportunity to go through this program every year," she says. "Right now, it's 10,000."

Funding is also the biggest constraint for programs like Second Story, whose executive director, Judith Dittman, is constantly scrabbling for dollars from a variety of federal, state, and local sources as well as from private philanthropy, while dozens of young women languish on the organization's waitlist, desperate for aid.

Dramatically raising investment in young people would not only benefit more youth in need of help; it would also more than pay for itself. The Forum for Youth Investment argues that an investment of $30,000 per young person would save taxpayers $65,230 in reduced expenditures for health care, welfare payments, and crime while also generating $105,500 in new tax revenues over that young person's lifetime.[5] In particular, the forum and its allies would like to see federal appropriations raised to the point where 1 million young people would benefit from education and job programs—or about triple what it is today.

Reaching 1 million young people should not mean, however, that Congress should indiscriminately raise funding across the board. Rather, this must also include efforts to deploy current dollars more effectively, as well as have more investments in research to help determine which programs work best and why. Some money should also be set aside for pilot projects and experiments in new approaches. The government should also consider revisiting programs, such as the Youth Opportunities Initiative that had a promising impact in Baltimore, as the White House Council on Community Solutions recommended in 2012.

Investments in new ways to streamline policy are also as important as investments in dollars. For instance, one laudable effort worth expanding is the Performance Partnership Pilots for Disconnected Youth (P3), authorized by Congress in 2014, which allowed states, tribes, and local and regional government to experiment with pooling funding from multiple federal sources into a single, more flexible pot of money. Among the benefits of this effort are more flexibility and less paperwork, as well as greater accountability for outcomes. For instance, instead of having to report separately to federal agencies, such as the Departments of Labor, Health and Human Services, and Education, each with its own procedures, performance targets, and limitations on funding, governments and grantees can pull together a single report on a common set of outcomes across all agencies. The P3 initiative has involved three rounds of pilots so far, and a 2017 report by the Government Accountability Office (GAO) concluded that the efforts have so far reduced the administrative burdens on agencies.[6] Among the pilots currently under way are efforts in California, Florida, Indiana, Louisiana, Texas, and New York, among others. In Los Angeles, for example, the city is proposing to serve up to eight thousand young people who are high school dropouts, in foster care, homeless, or on probation by expanding the employment and education services available through sixteen neighborhood YouthSource Centers located throughout the city.[7] Among other things, the pilot allows the city to lift the eligibility age for youth to receive services from twenty-one to twenty-four and waives some accounting requirements needed by the Department of Labor that would have restricted the use of funds. While these pilots are relatively new, they demonstrate the potential benefits of not just more money but also smart money as a way to serve more youth.

Step Three: Encourage More Businesses to Step Up

The availability of private-sector jobs with opportunities for advancement is enormously crucial to young people's success. The shortage of high-quality jobs available to young adults means that they aren't getting the early work experience they need or getting a foot in the door on a career path that will lead them to financial security.

While government-provided "summer jobs" programs can help fill the gap by providing work experience and income, they do not substitute for more valuable opportunities in the private sector, where the vast majority of workers will spend their careers. Nor is there yet conclusive evidence that public jobs for young adults lead to better outcomes on employment and earnings.[8]

Companies can and should do more to create more opportunities for young people and prioritize their hiring. It's unrealistic, however, to expect that simply exhorting companies to hire more youth will be enough to make it happen. Nor will it benefit young people in the long run if companies are encouraged to treat the hiring of youth as a charitable endeavor versus as a smart business decision that will benefit their companies. This is why organizations such as the Urban Alliance and Year Up can be critical in mediating the recruitment and hiring of young people, providing training in soft skills, and providing wraparound support to ensure that young people succeed in their placements. "We want companies to see this not as 'corporate social responsibility' but as a business practice," says Jonathan Hasak, Year Up's director of public policy.

Like the Urban Alliance, Year Up works to place young people in "supported" private-sector internships, where students receive classroom training in hard and soft skills before a six-month internship. Unlike the Urban Alliance, which works with high school students, Year Up works with young adults ages eighteen to twenty-four who have a high school diploma or a GED. According to a 2018 evaluation, Year Up graduates earned better than 50 percent more than members of a control group, an outcome that evaluators found to be "the largest reported to date for workforce programs."[9] Companies benefited as well, according to evaluators. "Several employers noted that experience with Year Up interns had led them to revamp career pathways in skilled technical occupations to create new career entry points at lower levels," the report noted. "One large firm heavily re-oriented its entry-level hiring practices to recruit sub-baccalaureate-level interns. For another, creating assignments for interns stimulated the realization that a substantial layer of tasks currently handled by mid-level employees could be performed by Year Up graduates."[10]

Founded in 2000, the year-long program currently operates in eight cities and served roughly 3,500 young people in 2013–14. Not only do programs like those offered by Year Up and the Urban Alliance deliver good results, they are cost-effective for taxpayers. In Year Up, for instance, fees from employers pay for 59 percent of program costs, while philanthropic and charitable dollars make up most of the rest, and only 2 percent comes from public money.[11]

Companies are beginning to step up on their own. Prudential Financial, for instance, announced in 2019 a $180 million global commitment to serving opportunity youth, while McDonald's launched in 2018 a global youth employment initiative, beginning stateside with a $2 million plan to help young people in Chicago.[12] In 2015, a coalition of companies and philanthropies, led by the Schultz Family Foundation and the Aspen Institute's Forum for Community Solutions, launched the 100,000 Opportunities Initiative, committed to hiring opportunity youth. Among the more than fifty companies now involved in the coalition are Chipotle, Walmart, Target, Starbucks, and CVS.[13] Monique Miles, director of the Aspen Institute's Opportunity Youth Incentive Fund, says that in addition to hiring, companies are also working to adapt their policies to better suit young people's needs, such as by providing scheduling flexibility for students who are working. More companies, including Starbucks, Google, and Uber,[14] are also moving to "ban the box"—i.e., declining to ask about a potential employee's criminal history—which puts them ahead of many states and localities in removing barriers to employment after a conviction.[15]

What could encourage more companies to step up to the plate is a targeted tax incentive, such as the Disconnected Youth Opportunity Tax Credit, which was part of the American Recovery and Reinvestment Act of 2009 and was available to employers who hired disconnected young adults in 2009 and 2010.[16] Tax incentives do, however, have a mixed record when it comes to incentivizing hiring that wouldn't have happened anyway, and they would likely need to be very generous to change companies' behavior. A better step might be to help expand high-quality internship and work-based learning programs such as Year Up and the Urban Alliance so that a company's decision as to whether to hire a young person is an easier one.

Step Four: Bring Opportunity Everywhere

Just as important as creating more opportunities is ensuring that all youth have adequate access to the means to move upward, wherever they live. Especially crucial is ensuring the eradication of "opportunity deserts," where young people are cut off from jobs and education, such as in rural areas or urban cores where manufacturing was once a middle-class mainstay but has since vanished. These areas often need access to both new jobs and better opportunities for higher education—for not only young people but also adults. Not surprisingly, disconnection among young people and older adults is intimately linked. Burd-Sharps and Lewis of Measure of America found that areas with low levels of adult education and employment and high levels of racial segregation were also much more likely to see higher rates of disconnection among the young. "These are likely areas where there's more unemployment and less economic opportunity overall," says Lewis. "But if adults are more tenuously attached to the labor market, they also don't have the connections, experience, or know-how to help their kids navigate the job market."

Carlos, the young man with the drug conviction in chapter 7 would likely agree.

"What you see is what you want to be," he says. "By the time I was thirteen or fourteen, I would say 'I don't want to go to school,' and my mom and dad would let me stay home. . . . If maybe I saw . . . my dad graduating high school and college, but the man wasn't working. I grew up, and I see what I see in the street, and to me that was faster than eight hours of school."

One promising new initiative that could help revitalize these communities was included in the 2017 tax legislation passed by Congress—perhaps the one bright spot in an otherwise dismal bill. Under this legislation, states can designate "Opportunity Zones," where private investments can be eligible for a variety of tax benefits, the biggest goodie being deferred taxation for up to ten years on unrealized capital gains reinvested in these zones.[17] According to the Economic Innovation Group (EIG), which developed the Opportunity Zone concept, as much as $6.1 trillion in unrealized gains held by both corporations and households is potentially available for investment, including in places like South Boston, Virginia, which was designated an Opportunity Zone by Gov. Ralph Northam. The challenge for state and local leaders will be to ensure that investment dollars actually flow to the communities that need it and that the investments made will help sustain these areas in the long term, rather than provide a temporary high that ultimately fades.

Recent innovations in rural higher education could also help solve the problem of higher education deserts, where 41 million Americans live.[18] Among the most promising of these developments is the establishment in several states of "higher education centers," which use a blend of technology and physical presence to bring college-level education to rural areas. In Pennsylvania, for instance, the state legislature authorized the creation of a "rural

regional college" tasked with bringing greater higher education opportunities to an area encompassing seven thousand square miles
over nine counties.[19] Initially launched as the Education Consortium of Upper Allegheny, with a budget of just $1.2 million, the
effort was expanded and rechristened the Northern Pennsylvania
Regional College (NPRC) in 2017.

The NPRC does not boast a typical college campus. Rather
than a single flagship location, the college operates six different
"hubs"—physical mini-campuses—scattered throughout the region, plus numerous "classrooms" using borrowed space from local
high schools, public libraries, and other community buildings.
When it launched, the NPRC didn't confer its own degrees; rather,
it provided the infrastructure for other accredited institutions to
extend their reach through "blended" offerings combining virtual
and in-person teaching. Founding president Joseph Nairn says the
college is working to expand its own offerings in the future.

Nairn says the institution's physical presence offers two benefits
over strictly online schools. First, it provides the many students
who don't have broadband internet at home a way to get online.
Second, requiring students to attend classes provides the structure
many need to stay on track. "The model of having students come
to a site and interact with teachers and students leads to better
outcomes," he says. "We are imposing discipline without requiring
people to commute some ungodly distance or requiring people to
pack up and move to a residential setting."[20]

Forest County, Pennsylvania, schools superintendent Amanda
Hetrick hopes institutions like NPRC can help her former students
build on the college experience they do have. "They have bits and
pieces," she says. "If we can get those bits and pieces together, we
can get them to an industry credential or an associate's degree."

Better local access to higher education could also improve the
chances of her current students succeeding in college, Hetrick says,
by enabling students to enroll in college courses while still in high
school. One reason so many rural students drop out of college, she
says, is that they leave for school unprepared for the coursework
and the environment. "With dual enrollment, we're exposing them

to college-level work," she says. "A lot of my kids are first-generation college goers. They don't know the language. When somebody says 'go see the registrar,' they don't know what that means."

These rural higher education centers can also serve to accelerate economic development as well as educate young rural students. In south central Virginia, for instance, the Southern Virginia Higher Education Center (SVHEC) in South Boston is following a model similar to the success of South Texas College in McAllen. SVHEC started life as a five-hundred-square-foot trailer in 1986 but now occupies 100,000 gleaming square feet of renovated space in its two repurposed tobacco warehouses. In addition to traditional classrooms, SVHEC offers hands-on lab space for its welding, IT, and mechatronics students. Its nursing training facilities include several mock patient rooms complete with mannequins for practicing procedures such as giving injections and taking vital signs. Recently, the center also opened an "innovation lab" to provide manufacturing and consulting services to local businesses. In early 2018, for instance, the lab was developing prototypes of recyclable wine barrels for a consortium of Virginia wineries. In 2017, says executive director Betty Adams, the center placed 173 students into new jobs. The region still has a long way to go before it matches it former prosperity, but it's a start.

"We get people in here who've never had success before, but they get a credential and it helps them get a job or a better job and then they start thinking, 'Wow, I want to come back and get another credential,' and it builds on itself," says Adams. "That's educational empowerment."

In addition to economic growth and better opportunities for higher education, a third important piece that young people living in opportunity deserts need is access to social capital, including the professional and social connections that a caring mentor can provide. Even in a community that is economically vibrant, young people need mentors who can help navigate the options available to them, get past obstacles, and provide both practical and emotional support.

These mentors are, however, in short supply. One survey of

young people conducted by Mary Bruce and John Bridgeland of Civic Enterprises finds that "one in three young people overall (34 percent) and even more at-risk youth (37 percent) report they never had an adult mentor of any kind (naturally occurring or structured) while they were growing up." What this means, Bridgeland further concludes, is that "approximately 16 million youth, including nine million at-risk youth, will reach age 19 without ever having a mentor."[21] Bruce and Bridgeland offer a variety of solutions for closing what they call "the mentoring gap," including expanded federal, state, and local funding for mentoring initiatives; better research into what makes a high-quality mentoring relationship; and better guidance and support for would-be mentors. They also point to promising efforts such as the NYC Success Mentors program, which works with "chronically absent" students who miss more than eighteen school days a year to overcome the obstacles that prevent them from being present. Launched in 2014 by Mayor Bill de Blasio, the city reports that Success Mentors now work with more than ten thousand chronically absent kids in 220 public schools, checking in with them throughout the school day and reaching out at least two to three times per week.[22] Each mentor manages a caseload of fifteen to twenty students, greets each mentee every morning, calls home if a student is absent, and meets with his or her students regularly just to check in. Mentors also celebrate successes "no matter how small," according to the program's practice guides. A big part of the program's impact might be the simple act of noticing whether a student is at school. "He's the only person that actually cared about me when it came to school," says one New York City high school student about her mentor in a video about the program.[23] "He's the only person that made me care more—the only person that made me come to school more . . . the only person that made me think positive rather than negative."

Step Five: Link Schools to Jobs and Careers

Far too many of the youth-serving interventions that exist today are after-the-fact efforts that aim to reconnect young people to jobs or school after the damage of disconnection has been done. As effective as these interventions can be, they can be costly, both for the public and for young people who will have lost valuable time and opportunities. The better approach is to prevent disconnection before it even occurs, such as by strengthening links to jobs and higher education while young people are in middle and high schools.

As earlier chapters have shown, a potentially effective strategy for keeping young people in school is to make it more relevant to future opportunities so that students have an incentive to stay in class. According to one survey of high school dropouts, also by John Bridgeland and Civic Enterprises, nearly half (47 percent) of students said they left school because it was "boring" and "classes were not interesting."[24] As noted earlier, some potentially promising ways to overcome this obstacle of boredom include career academies that blend academic learning with marketable vocational skills; early college and dual-enrollment programs that give students a head start on college while reducing their potential school debts; and supported internship programs that provide early exposure to work while imparting the "soft skills" young people need to succeed. These models should be broadly available to students, not isolated to the districts with forward-thinking leadership.

Models such as dual enrollment and early college also need to be carefully tailored to ensure that all students are able to participate. Dual enrollment, for instance, was originally conceived in the 1950s as a way for high-achieving students to get a jump-start on college. While most places that offer dual enrollment have broadened the reach of these programs to pupils of all levels, including through a focus on career and technical programs, students must still be ready for college-level work. This means that students in the worst-performing schools or those who've fallen behind academically are less likely to take advantage of these opportunities. "It's a rare program that works with students with severe deficits," says Adam Lowe of the National Alliance of Concurrent Enrollment Partnerships. States are also inconsistent in how generously they fund efforts like dual enrollment. Georgia, for example, leads with appropriations of $88 million a year, according to Lowe, while Massachusetts only spends between $600,000 and $800,000. As a result, many states ask parents and students to help finance dual-enrollment opportunities, which again can disadvantage poorer students. "Any time you have a program that's really good—if you're providing it only to those students who can afford it or who are already excelling, you're only going to worsen the gap among students rather than use that tool to reduce it," says Lowe.

One potentially obvious solution for reducing the costs of dual enrollment is to allow limited early access to federal student aid for high school students in dual enrollment, including Pell grants. One option, for example, could be to provide up to $1,000 a year in Pell funding for dual-enrollment students in accredited programs. Alternatively, students could be "advanced" the Pell funding they would otherwise qualify for were they already high school graduates. In addition to expanded student aid, states would also benefit from an infusion of federal dollars to support dual-enrollment programs.

Embracing new models that blur the lines between high school and college will also require some big shifts in the focus of K–12 education, including a rethinking of the outcomes that schools should be held accountable for. While No Child Left Behind prompted an important debate on the responsibility of all schools to deliver a high-quality education to all children, it also potentially created incentives for schools to "teach to the test," rather than to impart the knowledge and skills students need to succeed in the real world. Schools' incentives will need to be realigned to make room for priorities other than high-stakes testing. Schools should also stop overemphasizing four-year college preparation at the expense of career exploration and well-paying non-college options. While all students should be encouraged to think about four-year college, other paths should be presented as equally viable and attractive choices, particularly in skilled trades or in fields such as IT, where professional certifications can in many cases be more valuable than a degree.

"Students should be prepared to go on to advanced education, but they need to understand what kind of education they're investing in," says Monique Rizer, who recently succeeded Nathanial Cole as executive director of the Urban Alliance's D.C. program. "Is it going to exist ten years from now?" One way to ensure this, Rizer says, is to encourage much closer connections between community colleges and local employers. "Braiding some of these institutions together and having a softer handoff would make a huge difference," she says.

Step Six: Break the Pipeline to Disconnection from the Foster Care and Justice Systems

For the nation's most vulnerable young people—those emerging from the foster care and justice systems—the government owes no less than a top-to-bottom reform of these systems so that no young person suffers homelessness or extended disconnection.

At a minimum, these young people deserve much more generous transitional services and for a longer period of time than they do now. For foster youth, services should not end at age eighteen or at twenty-one, as they do in most states, but should continue to age twenty-four. Foster youth should also get greater help with housing and college tuition—the two resources that parents of youth in intact families often provide but to which foster youth have far less access. All states, for instance, should waive tuition at in-state colleges and community colleges for foster youth who have no other family financial support. States and the federal government should also greatly expand the resources available to combat youth homelessness and invest in initiatives to help former foster youth build up savings and financial security. One promising model, for example, is the "opportunity passport" program launched by the Jim Casey Youth Opportunities Initiative, which provides young people with financial literacy training, a bank account, and matched savings. Over the last fifteen years, the program has helped more than 3,800 young adults save more than $5.7 million toward the purchase of housing, cars, or higher education.[25] Ultimately, however, the goal should be long-term stability for every child in foster care.

As one young person with the Jim Casey Youth Opportunities says, "[I would have liked someone who would] sign a piece of paper and say, 'I'm going to be here for you no matter what. I'm going to get to know you and help you make better decisions so you can be successful in life.'"

For young people involved in the justice system, the greatest priority should be to divert as many young adults from entering the system in the first place. Diversion programs such as CASES deserve more support and replication, and detention should be a last-resort option. As author Cara Drinan argues, "[Y]outh detention not only reduces future productivity and earnings, but it also enhances the likelihood of future delinquency and recidivism." Rather, except under the most serious circumstances, justice-involved young adults deserve a second chance. "Precisely because children's brains are still in flux until late adolescence, they are more amenable to rehabilitation than adults," Drinan writes. "Studies have shown that probation and community service are more effective with juveniles than adults. This opportunity is lost when society exposes kids to harsh sentences rather than investing in their rehabilitation."

While states are making excellent progress on raising the age of criminal responsibility, thanks to organizations such as the Vera Institute for Justice, state laws that allow the transfer of juveniles to adult court must be reformed as well. Young people leaving the system also need better and more supports, including far better access to transition services that can reduce recidivism and help them connect to a job or to education. Young people also should not be haunted for the rest of their lives as a result of a youthful conviction. More states, for instance, should follow the lead of New York, which recently passed legislation to seal nonviolent offenders' criminal records after ten years of good behavior, and Louisiana, which in 2017 became the first state to ban public colleges from asking applicants about their criminal background.

Step Seven: Listen to Young People

Finally, policymakers must make an attitudinal shift toward young people and embrace their positive potential. All too often, youth—especially lower-income youth—are perceived as problems to be managed, rather than assets to be developed. Even more tragically, stereotypes about youth too often tip into criminalization. Many young people, writes Megan Alruth of the University of Texas–Austin, must contend with "dangerous assumptions and stereotypes by adults that youth are 'would-be thugs,' up to no good, and in need of armed containment. And, in many cases, young people are criminalized not just for their age, but also for the color of their skin, their gender identities, mental health challenges, and poverty or other traumatic experiences."[26]

In addition to good old-fashioned racism and classism, outdated notions of adolescent development are also to blame for these destructive attitudes toward young people. Until fairly recently, according to the pioneering youth development scholar Richard Lerner of Tufts University, developmental psychologists and researchers were heavily under the influence of G. Stanley Hall, who invented the study of adolescent development in the early 1900s.[27] Among Hall's beliefs, Lerner writes, was that adolescence was a period of "storm and stress" while individuals transitioned from "being beast-like to being civilized." Under this view, a "successful" adolescent was someone whose "beast-like" impulses didn't get the better of her or him—"someone who was not taking drugs or using alcohol, not engaging in unsafe sex, and not participating in crime or violence," Lerner writes. This "deficit-focused" view of young adults led to public policies primarily aimed at controlling young-adult behavior, including by criminalizing them.

By the early 1990s, however, Lerner and others began rejecting Hall's view and replacing it with the idea that all young people have strengths that can be nurtured through the "developmental assets" around them at home, at school, and in their communities—what Lerner calls the "social and ecological 'nutrients' for the growth of healthy youth." Under this approach, young people who get the right support not only naturally avoid bad behaviors but become positive contributors to the communities around them.

One example of a program that adheres to this model of "positive youth development" (PYD) is 4-H, which was also the subject of an intense evaluation by Lerner and his colleagues. 4-H provides young people with three things, according to Lerner: "Positive and sustained relationships between youth and adults," "activities that build important life skills," and "opportunities for youth to use these skills as participants and leaders in valued community activities."[28] In a long-term study of 4-Hers, Lerner and his colleagues found that kids participating in these programs were more likely to be civically active, more likely to pursue math and science, and more likely to engage in healthy behaviors, such as getting enough sleep and regular checkups.[29]

The approach of "positive youth development" is one that all policymakers should embrace, and it is the approach followed by all of the programs deeply profiled in this book. It is also the underlying premise behind the many laudable emerging efforts to give young people greater voice in their destiny and in the policies that affect them. Among the endeavors to engage youth perspectives are the Jim Casey Youth Opportunities Initiative mentioned earlier in this book, the Forum for Youth Investments' many convenings of opportunity youth, and the National Council of Young Leaders, organized under the sponsorship of YouthBuild. Young people are also taking the helm on justice reform—most notably with Black Lives Matter, but also through groups such as the Black Youth Project 100 and the YouthFirst Initiative, which are working to end youth incarceration.[30]

John Bridgeland, who coined the term "opportunity youth," says he was led to this term because of the perseverance he saw in the young people he met, and an optimism that was unshakable despite the challenges they were working to overcome. "I don't like buzz words, and I don't like terms of art that paper over vulnerabilities, but these young people were so optimistic and representative of a generation of extraordinary potential that was untapped," he says. "They know that employment and success in school and attachment to a decent-paying job were absolutely essential to a successful life. The term 'opportunity youth' shows the country these individuals aren't problems to be solved but potential to be fulfilled. We all have to do a better job of viewing them in the way they view themselves."

What's at Stake

The Urban Alliance's Monique Rizer is one example of how that potential can be fulfilled. She was an "opportunity youth" long before that phrase was coined. "My mom was a nineteen-year-old single mom and never finished college," she says. "I had five younger siblings, and four of them would not finish high school. I became pregnant myself at twenty and was faced with recreating the situation I grew up in." Rizer wanted something different for herself but didn't know how. "I wanted to go to college and do better than my parents, but I didn't know what that meant," she says. "I didn't have anyone around me to explain the path to the middle class or even what affluence looks like."

Rizer's years of near-disconnection came after high school. "For a couple years, I was very lost," she says. "My parents' financial situation became such that we had to leave our home. So we moved into a travel trailer with all the kids, and I was essentially on my own at seventeen." But what saved her from complete disconnection was the retail jobs she still managed to hold and her high school's dual-enrollment program with a local community college. "I did it because friends were doing it and it got me out of school half the day," she says. "But that one year alerted me to college. I thought I could just continue this and maybe go to a really good university one day."

That opportunity did in fact come, when Rizer, who grew up in Washington State, won a scholarship for promising low-income college students that had just been established by the Bill and Melinda Gates Foundation. As a Gates Foundation "Millennium Scholar" (now the Gates Scholarship), Rizer benefited from a full ride in college, along with mentors and other support services to help her through.[31] "The beautiful footnote to this is that my child is in college right now," she says. "He's on scholarship, he's serving in the National Guard, he's studying physics. It was so moving to think that, wow, I took this journey twenty years ago as a young parent, unsure I would even finish college, and here I am, doing work I love and sending my kid to school."

For at least the past forty years, the needs and demands of the baby boomers have dominated public policy as well as the federal budget. It's time now for a generational shift. What I have tried to argue in this book is that young adults for too long have been the missing link in our national conversation about opportunity, inequality, and the future of American prosperity. We can continue to ignore the more than one in ten young Americans who are currently disengaged from mainstream opportunities and pay the price for that loss of talent and energy as well as the inevitable consequences in added human misery. Or we can focus our attention on ensuring that every young adult gets a fair shot at a productive and independent adulthood, with a strong community and caring mentors around them, and abundant opportunities for upward advancement. The investment we make in our young adults is a reflection of our collective vision for the country's future. Let's not disappoint the aspirations of these young adults or rob the nation of its potential.

Acknowledgments

My deepest gratitude goes to the many young people who opened their hearts to share their stories with me for this book. Their generosity, optimism, and resilience were an inspiration, and I hope I have done their voices justice in these pages.

I am also indebted to the many passionate and dedicated advocates who guided my journey through the world of disconnection and lent me their experience and expertise, with special thanks to Thaddeus Ferber and Jo Ann Paanio at the Forum for Youth Investment; Monique Miles at the Aspen Institute Forum for Community Solutions; Kisha Bird at CLASP; Monique Rizer and Emily Rogers at the Urban Alliance; Joel Copperman, Loyal Miles, and Maceo June at CASES; Patrice Cromwell, Sandra Gasca-Gonzalez, Paula Young, Kathleen Holt-Whyte, and Alex Lohrbach of the Jim Casey Youth Opportunities Initiative; Shawn Terry-Young, Kerry Owings, and Ernest Dorsey at YO! Baltimore; Lori Kaplan, Doug Ierley, and Nicole Hanrahan of the Latin American Youth Center; Judith Dittman of Second Story; Matthew Morton of Chapin Hall; Darla Bardine at the National Network for Youth; Dorothy Stoneman at YouthBuild; and countless others who took the time to speak with me about their advocacy.

Heartfelt thanks are due to my professional mentors: Will Marshall at the Progressive Policy Institute, who launched my career in public policy, and Paul Glastris of the *Washington Monthly*, who taught me the power of narrative. I am also deeply grateful to Norris West of the Annie E. Casey Foundation, whose support and guidance throughout this project were invaluable; and Marc Favreau of The New Press, to whom I owe everything, but especially for the insight of his edits and for his bottomless well of patience for a novice author. Thanks also to the Annie E. Casey Foundation for its investment in this project and without whose support this book would not have been possible.

Last, but not least, thanks to my own family—my husband, Brian, and my two sons, Alex and Elliot—for their love, support, and encouragement.

Notes

Introduction

1. Shane Goldmacher and Jonathan Martin, "Alexandria Ocasio-Cortez Defeats Joseph Crowley in Major Democratic House Upset," *New York Times*, June 26, 2018.

2. Jenny Anderson, "The Students of Marjory Stoneman Douglas Are Going on a 20-State Bus Tour to Register Voters and Push Gun Reform," *Quartz*, June 4, 2018.

3. Gray Rohrer, "Florida Lawmakers Pass Historic Gun-Control Bill," *Orlando Sentinel*, March 7, 2018.

4. "Population Age 25 and Over by Educational Attainment, 1940–2018" (Infographic, Washington, D.C.: U.S. Census Bureau, 2019), https://www.census.gov/library/visualizations/time-series/demo/cps-historical-time-series.html.

5. Britt Hysen, "The Power of Millennial Entrepreneurship," *Huffington Post*, September 11, 2014.

6. Grant Trahant, "Causeartist Presents: The 36 Social Entrepreneurs to Watch for in 2018," *Causeartist.com*, http://www.causeartist.com/causeartist-presents-the-social-entrepreneurs-to-watch-for-in-2018.

7. Kristen Lewis, "Making the Connection: Transportation and Youth Disconnection" (report, New York: Measure of America, Social Science Research Council, 2019), https://ssrc-static.s3.amazonaws.com/moa/Making%20the%20Connection.pdf.

8. "Youth Not in Employment, Education or Training (NEET)" (Paris: Organisation for Economic Co-operation and Development, la st modified 2018), https://data.oecd.org/youthinac/youth-not-in-employment-education-or-training-neet.htm.

9. Jonathan Vespa, "The Changing Economics and Demographics of Young Adulthood: 1975–2016" (Washington, D.C.: U.S. Census Bureau, 2017).

1: Emergence and Divergence

1. Fanny Lyn Dolansky, "Coming of Age in Rome: The History and Social Significance of Assuming the Toga Virilis" (master's thesis, University of Victoria, 1999).

2. "Falling Through the Cracks: How Laws Allow Child Marriage to Happen in Today's America" (report, Falls Church, VA: Tahirih Justice Center, 2017).

3. Cara Drinan, *The War on Kids: How American Juvenile Justice Lost Its Way* (New York: Oxford University Press, 2018).

4. Selective Service Act of 1940, Pub. L. No. Public Law 772, 54 Stat. 889 (November 13, 1942); Selective Service Act of 1940, amendments, Public Law 772.

5. Jonathan Vespa, "The Changing Economics and Demographics of Young Adulthood: 1975–2016" (report, Washington, D.C.: U.S. Census Bureau, 2017).

6. Jeffrey Jensen Arnett, *Emerging Adulthood: The Winding Road from the Late Teens Through the Twenties* (New York: Oxford University Press, 2004).

7. U.S. Census Bureau, "Table MS-2. Estimated Median Age at First Marriage, by Sex: 1890 to the Present" (Historical Marital Status Tables; last modified November 2018), https://www.census.gov/data/tables/time-series /demo/families/marital.html; T.J. Mathews, M.S., and Brady E. Hamilton, Ph.D., U.S. Centers for Disease Control, "Mean Age of Mother, 1970–2000," *National Vital Statistics Reports* 51, no. 1 (Atlanta, December 2002).

8. Arnett (2017).

9. Ibid.

10. Gap Year Association, https://gapyearassociation.org/index.php.

11. "Gap Year Programs," Where There Be Dragons, https://www .wheretherebedragons.com/students/find-your-adventure/gap-year.

12. Harvard University, Harvard College Admissions and Financial Aid, "Should I Take Time Off?" (last modified 2017), https://college.harvard.edu /admissions/preparing-college/should-i-take-time.

13. Ibid.

14. Katherine Skiba, "Malia Obama's Gap Year About to End as She Goes to Harvard," *Chicago Tribune*, August 18, 2017.

15. Harvard University, Center on the Developing Child, "Experiences Build Brain Architecture," https://developingchild.harvard.edu/resources /experiences-build-brain-architecture.

16. Harvard University, Center on the Developing Child, "Brain Architecture," https://developingchild.harvard.edu/science/key-concepts/brain -architecture.

17. Frances E. Jensen, M.D., and Amy Ellis Nutt. *The Teenage Brain: A Neuroscientist's Survival Guide to Raising Adolescents and Young Adults* (New York: HarperCollins Publishers, 2015).

18. Ibid.

19. Arnett (2017).

20. Betty Hart and Todd Risley, *Meaningful Differences in the Everyday Experiences of Young Children* (Baltimore, MD: Paul H. Brookes Publishing Co.,1995).

21. Harvard University, Center on the Developing Child, "Five Numbers to Remember About Early Childhood Development," https://developingchild .harvard.edu/resources/five-numbers-to-remember-about-early-childhood -development/#note.

22. Annette Lareau, *Unequal Childhoods: Class, Race and Family Life*, 2d ed. (Berkeley and Los Angeles: University of California Press, 2011).

23. Ibid.

24. "How America Pays for College 2017" (report, Washington, D.C.: Sallie Mae and Ipsos Research, 2017).

25. Ben Miller, "Who Are Student Loan Defaulters?" (report, Washington, DC: Center for American Progress, 2017).

26. College Board, "Completion Rates by Family Income and Parental Education Level: Figure 2.5a: Percentage of 1999 Entrants at Flagship Universities Graduating Within Six Years, by Parental Education Level and Family Income, Adjusted for Student Characteristics" (Chart, Trends in Higher Education, 2016), https://trends.collegeboard.org/education-pays/figures-tables /completion-rates-family-income-and-parental-education-level.

27. Anthony Carnevale and Ban Cheah, "Five Rules of the College and Career Game" (report, Washington, D.C.: Georgetown University Center on Education and the Workforce, 2018).

28. Robert F. Schoeni and Karen E. Ross, "Material Assistance from Families During the Transition to Adulthood," in *On the Frontier of Adulthood: Theory, Research and Public Policy*, edited by Richard A. Settersten Jr., Frank F. Furstenberg Jr., and Ruben G. Rumbaut (Chicago: University of Chicago Press, 2005).

29. Author's calculations, "CPI Inflation Calculator," U.S. Bureau of Labor Statistics, https://www.bls.gov/data/inflation_calculator.htm.

30. Board of Governors of the Federal Reserve System, "Experiences and Perspectives of Young Workers 2016" (report: Washington, D.C.: Federal Reserve, 2016).

31. Hannah Seligson, "The New 30-Something," *New York Times*, March 2, 2019.

32. Vespa (2017).

33. Kim Parker, "The Boomerang Generation" (Pew Social and Demographic Trends Report, Washington, D.C.: Pew Research Center, 2012).

34. "The State of the Nation's Housing 2018" (report, Boston, MA: Joint Center for Housing Studies of Harvard University, 2018).

35. Richard V. Reeves, *Dream Hoarders: How the American Upper Middle Class Is Leaving Everyone Else in the Dust, Why That Is a Problem, and What to Do About It* (Washington, D.C.: Brookings Institution Press, 2017).

36. Nathalie Saltikoff, "The Positive Implications of Internships on Early Career Outcomes," *NACE Journal*, May 2017, https://www.naceweb.org/job-market/internships/the-positive-implications-of-internships-on-early-career-outcomes.

37. Carlos Vera and Daniel Jenab, "Experience Doesn't Pay the Bills" (report, Washington, D.C.: Pay Our Interns, 2017).

38. Ibid.

39. "A Week in New York City on $25/Hour and $1k Monthly Allowance," Refinery29.com, July 15, 2018, https://www.refinery29.com/en-us/money-diary-new-york-city-marketing-intern-income.

40. Reeves (2017).

41. "Upside Down—$500 Billion in Tax Incentives to Build Wealth in 2013," ProsperityNow.com, January 6, 2014.

42. Richard V. Reeves and Nathan Joo, "A Tax Break for 'Dream Hoarders': What to Do About 529 College Savings Plans" (report, Washington, D.C.: Brookings Institution, 2017).

43. Margot L. Crandall-Hollick and Gene Falk, "R45035: The Child and Dependent Care Credit: Impact of Selected Policy Options" (report, Washington, D.C.: Congressional Research Service, 2017).

44. Raj Chetty, Nathaniel Hendren, Patrick Kline, and Emmanuel Saez, "Where Is the Land of Opportunity? The Geography of Intergenerational Mobility in the United States," *Quarterly Journal of Economics* 129, no. 4 (2014): 1553–1623.

45. Raj Chetty, David Grusky, Maximilian Hell, Nathaniel Hendren, Robert Manduca, and Jimmy Narang, "The Fading American Dream: Trends in Absolute Income Mobility Since 1940" (NBER Working Paper No. 22910, December 2016).

46. Robert Putnam, *Our Kids: The American Dream in Crisis* (New York: Simon and Schuster, 2015).

47. Centers for Medicare and Medicaid Services, "Eligibility," Medicaid.gov, https://www.medicaid.gov/medicaid/eligibility/index.html.

48. "Eligibility for Assistance and Occupancy," in *HUD Occupancy Handbook* (Washington, D.C.: U.S. Department of Housing and Urban Development, 2007). Generally speaking, adult children can remain in public housing with their parents after they are age eighteen and no longer "dependents" only if they are full-time students, disabled, or qualify as a "live-in aide" who is "essential to the care or well-being of the elderly parent(s)."

49. Work requirements apply to so-called ABAWDs (able-bodied adults without dependents) in order for continued eligibility for SNAP. "Supplemental

Nutrition Assistance Program (SNAP)—Facts About SNAP," United States Department of Agriculture, Food and Nutrition Service (last modified September 13, 2017), https://www.fns.usda.gov/snap/facts-about-snap.

50. Stephen J. Rose, "The Growing Size and Incomes of the Upper Middle Class" (report, Washington, D.C.: Urban Institute, 2016).

51. Economic Mobility Project, "Pursuing the American Dream: Economic Mobility Across Generations" (report, Washington, D.C.: The Pew Charitable Trusts, 2012).

2: An Epidemic of Disconnection

1. Michael E. Ruane, "Fifty Years Ago Some Called D.C. 'The Colored Man's Paradise.' Then Paradise Erupted," *Washington Post*, March 26, 2018.

2. Jack Moore, "'Everything Was on fiRe'—Remembering the D.C. Riots 50 Years Later," WTOP.com, April 2, 2018.

3. M.H. Morton, A. Dworsky, and G.M. Samuels, "Missed Opportunities: Youth Homelessness in America, National Estimates" (report, Chicago, IL: Chapin Hall at the University of Chicago, 2017).

4. The federal government arguably severely undercounts homeless youth. On one cold night every year in January, volunteers fan out across the country in an effort to take a "census" of homeless people in America. Young people are rarely included in the count because they are less likely to be sleeping out in the open or in adult homeless shelters, out of fear for their safety. As the Chapin Hall research found, youth homelessness is often characterized by "couch surfing," which the U.S. Department of Housing and Urban Development does not consider "homelessness." For more on the undercount on youth homelessness (and more on Trevor's story), see Anne Kim, "For Homeless Youth, Statistics and Reality Are Miles Apart," TalkPoverty.org, Jan. 24, 2018, https://talkpoverty.org/2018/01/24/homeless-youth-statistics-reality-miles-apart.

5. Laura T. Murphy, "Labor and Sex Trafficking Among Homeless Youth: A Ten-City Study" (report, New Orleans: Loyola University, 2017).

6. Charlie Savage and Timothy Williams, "U.S. Seizes Backpage.com, a Site Accused of Enabling Prostitution," *New York Times*, April 7, 2018.

7. Kristen Lewis, "Making the Connection: Transportation and Youth Disconnection" (report, New York: Measure of America, Social Science Research Council, 2019), https://ssrc-static.s3.amazonaws.com/moa/Making%20the%20Connection.pdf.

8. Mark S. Granovetter, "The Strength of Weak Ties," *American Journal of Sociology* 78, no. 6 (May 1973): 1360–80.

9. Kimberlee Morrison, "Survey: 92% of Recruiters Use Social Media to Find High-Quality Candidates," *Adweek*, September 22, 2015.

10. Kristen Lewis and Rebecca Gluskin, "Two Futures: The Economic Case for Keeping Youth on Track" (report, New York: Measure of America, Social Science Research Council, 2018).

11. Kayla Fontenot, Jessica Semega, and Melissa Kollar, "Income and Poverty in the United States: 2017" (report, Washington, D.C.: U.S. Census Bureau, September 2018).

12. "Youth Not in Employment, Education or Training (NEET) (Indicator)," OECD, 2018, doi: 10.1787/72d1033a-en.

13. Jeremy W. Bray, Brooks Depro, Doren McMahon, Marion Siegel, and Lee Mobley, "Disconnected Geography: A Spatial Analysis of Disconnected Youth in the United States" (report, Washington, D.C.: Center for Economic Studies, U.S. Census Bureau, August 2016).

14. Interactive data by state, county, and congressional district are available at Measure of America's interactive tool: http://www.measureofamerica.org/DYinteractive/#Metro.

15. Semega et al. (2017).

16. Camille L. Ryan and Kurt Bauman, "Educational Attainment in the United States: 2015" (report, Washington, D.C.: U.S. Census Bureau, March 2016).

17. Lewis (2019). In particular, Lewis finds that "18.9 percent of disconnected black boys and young men are institutionalized, nearly three times the rate for disconnected white boys and men." Even more troubling, she finds that a whopping 36.2 percent of disconnected black boys ages 16 and 17 are not living with either of their parents.

3: Marooned: Place and Opportunity

1. "Allegheny National Forest" United States Department of Agriculture, Forest Service, https://www.fs.usda.gov/allegheny.

2. "Quick Facts, Warren County, Pennsylvania; Forest County, Pennsylvania," U.S. Census Bureau, https://www.census.gov/quickfacts/fact/table/warrencountypennsylvania, forestcountypennsylvania/PST045218.

3. Camille L. Ryan and Kurt Bauman, "Educational Attainment in the United States: 2015" (report, Washington, D.C.: U.S. Census Bureau, March 2016).

4. Pennsylvania Department of Corrections Monthly Population Report as of June 30, 2018, https://www.cor.pa.gov/About%20Us/Statistics/Documents/Current%20Monthly%20Population.pdf.

5. "Youth Disconnection by County," Measure of America, Social Sciences Research Council, http://www.measureofamerica.org/DYinteractive/#County.

6. "Historic PA Lumber Photos," Pennsylvania Lumber Museum, http://lumbermuseum.org/historic-pa-logging-photos.

7. "Timber Harvesting in Pennsylvania: Information for Citizens and Local Government Officials," Pennsylvania State University Extension, https://ex tension.psu.edu/timber-harvesting-in-pennsylvania-information-for-citizens -and-local-government-officials.

8. Bureau of Labor Statistics, U.S. Department of Labor, *Occupational Outlook Handbook, Logging Workers*, https://www.bls.gov/ooh/farming-fishing -and-forestry/logging-workers.htm (visited July 20, 2018).

9. Bill Bishop, *The Big Sort: Why the Clustering of Like-Minded America Is Tearing Us Apart* (First Mariner Books, 2009).

10. Richard Florida, "Why America's Richest Cities Keep Getting Richer," *The Atlantic*, April 12, 2017, https://www.theatlantic.com/business /archive/2017/04/richard-florida-winner-take-all-new-urban-crisis/522630.

11. Jessica Tyler and Mary Hanbury, "Arlington, Virginia, Will Soon Be Home to Part of Amazon's HQ2. Here Are Some Reasons It Won the E-Commerce Giant Over," *Business Insider*, November 17, 2018.

12. "2017 Distressed Communities Index," Economic Innovation Group, https://eig.org/wp-content/uploads/2017/09/2017-Distressed-Communities -Index.pdf.

13. "Social Capital Project," United States Congress, Joint Economic Committee, 2019, https://www.lee.senate.gov/public/socialcapitalproject.

14. Raj Chetty, Nathaniel Hendren, Maggie R. Jones, and Sonya Porter, "Race and Economic Opportunity in the United States," 2018, http://www .equality-of-opportunity.org/assets/documents/race_slides.pdf.

15. "2017 Distressed Communities Index"; U.S. Joint Economic Committee, "The Geography of Social Capital in America" (report, Washington, D.C.: U.S. JEC, 2018).

16. "Startup! Winners Get Money to Launch Downtown Ventures," So VaNow.com, April 27, 2017, http://www.sovanow.com/index.php?/news/article /start-up_winners_get_money_to_launch_downtown_ventures.

17. "Abandoned Burlington Plant Set to Be Razed," SoVaNow.com, October 11, 2012, accessible at http://thenewsrecord.com/index.php?/news /article/abandoned_burlington_plant_set_to_be_razed; "Things Really Do Change in 100 Years," SoVaNow.com, December 26, 2012, accessible at http://www.sovanow.com/index.php?/news/article/things_really_do_change _in_100_years.

18. *Local Legacies: National Tobacco Festival*, Library of Congress, accessible at http://memory.loc.gov/diglib/legacies/loc.afc.afc-legacies.200003623.

19. "Developing a Diverse Economy in Southern and Southwest Virginia," Virginia Tobacco Region Revitalization Commission, https://www.revitalize va.org; "Master Settlement Agreement," Naag.org, http://www.naag.org/assets /redesign/files/msa-tobacco/MSA.pdf.

20. "Opportunity Zones," Virginia Department of Housing and Community Development, available at http://www.dhcd.virginia.gov/index.php/component/content/article/346.html.

21. "Quick Facts: South Boston Town, Virginia; Halifax County, Virginia" (Washington, D.C.: U.S. Census Bureau, 2018), https://www.census.gov/quickfacts/fact/table/southbostontownvirginia,halifaxcountyvirginia/PST045217?.

22. Michael Slackman, "Bank Sues to Force Insurers to Declare Tower 9/11 Loss," New York Times, August 12, 2003.

23. Fabienne Waks, "Generation AXA: 1985–2010, 25 Years in the History of AXA," AXA Group, 2011, https://axa-prod.s3.amazonaws.com/www-axa-com%2F7eef184e-5bb1-4173-a0b4-93ba3eac1745_axa_generation_axa_va.pdf.

24. Elyse Ashburn, "The Cautionary Tale of a Short-Lived College," Chronicle of Higher Education, November 21, 2010.

25. "Quick Facts," 2018.

26. Victoria Rosenboom and Kristin Blagg, "Three Million Americans Are Disconnected from Higher Education," Urban Institute, February 1, 2018, https://www.urban.org/urban-wire/three-million-americans-are-disconnected-higher-education.

27. Victoria Rosenboom and Kristin Blagg, "Disconnected from Higher Education: How Geography and Internet Speed Limit Access to Higher Education" (report, Washington, D.C.: Urban Institute, 2018), https://www.urban.org/sites/default/files/publication/96191/disconnected_from_higher_education_2.pdf.

28. "High School Benchmarks 2017: National College Progression Rates," National Student Clearinghouse Research Center (report, Herndon, Virginia: National Student Clearinghouse, 2017), https://nscresearchcenter.org/wp-content/uploads/2017HSBenchmarksReport-1.pdf.

29. "Rural Education," United States Department of Agriculture, Economic Research Service, 2019, https://www.ers.usda.gov/topics/rural-economy-population/employment-education/rural-education.

30. Ibid.

31. "Escape Velocity: How Elite Communities Are Pulling Away in the 21st Century Race for Jobs, Businesses, and Human Capital," Economic Innovation Group (report, Washington, D.C.: Economic Innovation Group, 2018), https://eig.org/wp-content/uploads/2018/05/Escape-Velocity-Report.pdf.

32. "Population Estimate as of July 31, 2017," American FactFinder (Washington, D.C: U.S. Census Bureau, 2017).

33. "Mecklenburg County Tapped for AP Computer Science Grant," SoVa Now.com, May 3, 2017.

4: An Urban Opportunity Desert

1. "Market Overview," Economic Alliance of Greater Baltimore, http://www.greaterbaltimore.org/advantage/market-overview.

2. "Baltimore City Economic Indicator Report—Third Quarter 2018" (report, Baltimore, MD: Bureau of the Budget and Management Research, City of Baltimore, 2018); "Existing Home Sales Overview," National Association of Realtors (last modified 2019), https://www.nar.realtor/research-and-statistics/housing-statistics/existing-home-sales.

3. "Living Here," Economic Alliance of Greater Baltimore, http://www.greaterbaltimore.org/assistance/living-here.

4. Christina Tkacik, "Remembering the Baltimore Riots After Freddie Gray's Death, Three Years Later," *Baltimore Sun*, April 27, 2018.

5. Jeremy Ashkenas, Larry Buchanan, Alicia Desantis, Haeyoun Park, and Derek Watkins, "A Portrait of the Sandtown Neighborhood in Baltimore," *New York Times,* May 3, 2015.

6. Tanika White, "Douglass Still Struggling," *Baltimore Sun,* May 18, 2004.

7. Michael Yockel, "100 Years: The Riots of 1968," *Baltimore* (May 2007).

8. Ashkenas et al. (2015).

9. "Baltimore City 2017 Neighborhood Health Profile—Sandtown-Winchester/Harlem Heights" (report, Baltimore, MD: Baltimore City Health Department, 2017).

10. Sherry L. Murphy, Jiaquan Xu, Kenneth D. Kochanek, and Elizabeth Arias, Baltimore City Health Department, U.S. Centers for Disease Control and Prevention, National Center for Health Statistics, "Mortality in the United States, 2017" (NCHS Data Brief 328, Washington, D.C.: U.S. Department of Health and Human Services, 2018).

11. Lee Bruno and Carol Pistorino, "Youth Opportunity Grant Initiative: Process Evaluation Final Report" (Employment and Training Administration, U.S. Department of Labor, Washington, D.C., August 2007).

12. "Changing Minds, Changing Lives: Baltimore's Youth Opportunity 2000–2007" (report, Baltimore, MD: Mayor's Office of Economic Development).

13. Peter Rosenblatt and Stefanie DeLuca, "What Happened in Sandtown-Winchester? Understanding the Impacts of a Comprehensive Community Initiative," *Urban Affairs Review* 53, no. 3 (December 16, 2015): 463–94.

14. Ibid.

15. Maxine J. Wood, "Highlighting the History of Housing Segregation in Baltimore, Maryland, and Its Impact on the Events of April 27, 2015, and Beyond" (The Pathways from Poverty Consortium, Johns Hopkins School of Education, Baltimore, MD, July 1, 2015).

16. "Frederick Douglass High 2017–18 School Report Card" (Baltimore: Maryland State Department of Education), http://reportcard.msde.maryland.gov/Graphs/#/ReportCards/ReportCardSchool/3/17/6/30/0450.

17. "Towson High Law and Public Policy 2017–18 School Report Card" (Baltimore: Maryland State Department of Education), http://reportcard.msde.maryland.gov/Graphs/#/ReportCards/ReportCardSchool/3/17/6/03/0971.

18. Robert Balfanz and Nettie Legters, "Locating the Dropout Crisis" (report, Baltimore, MD: Johns Hopkins University, 2004). In this landmark report, Balfanz and Legters discovered nearly two thousand high schools nationwide that at the time were graduating fewer than 60 percent of their students.

19. "Why It Matters," Power to Decide, 2019, https://powertodecide.org/what-we-do/information/why-it-matters.

20. Nathan Sick, Shayne Spaulding, and Yuju Park, "Understanding Young-Parent Families" (report, Washington, D.C.: Urban Institute, February 2018).

21. Ibid.

22. Marybeth J. Mattingly, Andrew Schaefer, and Jessica Carson, "Child Care Costs Exceed 10 Percent of Family Income for One in Four Families" (National Issue Brief 109, Durham, NH: University of New Hampshire Carsey School of Public Policy, 2016).

23. Fact Sheet, "Child Care in the FY2018 Omnibus Spending Bill" (Washington, D.C.: CLASP, March 2018), https://www.clasp.org/sites/default/files/publications/2018/03/Child%20Care%20in%20the%20FY%202018%20Omnibus.pdf.

24. David Reich and Chloe Cho, "Unmet Needs and the Squeeze on Appropriations" (report, Washington, D.C.: Center on Budget and Policy Priorities, May 19, 2017), https://www.cbpp.org/research/federal-budget/unmet-needs-and-the-squeeze-on-appropriations.

25. Sick et al. (2018).

26. "Child Care Subsidy Program," Maryland Department of Education, Division of Early Childhood, Maryland.gov, https://earlychildhood.marylandpublicschools.org/child-care-subsidy-program.

27. Daniel Princiotta, "How Many 'Sandtowns' Are There Nationwide?" (The Pathways from Poverty Consortium, Johns Hopkins School of Education, Baltimore, MD, July 1, 2015).

5: When Work Disappears

1. Andrew Sum, Ishwar Khatiwada, Mykhaylo Trubskyy, and Martha Ross, with Walter McHugh and Sheila Palma, "The Plummeting Labor Market Fortunes of Teens and Young Adults" (report, Washington, D.C.: Brookings Institution, March 2014), https://assets.rockefellerfoundation.org/app/uploads

/20150310143832/The-Plummeting-Labor-Market-Fortunes-of-Teends-and
-Young-Adults1.pdf.

2. Ben Leubsdorf, "Economists Think the U.S. Economy Is at or Near Full
Employment," *Wall Street Journal*, January 11, 2018.

3. "Economic News Release: Table A-1. Employment Status of the Civilian
Population by Sex and Age" (Washington, D.C.: U.S. Bureau of Labor Sta-
tistics, 2019), https://www.bls.gov/webapps/legacy/cpsatab1.htm; Shobhana
Chandra, "Corporate Earnings Climb 7.7%, Reflecting Tax Windfall and
Strong Economy," *Bloomberg*, August 9, 2018.

4. "Economic News Release: Employment Situation Summary" (Washington, D.C.: Bureau of Labor Statistics, May 3, 2019), https://www.bls.gov
/news.release/empsit.nr0.htm.

5. U.S. Bureau of Labor Statistics, "Unemployment Rate 2.7 Percent for
People Ages 45 to 54, 8.3 Percent for 16 to 24 in October 2018," *TED: The
Economics Daily* (last modified November 7, 2018), https://www.bls.gov
/opub/ted/2018/unemployment-rate-2-point-7-percent-for-people-ages-45-to
-54-8-point-3-percent-for-ages-16-to-24-in-october-2018.htm.

6. BLS Data Viewer, "Unemployment Rate, 16–24 Years" (Washington,
D.C.: Bureau of Labor Statistics), data for April 2019, https://beta.bls.gov
/dataViewer/view/timeseries/LNS14024887.

7. Sum et al. (2014).

8. BLS Data Viewer, "Labor Force Participation Rate, 16–24 Years, Not
Enrolled in School" (Washington, D.C.: U.S. Bureau of Labor Statistics),
data for April 2000 to 2019, https://beta.bls.gov/dataViewer/view/timeseries
/LNU01323016.

9. BLS Data Viewer, "Labor Force Participation Rate, Not Enrolled in
School, Less Than a High School Diploma, 16–24 Years" (Washington, D.C.:
Bureau of Labor Statistics), data for 1st quarter 2019, https://beta.bls.gov
/dataViewer/view/timeseries/LNU01323019Q.

10. Bureau of Labor Statistics, "School's Out" (Spotlight on Statistics,
Washington, D.C.: U.S. BLS, 2011).

11. In particular, a Federal Reserve survey found that "[s]eventy-nine
percent of employees who worked for pay during high school and 90 percent of employees who worked for pay during college have a full-time job.
Furthermore, 94 percent of those who held a paid internship during college
have a full-time job." Board of Governors of the Federal Reserve System,
"Experiences and Perspectives of Young Workers 2016" (report, Washington,
D.C.: Federal Reserve Board, 2016), https://www.federalreserve.gov/econ
resdata/2015-experiences-and-perspectives-of-young-workers-201612.pdf.
Andrew Sum and his colleagues (2014) also find that teens and older young
adults with work experience are more likely to find jobs the following year.

12. Sum et al. (2014).

13. BLS Data Viewer, "Labor Force Participation Rate, 16–24 Years, Black or African-American" (Washington, D.C.: U.S. Bureau of Labor Statistics), data for April 2019, https://beta.bls.gov/dataViewer/view/timeseries /LNU01324931; BLS Data Viewer, "Unemployment Rate, 16–24 Years, Black or African-American" (Washington, D.C.: Bureau of Labor Statistics), data for April 2019, https://beta.bls.gov/dataViewer/view/timeseries/LNU04024931.

14. BLS Data Viewer, "Unemployment Rate, 16–24 Years, White" (Washington, D.C.: Bureau of Labor Statistics), data for April 2019, https://beta.bls .gov/dataViewer/view/timeseries/LNU04024893; BLS Data Viewer, "Labor Force Participation Rate, 16–24 Years, White" (Washington, D.C.: Bureau of Labor Statistics), data for April 2019, https://beta.bls.gov/dataViewer/view /timeseries/LNU01324893.

15. Teresa L. Cordova and Matthew D. Wilson, "Abandoned in Their Neighborhoods: Youth Joblessness Amidst the Flight of Industry and Opportunity" (report, Chicago, IL: Great Cities Institute, University of Illinois at Chicago, January 2017).

16. Margaret Simms and Marla McDaniel, "The Black–White Jobless Gap" (brief, Washington, D.C.: Urban Institute, September 2010), https:// www.urban.org/sites/default/files/publication/29676/901378-The-Black -White-Jobless-Gap.pdf.

17. Ibid.

18. Board of Governors of the Federal Reserve System, "Experiences and Perspectives of Young Workers 2016," https://www.federalreserve.gov/econres data/2015-experiences-and-perspectives-of-young-workers-201612.pdf.

19. Ibid.

20. Ibid.

21. Ibid.

22. Ibid.

23. "Table 3. Median Usual Weekly Earnings of Full-Time Wage and Salary Workers by Age, Race, Hispanic or Latino Ethnicity, and Sex, First Quarter 2019 Averages, Not Seasonally Adjusted (Washington, D.C.: U.S. Bureau of Labor Statistics, last modified April 19, 2019).

24. Ibid.

25. Board of Governors of the Federal Reserve System (2016).

26. David Bensman and Mark R. Wilson, "Iron and Steel," *Encyclopedia of Chicago*, Chicago Historical Society, 2005, http://www.encyclopedia.chicago history.org/pages/653.html.

27. Ibid.

28. Ibid.

29. Rod Sellers, "Chicago's Southeast Side Industrial History" (report, Chicago, IL: Southeast Historical Society, March 2006), https://www.csu .edu/cerc/researchreports/documents/ChicagoSESideIndustrialHistory.pdf.

30. Bensman and Wilson (2005).

31. Sellers (2006).

32. Roxann Lopez, "Has Chicago Forgotten Its Southeast Side?" *Chicago Tribune,* August 1, 2018.

33. "Loop Chicago: Do Business," Chicago Loop Alliance, 2019, http://loopchicago.com/work.

34. Anthony Carnevale, Tamara Jayasundera, and Artem Gulish, "Six Million Missing Jobs: The Lingering Pain of the Great Recession" (report, Washington, D.C.: Georgetown University: Center on Education and the Workforce, 2015).

35. John M. Bridgeland and Jessica A. Milano, "Opportunity Road: The Promise and Challenges of America's Forgotten Youth" (report, Washington, D.C.: Civic Enterprises and America's Promise Alliance, 2012).

36. Strada Education Network and Gallup, "2017 College Student Survey: A Nationally Representative Survey of Currently Enrolled Students" (report, Indianapolis, Indiana: Strada-Gallup, 2018).

37. Board of Governors of the Federal Reserve System (2016).

38. Association for Career and Technical Education, "Career Exploration in Middle School: Setting Students on the Path to Success" (report, Alexandria, VA: ACTE, 2017), https://www.acteonline.org/wp-content/uploads/2018/02/ACTE_CC_Paper_FINAL.pdf.

39. Rachel Bird Niebling and Philip Lovell, "Never Too Late: Why ESEA Must Fill the Missing Middle" (report, Washington, D.C.: Alliance for Excellent Education, May 2015), https://all4ed.org/wp-content/uploads/2015/05/NeverTooLate.pdf.

40. Board of Governors of the Federal Reserve System (2016).

41. Specifically, Advance CTE finds that CTE-focused students have a graduation rate of 93 percent, or about 10 percentage points higher than non-CTE students. Advance CTE, "The Value and Promise of Career Technical Education" (report, Silver Spring, MD: Advance CTE, 2017), https://cte.careertech.org/sites/default/files/files/resources/The_Value_Promise_Career_Technical_Education_2017.pdf.

42. Deberae Culpepper, "The Development of Tracking and Its Historical Impact on Minority Students" (report, Minneapolis, MN: Walden University, 2012), https://scholarworks.waldenu.edu/cgi/viewcontent.cgi?referer=&https redir=1&article=1998&context=dissertations.

43. Brian A. Jacob, "What We Know About Career and Technical Education in High School" (Washington, D.C.: Brookings Institution, October 5, 2017).

44. National Skills Coalition, "United States' Forgotten Middle" (fact sheet, Washington, D.C.: National Skills Coalition, 2017), https://www.national skillscoalition.org/resources/publications/2017-middle-skills-fact-sheets/file/United-States-MiddleSkills.pdf.

45. Advance CTE, "Legislative Summary and Analysis: Strengthening Career and Technical Education for the 21st Century Act (Perkins V)" (report, Silver Springs, MD: Advance CTE, August 6, 2018), https://www.acteonline.org/wp-content/uploads/2018/08/AdvanceCTE_ACTE_P.L.115-224Summary_Updated080618.pdf.

46. National Center for Education Statistics, "Fast Facts: Career and Technical Education, U.S. Department of Education" (Washington, D.C.: NCES 2013), https://nces.ed.gov/fastfacts/display.asp?id=43.

47. Robert Balfanz and Nettie Legters, "Which High Schools Produce the Nation's Dropouts? Where Are They Located? Who Attends Them?" (report, Baltimore, MD: Johns Hopkins University, September 2004), https://files.eric.ed.gov/fulltext/ED484525.pdf.

48. Jennifer L. DePaoli, Robert Balfanz, Matthew N. Atwell, and John Bridgeland, "Building a Grad Nation: Progress and Challenge in Raising High School Graduation Rates" (report, Baltimore, MD: Civic Enterprises and Everyone Graduates Center at the School of Education at Johns Hopkins University, 2018).

49. Ibid.

50. National Center for Education Statistics, "Findings: Post-Secondary/College," https://nces.ed.gov/surveys/ctes/figures/fig_2016083-1.asp.

51. Ibid.

52. S.A. Ginder, J.E. Kelly-Reid, and F.B. Mann, "Postsecondary Institutions and Cost of Attendance in 2017–18"; "Degrees and Other Awards Conferred, 2016–17"; and "12-Month Enrollment, 2016–17: First Look (Preliminary Data) (NCES 2018-060)" (Washington, D.C.: U.S. Department of Education, National Center for Education Statistics, 2018), http://nces.ed.gov/pubsearch.

6: Abandoned by the State: "Aging Out"

1. Child Welfare Information Gateway, "Foster Care Statistics 2016" (fact sheet, Washington, D.C.: U.S. Department of Health and Human Services, Children's Bureau, 2017).

2. Mark E. Courtney and Darcy Hughes Heuring, "The Transition to Adulthood for Youth 'Aging Out' of the Foster Care System," in *On Your Own Without a Net: The Transition to Adulthood for Vulnerable Populations*, D. Wayne Osgood, E. Michael Foster, Constance Flanagan, and Gretchen R. Ruth, eds. (Chicago, IL: University of Chicago Press, 2005).

3. "Child Welfare Outcomes, 2015: Report to Congress," (Washington, D.C.: U.S. Department of Health and Human Services, Administration for Children and Families, Administration on Children, Youth, and Families, Children's Bureau, June 13, 2018), https://www.acf.hhs.gov/sites/default/files/cb/cwo2015.pdf.

4. Sara Rimer, "From Foster Homes to Life on New York Streets: 3 Case Studies in Failure," *New York Times*, July 19, 1985.

5. *Palmer v. Cuomo*, 121 A.D.2d 194 (1986).

6. MaryLee Allen and Robin Nixon, "The Foster Care Independence Act and John H. Chafee Foster Care Independence Program: New Catalysts for Reform for Young People Aging Out of Foster Care," *Clearinghouse Review: Journal of Poverty Law and Policy* 34, no. 3–4 (July–August 2000): 197–216.

7. Ibid.

8. Child Welfare Information Gateway, "Working with Youth to Develop a Transition Plan" (Washington, D.C.: U.S. Department of Health and Human Services, Children's Bureau, 2013).

9. "Services to Children: Youth Transitions Procedure" (procedure manual, Salem, OR: Oregon Department of Human Services, rev. September 2018), http://www.dhs.state.or.us/caf/safety_model/procedure_manual/ch04/ch4 -section29.pdf.

10. Adrienne L. Fernandes-Alcantara, "Youth Transitioning from Foster Care: Background and Federal Programs" (RL34499, Washington, D.C.: Congressional Research Service, September 8, 2017).

11. Ibid.

12. Child Welfare Information Gateway, "Major Federal Legislation Concerned with Child Protection, Child Welfare, and Adoption (Washington, D.C.: U.S. Department of Health and Human Services, Children's Bureau, 2016); NCSL, "Extending Foster Care Beyond Age 18" (Washington, D.C.: National Conference of State Legislatures, July 2017), http://www.ncsl.org /research/human-services/extending-foster-care-to-18.aspx.

13. Child Welfare Information Gateway (2016).

14. U.S. Department of Health and Human Services, Administration for Children and Families, "Evaluation of the Life Skills Training Program: Los Angeles County" (Washington, D.C.: U.S. Dept. HHS, July 2008).

15. M. Courtney, A. Zinn, R. Koralek, and R. Bess, "Evaluation of the Independent Living—Employment Services Program, Kern County, California: Final Report" (OPRE Report #2011?13, Washington, D.C.: Office of Planning, Research, and Evaluation, Administration for Children and Families, U.S. Department of Health and Human Services, 2011).

16. Isaiah, "I Will Be Exiting Foster Care in 26 More Days," Fosterclub .com, December 7, 2009, https://www.fosterclub.com/blog/youth-perspective /i-will-be-exiting-foster-care-26-more-days.

17. "Comparing Outcomes Reported by Young People at Ages 17 and 19 in NYTD Cohort 2," National Youth in Transition Database, Data Brief #6 (Washington, D.C.: U.S. Department of Health and Human Services, Administration for Children and Families, November 2017), https://www.acf .hhs.gov/sites/default/files/cb/nytd_data_brief_6.pdf.

18. Mark E. Courtney, Amy Dworsky, Adam Brown, Colleen Cary, Kara Love, and Vanessa Vorhies, "Midwest Evaluation of the Adult Functioning of Former Foster Youth: Outcomes at Age 26" (report, Chicago, IL: Chapin Hall at the University of Chicago, 2011), available at https://www.chapinhall.org /wp-content/uploads/Midwest-Eval-Outcomes-at-Age-26.pdf.

19. Camille L. Ryan and Kurt Bauman, "Educational Attainment in the United States: 2015" (report, Washington, D.C.: U.S. Census Bureau, March 2016).

20. "Comparing Outcomes" (2017).

21. Courtney et al. (2011).

22. "Child Welfare Outcomes, 2015: Report to Congress" (Washington, D.C.: U.S. Department of Health and Human Services Administration for Children and Families Administration on Children, Youth and Families Children's Bureau, June 13, 2018), https://www.acf.hhs.gov/sites/default/files/cb /cwo2015.pdf.

23. Ibid.

24. Mark E. Courtney and Darcy Hughes Heuring, "The Transition to Adulthood for Youth 'Aging Out' of the Foster Care System," in *On Your Own Without a Net: The Transition to Adulthood for Vulnerable Populations*, D. Wayne Osgood, E. Michael Foster, Constance Flanagan and Gretchen R. Ruth, eds. (Chicago, IL: University of Chicago Press, 2005).

25. FC Steve, "Foster Youth Who 'Age Out' Are Forced to Become Adults Before They Are Ready," Fosterclub.com, December 2, 2008, https://www .fosterclub.com/blog/real-stories/foster-youth-who-age-out-are-forced-become -adults-they-are-ready.

26. Sara Edelstein and Christopher Lowenstein, "Supporting Youth Transitioning out of Foster Care, Issue Brief 2: Financial Literacy and Asset Building Programs" (OPRE Report #2014-69, Washington, D.C.: Office of Planning, Research, and Evaluation, Administration for Children and Families, U.S. Department of Health and Human Services, 2014).

27. Ibid.

28. Qiana Torres Flores and Aubrey Hasvold, "Individual Development Accounts for Foster Youth" (National Conference of State Legislatures, March 2014), *Legisbrief* 22, no. 9.

29. "John H. Chafee Foster Care Independence Program," U.S. Department of Health and Human Services, Administration for Children and Families, 2012, https://www.acf.hhs.gov/cb/resource/chafee-foster-care-program; S.A. Ginder, J.E. Kelly-Reid, and F.B. Mann, "Postsecondary Institutions and Cost of Attendance in 2017–18" (Washington, D.C.: U.S. Department of Education, National Center for Education Statistics, 2018), http://nces.ed.gov /pubsearch.

30. Emily Parker and Molly Sarubbi, "Tuition Assistance Programs for Foster Youth Pursuing Postsecondary Education" (report, Denver, CO: Education Commission of the States, March 2017).

31. Robin Dion, Amy Dworsky, Jackie Kauff, and Rebecca Kleinman, "Housing for Youth Aging Out of Foster Care" (report, Washington, D.C.: U.S. Department of Housing and Urban Development, Office of Policy Development and Research, May 2014).

32. Anne Kim, "For Homeless Youth, Statistics and Reality Are Miles Apart," TalkPoverty.org, January 24, 2018, https://talkpoverty.org/2018/01/24/homeless-youth-statistics-reality-miles-apart.

7: "Justice"

1. "Annual Estimates of the Resident Population: April 1, 2010 to July 1, 2017," American FactFinder (Washington D.C.: U.S. Census Bureau), 2017, https://factfinder.census.gov/faces/tableservices/jsf/pages/productview.xhtml?pid=PEP_2017_PEPANNRES&prodType=table.

2. Drug-related offenses are the most common reason for arrest, according to the FBI. Of the estimated 10,662,252 arrests in 2016, 1,572,579 were for drug offenses—three times the number of arrests for violent crimes such as murder and rape (515,151 arrests). "Uniform Crime Report: Crime in the United States, 2016" (report ,Washington, D.C.: Federal Bureau of Investigation, 2017), https://ucr.fbi.gov/crime-in-the-u.s/2016/crime-in-the-u.s.-2016/cius-2016/topic-pages/persons-arrested?55.

3. In 1995, criminologist John DiIulio (wrongly) predicted a wave of juvenile criminal violence led by violent so-called super-predator youth. His predictions—tragically—helped usher in the highly destructive era of mass incarceration and "zero tolerance" that society is now trying to reverse. For background, see DiIulio's original piece, "The Coming of the Super-Predators," *Weekly Standard*, November 27, 1995, https://www.weeklystandard.com/john-j-dilulio-jr/the-coming-of-the-super-predators.

4. New York State Department of Corrections and Community Supervision, "New York State Jail Population 10 Year Trends: 2008–2017," http://www.criminaljustice.ny.gov/crimnet/ojsa/jail_pop_y.pdf; New York State Department of Corrections and Community Supervision, "Under Custody Report: Profile of Under Custody Population as of January 1, 2017," http://www.doccs.ny.gov/Research/Reports/2017/Under%20Custody%20Report%202017.pdf.

5. "Improving Approaches to Serving Young Adults in the Justice System" (report, Washington, D.C.: Justice Policy Institute, December 2016). This proportion holds true nationally, according to the Vera Institute for Justice, which finds that young people ages eighteen to twenty-four make up 21 percent of the population admitted to adult prisons every year. Alex Frank, "Why

Reimagining Prison for Young Adults Matters" (New York: Vera Institute of Justice, February 28, 2017).

6. "Improving Approaches to Serving Young Adults" (2016).

7. "Arrests by Age, 2016," Federal Bureau of Investigation, https://ucr.fbi .gov/crime-in-the-u.s/2016/crime-in-the-u.s.-2016/tables/table-20.

8. Danielle Kaeble and Mary Cowhig, "Correctional Populations in the United States, 2016" (bulletin, Washington, D.C.: U.S. Department of Justice, Bureau of Justice Statistics, April 2018), https://www.bjs.gov/content/pub /pdf/cpus16.pdf.

9. "Why We Need Pretrial Reform," Pretrial Justice Institute, https://www .pretrial.org/get-involved/learn-more/why-we-need-pretrial-reform.

10. Ibid.

11. "Improving Approaches to Serving Young Adults" (2016).

12. Cara Drinan, *The War on Kids: How American Juvenile Justice Lost Its Way* (New York: Oxford University Press, 2018), 74.

13. "Effects on Violence of Laws and Policies Facilitating the Transfer of Youth from the Juvenile to the Adult Justice System" (Morbidity and Mortality Weekly Report, Vol. 56 / No. RR-9, Atlanta, GA: U.S. Centers for Disease Control, Nov. 30, 2007), https://www.cdc.gov/mmwr/pdf/rr/rr5609.pdf.

14. Amanda Burgess-Proctor, Kendal Holtrop, and Francisco A. Villarruel, "Youth Transferred to Adult Court: Racial Disparities" (Adultification Policy Brief 2, Washington, D.C.: Campaign for Youth Justice, n.d.).

15. "Raising the Age: Shifting to a Safer and More Effective Juvenile Justice System" (report, Washington, D.C.: Justice Policy Institute, 2017).

16. Bipartisan members of Congress now say they would consider lifting the ban on "Pell for prisoners," and legislation to make this happen could be part of the next Higher Education Act authorization. Erica L. Green, "Senate Leaders Reconsider Ban on Pell Grants for Prisoners," *New York Times*, February 15, 2018. As of this writing, the Trump administration has also called for "Second Chance Pell" pilots, which allow a limited number of institutions to award Pell grants to incarcerated students, to be made permanent.

17. Richard A. Mendel, "No Place for Kids: The Case for Reducing Juvenile Incarceration" (report, Baltimore, MD: Annie E. Casey Foundation, 2011).

18. Barry Holman and Jason Zeidenberg, "The Dangers of Detention: The Impact of Incarcerating Youth in Detention and Other Secure Facilities" (report, Washington, D.C.: Justice Policy Institute, 2006).

19. "Raising the Age" (2017).

20. Holman and Zeidenberg (2006).

21. Mendel (2011).

22. Stephen Raphael, "Early Incarceration Spells and the Transition to Adulthood," in *The Price of Independence: The Economics of Early Adulthood*, Sheldon Danziger and Cecilia Rouse, eds. (New York: Russell Sage Foundation, 2007).

23. Holman and Zeidenberg (2006).

24. Teresa Wilitz, "Children Still Funneled Through Adult Prisons, but States Are Moving Against It," *USA Today*, June 17, 2017.

25. "Fact Sheet: Black Disparities in Youth Incarceration" (Washington, D.C.: The Sentencing Project, 2017).

26. Paul Del Muro, "Consider the Alternatives: Planning and Implementing Detention Alternatives" (report, Baltimore, MD: Annie E. Casey Foundation, 1999).

27. Alex Woodward, "New Orleans Youth Who Commit Minor Crimes Will Face Warnings or Summonses Instead of Arrests," TheAdvocate.com, August 24, 2017.

28. Cara Drinan, *The War on Kids: How American Juvenile Justice Lost Its Way* (New York: Oxford University Press, 2017).

29. Ibid.

30. Ibid.

31. "Archived Indicator: Young Adults in Jail or Prison," ChildTrends, https://www.childtrends.org/indicators/young-adults-in-jail-or-prison.

32. Burgess-Proctor et al. (n.d.).

33. "Fact Sheet: Black Disparities in Youth Incarceration" (2017).

34. E.J. Smith and S.R. Harper, "Disproportionate Impact of K–12 School Suspension and Expulsion on Black Students in Southern States" (report, Philadelphia: University of Pennsylvania, Center for the Study of Race and Equity in Education, 2015).

35. Ibid.

36. Nicholas Fandos, "Senate Passes Bipartisan Criminal Justice Bill," *New York Times*, December 18, 2018.

37. "Alternatives to Incarceration," CASES, https://www.cases.org/alternatives-to-incarceration.

8: Throwing Lifelines

1. Administration for Children and Families, Families and Youth Services Bureau, "Transitional Living Program Fact Sheet" (Washington, D.C.: U.S. Department of Health and Human Services, last modified April 26, 2018), https://www.acf.hhs.gov/fysb/resource/tlp-fact-sheet.

2. M.H. Morton, A. Dworsky, and G.M. Samuels, "Missed Opportunities: Youth Homelessness in America: National Estimates" (policy brief, Chicago, IL: Chapin Hall at the University of Chicago, 2017).

3. Maureen Costantino and Leigh Angres, "The Federal Budget in 2015" (graphic, Washington, D.C.: Congressional Budget Office, 2016), https://www.cbo.gov/sites/default/files/114th-congress-2015-2016/graphic/51110-budget1overall.pdf.

4. Ibid.

5. Thaddeus Ferber, Jo Ann Paanio, Caitlin Johnson, and Caitlin Kawaguchi, "The Reconnecting Youth Campaign" (report, Washington, D.C.: Forum for Youth Investment, 2018).

6. "Reconnecting Youth Campaign: Unleashing Limitless Potential," Spark Action, 2019, https://sparkaction.org/reconnecting-youth/solution.

7. U.S. Department of Labor, "FY 2019 Department of Labor Budget in Brief" (report, Washington, D.C.: U.S. Department of Labor, 2018).

8. "ROI for Reconnecting Opportunity Youth in Each Congressional District" (report, Washington, D.C.: Forum for Youth Investment, March 28, 2016), http://forumfyi.org/files/roi_for_reconnecting_opportunity_youth_in_each_congressional_district.pdf.

9. Kristina Rosinsky and Dana Connelly, "Child Welfare Financing SFY 2014: A Survey of Federal, State, and Local Expenditures," ChildTrends, December 2016, https://www.childtrends.org/wp-content/uploads/2016/10/2016-53ChildWelfareFinancingSFY2014-1.pdf.

10. Ibid.

11. Cris Beam, *To the End of June: The Intimate Life of American Foster Care* (Boston, MA: Mariner Books, 2014).

12. Clive R. Belfield and Henry M. Levin, "The Economics of Investing in Opportunity Youth" (report, Washington, D.C.: Civic Enterprises, September 2012).

13. "Reconnecting Youth Campaign: Unleashing Limitless Potential," Spark Action.

9: Intensive Care

1. "Quick Facts—Fairfax County, Virginia," U.S. Census Bureau (last modified July 1, 2017), https://www.census.gov/quickfacts/fact/table/fairfaxcountyvirginia/PST045217.

2. "Information for Homeless Families," Fairfax County Public Schools, https://www.fcps.edu/resources/family-engagement/information-homeless-families.

3. "Training Futures," Northern Virginia Family Service, https://www.nvfs.org/our-services/workforce-development/training-futures.

4. "39 ChalleNGe Sites and Counting," National Guard Youth Foundation, http://www.ngyf.org/challenge-near-you.

5. Cynthia Miller, Megan Millenky, Lisa Schwartz, Lisbeth Goble, and

Jillian Stein, "Building a Future: Interim Impact Findings from the Youth-Build Evaluation" (report, New York: MDRC, 2016).

6. Megan Millenky, Dan Bloom, Sara Muller-Ravett, and Joseph Broadus, "Staying on Course: Three-Year Results of the National Guard Youth ChalleNGe Evaluation" (paper, New York: MDRC, 2011).

7. Miller et al. (2016).

8. Administration for Children and Families, Office of Planning, Research, and Evaluation, "Transitional Living Program Evaluation Studies, 2014–2019: Project Overview," U.S. Department of Health and Human Services, https://www.acf.hhs.gov/opre/research/project/transitional-living -program-evaluation-studies.

9. Melanie Skemer and Erin Jacobs Valentine, "Striving for Independence: Two-Year Impact Findings from the Youth Villages Transitional Living Evaluation" (report, New York: MDRC, 2016).

10. Family and Youth Services Bureau, "Transition Living Program Fact Sheet" (U.S. Department of Health and Human Services, Administration for Children and Families, last modified April 25, 2018), https://www.acf.hhs .gov/fysb/resource/tlp-fact-sheet.

11. Millenky et al. (2011).

10: Super Mentors

1. John Rampton, "10 Reasons Why a Mentor Is a Must." *Inc.*, January 9, 2016.

2. Emily Forrest Cataldi, Christopher T. Bennett, and Xianglei Chen, National Center for Education Statistics, "First-Generation Students: College Acmes, Persistence and Postbachelor Outcomes" (Stats in Brief NCES 2018-421, Washington, D.C.: U.S. Department of Education, 2018).

3. "What We Do," Thread.org, https://www.thread.org/what-we-do.

4. David Bornstein, "For Vulnerable Teenagers, a Web of Support," *New York Times*, March 8, 2016.

5. Brett Theodos, Michael R. Pergamit, Alexandra Derian, Sara Edelstein, and Allison Stolte, "Solutions for Youth: An Evaluation of the Latin American Youth Center's Promotor Pathway Program" (report, Washington, D.C.: Urban Institute, 2016).

6. Mary Bruce and John Bridgeland, "The Mentoring Effect: Young People's Perspectives on the Outcomes and Availability of Mentoring" (report, Washington, D.C.: Civic Enterprises in association with Hart Research Associates, 2014).

7. Theodos et al.(2016).

8. Ibid.

11: The Apprentice and the Intern

1. Miller is also getting his education for free, thanks to his employer and the New Economy Workforce Credential Grant, an innovative workforce development grant program sponsored by the commonwealth of Virginia. Under the grant program, the commonwealth pays for two-thirds of the cost of approved training and education programs aimed at filling high-needs jobs. Anne Kim, "The Road to a Stable Job—Without Crippling Student Debt," *Washington Monthly*, September 21, 2017.

2. "FACT SHEET: Investing More Than $50 Million Through Apprentice-shipUSA to Expand Proven Pathways into the Middle Class," White House news release, October 21, 2016, https://obamawhitehouse.archives.gov/the-press-office/2016/10/21/fact-sheet-investing-more-50-million-through-apprenticeshipusa-expand.

3. Glenn Thrush, "Amid Worker Shortage, Trump Signs Job Training Order," *New York Times*, July 19, 2018.

4. "Registered Apprenticeship National Results Fiscal Year (FY) 2017 (10/01/2016 to 9/30/2017)" (report, Washington, D.C.: United States Department of Labor Employment and Training Association, last modified April 4, 2018), https://doleta.gov/oa/data_statistics.cfm.

5. Tamar Jacoby, "Why Germany Is So Much Better at Training Its Workers," *The Atlantic*, October 16, 2014.

6. Federal Ministry of Education and Research, "Report on Vocational Education and Training 2015" (Federal Republic of Germany: Division of Basic Policy Issues of Initial and Continuing Vocational Training, 2015).

7. Megan Dunn and James Walker, Bureau of Labor Statistics, "Union Membership in the United States" (Spotlight on Statistics, Washington, D.C.: U.S. Department of Labor, 2016).

8. Brett Theodos, Michael R. Pergamit, Devlin Hanson, Sara Edelstein, Rebecca Daniels, and Tanaya Srini, "Pathways After High School: Evaluation of the Urban Alliance High School Internship Program" (report, Washington, D.C.: Urban Institute, 2017).

9. "Experiences and Perspectives of Young Workers 2016," Board of Governors of the Federal Reserve System, https://www.federalreserve.gov/econresdata/2015-experiences-and-perspectives-of-young-workers-201612.pdf.

10. Anne Rader and Mark Elliott, "A Promising Start: Year Up's Initial Impacts on Low-Income Young Adults' Careers" (report, New York: Economic Mobility Corporation, April 2011).

11. D. Fein and J. Hamadyk, "Bridging the Opportunity Divide for Low-Income Youth: Implementation and Early Impacts of the Year Up Program" (OPRE Report #2018-65, Washington, D.C.: Office of Planning, Research, and Evaluation, Administration for Children and Families, U.S. Department of Health and Human Services, 2018).

12. "2015 FDIC National Survey of Unbanked and Underbanked Households" (report, Washington, D.C.: Federal Deposit Insurance Corporation, October 20, 2016).

13. Mark S. Granovetter, "The Strength of Weak Ties," *American Journal of Sociology* 78, no. 6 (May 1973): 1360–80, https://www.jstor.org/stable/2776392.

14. Ibid., 201–33, https://www.jstor.org/stable/202051?origin=JSTOR-pdf.

15. Ibid.

12: A Texas Turnaround to Make Schools Work

1. Atul Gawande, "The Cost Conundrum," *New Yorker*, June 1, 2009.

2. "Children Crying at U.S. Border and Sitting in Cages: Trump's Separation Policy in Pictures," *Newsweek*, June 2018, https://www.newsweek.com /children-crying-us-border-and-sitting-cages-trumps-separation-policy-pictures -985689.

3. "QuickFacts, McAllen City, Texas," U.S. Census Bureau, https://www .census.gov/quickfacts/fact/table/mcallencitytexas,US/PST045217.

4. "Youth Disconnection by Metro Area," Measure of America, Social Science Research Council, www.measureofamerica.org/DYinteractive /#Metro.

5. "Economy at a Glance: McAllen-Edinburg-Mission, TX Metropolitan Statistical Area, Series ID: LAUMT483258000000003" (table, Washington, D.C.: Bureau of Labor Statistics, 2019).

6. "QuickFacts, McAllen City, Texas."

7. David Maraniss, "Texas Citrus Growers Fear Crop Is Destroyed," *Washington Post*, December 24, 1989, https://www.washingtonpost.com/archive /politics/1989/12/24/texas-citrus-growers-fear-crop-is-destroyed/64ae8225 -db31-44f5-94b6-8676c322f589.

8. Joseph A. Witt Jr., "The Mexican Peso Crisis," *Economic Review* 81, no. 1 (Jan/Feb 1996).

9. "Texas Colonias: A Thumbnail Sketch of the Conditions, Issues, Challenges and Opportunities" (report, Dallas, TX: Federal Reserve Bank of Dallas, 1995).

10. "About La Plaza Mall," Simon Malls, https://www.simon.com/mall/la -plaza-mall/about.

11. "Tres Lagos Master Plan," Tres Lagos, https://www.treslagosmcallen .com/master-plan/education.

12. "Fact Sheet," South Texas College, https://www.southtexascollege.edu /about/pdf/fact-sheet.pdf.

13. "Industrial Clusters," McAllen EDC, http://www.mcallenedc.org /doing-business-here/industrial-clusters.

14. Steve Taylor, "Established Maquilas in Reynosa Expanding but Not as Many New Ones Opening," *Rio Grande Guardian*, October 6, 2017, https://

riograndeguardian.com/established-maquilas-expanding-in-reynosa-but-not -as-many-new-ones-opening.

15. Luis Ribera and Flynn Adcock, "Increase in U.S. Imports of Fresh Produce from Mexico" (CNAS Issue Brief 2017-03, College Station, TX: Center for North American Studies, November 2017), http://cnas.tamu.edu/Index /Produce%20Inflow%20from%20Mexico%20November%202017.pdf.

16. "Business Administration," South Texas College, https://bt.southtexas college.edu/ba.

17. "Inside PSJA ID," Pharr-San Juan-Alamo Independent School District, https://www.psjaisd.us/Page/35.

18. "Striving for Excellence: A Profile of Seven Economically Damaged School Districts," State of Texas Legislative Budget Board, http://www.lbb .state.tx.us/Documents/Publications/School_Performance_Review/SPR /Pharr/Pharr_ISD.pdf.

19.Jeremy Roebuck and Andres Martinez, "PSJA School Officials Charged," *Valley Morning Star*, June 6, 2007, https://www.valleymorningstar.com/news /local_news/psja-school-officials-charged/article_04f11192-562a-5204-8b78 -763acb2be8e2.html.

20. "Public Schools Explorer: Pharr-San Juan-Alamo ISD," *Texas Tribune*, https://schools.texastribune.org/districts/pharr-san-juan-alamo-isd.

21. Hidalgo Independent School District, https://www.hidalgo-isd.org /domain/129.

22. James J. Kemple, "Career Academies: Long-term Impacts on Labor Market Outcomes, Educational Attainment and Transitions to Adulthood" (report, New York: MDRC, June 2008).

23. "About Career Academies," National Career Academy Coalition, https://www.ncacinc.com/nsop/academies.

24. "About PSJA ISD—Points of Pride," PSJA ISD, https://www.psjaisd .us/Page/37.

25. "Fast Facts About Dual and Concurrent Enrollment," National Alliance of Concurrent Enrollment Partnerships, http://www.nacep.org/research -policy/fast-facts.

26. Tom North and Jonathan Jacobs, "Dual Credit in Oregon: 2010 Followup" (report, Monmouth, OR: Office of Institutional Research, Oregon University System, September 21, 2010).

27. "What We Know About Dual Enrollment" (New York: Community College Research Center, Columbia University, February 2012), http://ccrc.tc .columbia.edu/media/k2/attachments/dual-enrollment-research-overview.pdf.

28. Brenda Bautsch, "The Effects of Concurrent Enrollment on the College-Going and Remedial Education Rates of Colorado's High School Students" (report, Denver, CO: Colorado Department of Higher Education, March 27, 2014).

29. Andrea Berger, Lori Turk-Bicakci, Michael Garet, Joel Knudson, and Gur Hoshen, "Early College, Continued Success: Early College High School Initiative Impact Study" (report, Washington, D.C.: American Institutes for Research, 2014).

30. "Las Colonias in the 21st Century: Progress Along the Texas-Mexico Border" (report, Dallas, TX: Federal Reserve Bank of Dallas, April 2015).

13: The "Fierce Urgency of Now"

1. "Final Report: Community Solutions for Opportunity Youth" (report, Washington, D.C.: White House Council for Community Solutions, June 2012).

2. "WIOA Overview," U.S. Department of Labor, Employment, and Training Administration, https://www.doleta.gov/WIOA/Overview.cfm. In particular, WIOA raised the share of state and local youth funds going to out-of-school youth to 75 percent (from 30 percent) and increased the age of eligibility from twenty-one to twenty-four. See also Farhana Hossain, "Serving Out-of-School Youth Under the Workforce Innovation and Opportunity Act (2014)" (report, New York: MDRC, June 2015).

3. Chad Stone, Danilo Trisi, Arloc Sherman, and Roderick Taylor, "A Guide to Statistics on Historical Trends in Income Inequality" (Washington, D.C.: Center on Budget and Policy Priorities, August 29, 2019), https://www.cbpp.org/research/poverty-and-inequality/a-guide-to-statistics-on-historical-trends-in-income-inequality.

4. Melissa Schettini Kearney, "Testimony Before the Joint Economic Committee: Income Inequality in the United States," January 16, 2014, available at https://www.brookings.edu/wp-content/uploads/2016/06/16-income-inequality-in-america-kearney-1.pdf.

5. F. Cingano, "Trends in Income Inequality and Its Impact on Economic Growth" (OECD Social, Employment, and Migration Working Papers, No. 163, Paris: OECD Publishing, 2014), https://doi.org/10.1787/5jxrjncwxv6j-en.

6. "Indicators of Higher Education Equity in the United States: 2016 Historical Trend Report" (report, Washington, D.C.: The Pell Institute for the Study of Opportunity in Higher Education and the University of Pennsylvania Alliance for Higher Education and Democracy, 2016), http://www.pellinstitute.org/downloads/publications-Indicators_of_Higher_Education_Equity_in_the_US_2016_Historical_Trend_Report.pdf.

7. Chris Chamberlain and Guy Johnson, "Pathways into Adult Homelessness," *Journal of Sociology* 49, no. 1: 60–77, DOI:10.1177/1440783311422458.

8. Khary K. Rigg and Shannon M. Monnat, "Urban vs. Rural Differences in Prescription Opioid Misuse Among Adults in the United States: Informing Region Specific Drug Policies and Interventions," *International Journal of Drug Policy* 26, no. 5: 484–91.

9. "Unemployment, Youth Total (% of Labor Force Ages 15–24) (Modeled ILO Estimate)," World Bank, https://data.worldbank.org/indicator/SL .UEM.1524.ZS?year_high_desc=true; "Strategy for the Global Initiative on Decent Jobs for Youth," International Labour Organization, October 22, 2015, https://www.unsceb.org/CEBPublicFiles/Global%20Initiative%20on %20Decent%20Jobs%20for%20Youth%20Strategy%20Document%20Oct %202015.pdf.

10. "Youth Employment," International Labour Organization, https://www .ilo.org/global/topics/youth-employment/lang—en/index.htm.

11. "Global Risks 2014" (report, Geneva: World Economic Forum, 2014).

12. Anne Kim, "For Homeless Youth, Statistics and Reality Are Miles Apart," TalkPoverty.org, January 24, 2018, https://talkpoverty.org/2018/01/24/home less-youth-statistics-reality-miles-apart.

13. See, e.g., Ana J. Montalvo and Amy O'Hara, "A Profile of the Idle Youth in the U.S." (report, Washington, D.C.: Housing and Household Economics Statistics Division, U.S. Census Bureau, April 2008), http://paa2008.prince ton.edu/papers/81066.

14. "Youth Voting: Indicators of Child and Youth Well-Being" (Bethesda, MD: ChildTrends Data Bank, December 2015).

15. Ibid.

16. Thom File, "Voting in America: A Look at the 2016 Presidential Election" (blog post, Washington, D.C.: U.S. Census Bureau, May 10, 2017).

17. Ibid.

18. Peter Schochet, John Burghardt, and Sheena McConnell, "Does Job Corps Work? Impact Findings from the National Job Corps Study," *American Economic Review* 98, no. 5 (2008): 1864–86, http://www.aeaweb.org/articles .php?doi=10.1257/aer.98.5.1864.

19. "Job Corps Could Not Demonstrate Beneficial Training Outcomes" (Report to the Employment and Training Administration, Report No. 04-18-001-03-370, Washington, D.C.: Office of Inspector General, March 30, 2018).

20. Ibid.

21. John M. Bridgeland, Erin S. Ingram, and Matthew Atwell, "A Bridge to Reconnection: A Plan for Reconnecting One Million Opportunity Youth Each Year Through Federal Funding Streams" (report, Washington, D.C.: Civic Enterprises, 2016).

14: Seven Steps for Ending Disconnection

1. "Statistical Bulletin: Young People Not in Education, Employment or Training (NEET): May 2019," UK, Office for National Statistics, 2019, https://www.ons.gov.uk/employmentandlabourmarket/peoplenotinwork

/unemployment/bulletins/youngpeoplenotineducationemploymentortraining
neet/may2019.

2. "About the American Community Survey," U.S. Census Bureau, https://
www.census.gov/programs-surveys/acs/about.html.

3. See endnote 4 in chapter 2. "Methodological Note," Measure of America, https://ssrc-static.s3.amazonaws.com/moa/dy18.method.note.pdf.

4. Here's how the United Kingdom's Office of National Statistics defines
education and employment for purposes of determining who is "NEET": "A
person is considered to be in education or training if any of the following apply:

• they are enrolled on an education course and are still attending or
waiting for term to (re)start
• they are doing an apprenticeship
• they are on a government-supported employment or training
programme
• they are working or studying towards a qualification
• they have had job-related training or education in the last four weeks

'In employment' includes all people in some form of paid work, including
those working part-time. People not in employment are classed as either unemployed or economically inactive. Unemployed people are those who have
been looking for work in the past four weeks and who are available to start
work within the next two weeks. Economically inactive people are those who
have not been looking for work and/or who are not available to start work.
Examples of economically inactive people include those not looking for work
because they are students and those who are looking after dependents at
home. These definitions are based on those recommended by the International Labour Organisation (ILO)."

5. "ROI for Reconnecting Opportunity Youth in Each Congressional District," Forum for Youth Investment, March 28, 2016, http://forumfyi.org
/files/roi_for_reconnecting_opportunity_youth_in_each_congressional_dis
trict.pdf.

6. "Performance Partnerships: Agencies Need to Better Identify Resource
Contributions to Sustain Disconnected Youth Pilot Programs and Data to
Assess Pilot Results" (report, Washington, D.C.: Government Accountability
Office, April 2017).

7. "Performance Partnership Pilots for Disconnected Youth: First Annual
Report to Congress," Youth.gov, June 2017, https://youth.gov/youth-topics
/reconnecting-youth/performance-partnership-pilots/report-to-congress-2017.

8. Martha Ross and Richard Kazis, "Youth Summer Jobs Programs: Align-
ing Means and Ends" (report, Washington, D.C.: Brookings Institution,
July 14, 2016).

9. D. Fein and J. Hamadyk, "Bridging the Opportunity Divide for Low-Income Youth: Implementation and Early Impacts of the Year Up Program" (OPRE Report #2018-65, Washington, D.C.: Office of Planning, Research, and Evaluation, Administration for Children and Families, U.S. Department of Health and Human Services, 2018).

10. Ibid.

11. Ibid.

12. "Prudential Financial Announces $180 Million Global Investment to Solve Complex Challenges Facing Opportunity Youth, Promoting Financial Wellness of the Next Generation," press release, Prudential Financial, Inc., April 23, 2019, http://news.prudential.com/prudential-financial-announces -180-million-global-investment-to-solve-complex-challenges-facing-opportunity -youth-promoting-financial-wellness-next-generation.htm; David Pan, "McDonald's to Spend $2 Million on Helping Young People in Chicago," *USA Today*, August 22, 2018.

13. "Employers," 100,000 Opportunities Initiative, last modified 2019, https://www.100kopportunities.org/employers.

14. Carimah Townes, "Numerous Major Corporations Join White House Initiative to Ban the Box," ThinkProgress, April 12, 2016, https://thinkprogress .org/numerous-major-corporations-join-white-house-initiative-to-ban-the-box -65756e240e52.

15. According to the National Conference of State Legislatures, twenty-one states and the District of Columbia currently regulate when employers can ask about a criminal conviction. Most of these laws, however, apply to public employers and government contractors. "Criminal Records and Employment: Legislative Trends," National Conference of State Legislatures, last modified 2016, https://comm.ncsl.org/productfiles/83136608/second_chance_handout .pdf.

16. American Recovery and Reinvestment Act of 2009, 26 U.S.C. 1 et seq. Section 1221.

17. "Opportunity Zones: A New Incentive for Investing in Low-Income Communities," Economic Innovation Group, https://eig.org/wp-content/up loads/2018/02/Opportunity-Zones-Fact-Sheet.pdf.

18. See chapter 3.

19. Pennsylvania General Assembly Legislative Budget and Finance Committee, "An Interim Report on the Establishment of the Northern Pennsylvania Regional College" (report, Harrisburg, PA: Pennsylvania General Assembly, 2018), http://lbfc.legis.state.pa.us/Resources/Documents/Reports /626.pdf.

20. One of the students who benefited from this model is Tesla Rae Moore, whom we met in chapter 3. For more on her story, see Anne Kim, "An Innovative Fix for Rural Higher Education Deserts," *Washington Monthly*,

September/October 2018, https://washingtonmonthly.com/magazine/sep
tember-october-2018/degrees-of-separation.

21. Mary Bruce and John Bridgeland, "The Mentoring Effect: Young People's Perspectives on the Outcomes and Availability of Mentoring" (report, Washington, D.C.: Civic Enterprises in association with Hart Associates, 2014).

22. New York City Department of Education, *Success Mentor Guide 2018–2019: Connecting Chronically Absent Students with Caring Adults* (New York: New York City Department of Education, 2018), https://drive.google.com/file/d/1BmJreHkk8dKOmwAHG_IrSujpOFMzzN06/view.

23. "Success Mentors," New York City Department of Education, New York City Community Schools, last modified 2016, https://sites.google.com/mynyc school.org/newyorkcitycommunityschools/resources/attendance-resources/success-mentors.

24. John M. Bridgeland, John J. Dilulio Jr., and Karen Burke Morison, "The Silent Epidemic: Perspectives of High School Dropouts" (report, Washington, D.C.: Civic Enterprises, 2006).

25. "The Opportunity Passport: A Pathway to Economic Security for Youth in Foster Care," Jim Casey Youth Opportunities Initiative, https://www.aecf.org/m/resourcedoc/aecf-opportunitypassportexplainer-2017.pdf.

26. Megan Alrutz, "The Criminalization of Youth," *Pacific Standard*, March 17, 2015.

27. Richard M. Lerner, "Promoting Positive Youth Development: Theoretical and Empirical Bases" (white paper, Somerville, MA: Institute for Applied Research in Youth Development, Tufts University, 2005).

28. Richard M. Lerner and Jacqueline V. Lerner, "The Positive Development of Youth: Comprehensive Findings from the 4-H Study of Positive Youth Development" (report, Somerville, MA: Institute for Applied Research in Youth Development, Tufts University, 2016).

29. Ibid.

30. "About BYP100," BYP100.org, https://byp100.org/about-byp100; "Youth First," Youth First Initiative, http://www.youthfirstinitiative.org.

31. "The Gates Scholarship," Gates Scholarship, last modified 2016, https://www.thegatesscholarship.org/scholarship.

INDEX

About the Author

Anne Kim is a contributing editor to *Washington Monthly*. Her writings on economic opportunity, social policy, and higher education have appeared in numerous national outlets, including the *Washington Monthly*, the *Washington Post*, *Governing*, and TheAtlantic.com, among others. She is a veteran of the think tanks Third Way and the Progressive Policy Institute as well as of Capitol Hill, where she worked for Rep. Jim Cooper (D-TN). Kim has a law degree from Duke University and a bachelor's in journalism from the University of Missouri-Columbia. She lives in northern Virginia.

Publishing in the Public Interest

Thank you for reading this book published by The New Press. The New Press is a nonprofit, public interest publisher. New Press books and authors play a crucial role in sparking conversations about the key political and social issues of our day.

We hope you enjoyed this book and that you will stay in touch with The New Press. Here are a few ways to stay up to date with our books, events, and the issues we cover:

- Sign up at www.thenewpress.com/subscribe to receive updates on New Press authors and issues and to be notified about local events
- Like us on Facebook: www.facebook.com/newpress books
- Follow us on Twitter: www.twitter.com/thenewpress

Please consider buying New Press books for yourself; for friends and family; or to donate to schools, libraries, community centers, prison libraries, and other organizations involved with the issues our authors write about.

The New Press is a 501(c)(3) nonprofit organization. You can also support our work with a tax-deductible gift by visiting www.thenewpress.com/donate.